LIBRARY OF NEW TESTAMENT STUDIES

397

FORMERLY THE JOURNAL FOR THE STUDY OF THE NEW TESTAMENT

SUPPLEMENT SERIES

Editor
Mark Goodacre

READING DREAMS

An Audience-Critical Approach to the Dreams in the
Gospel of Matthew

DEREK S. DODSON

t&t clark

Published by T&T Clark International
A Continuum imprint
The Tower Building, 11 York Road, London SE1 7NX
80 Maiden Lane, Suite 704, New York, NY 10038

www.continuumbooks.com

British Library Cataloguing-in-Publication Data
A catalogue record for this book is available from the British Library

ISBN: 978-0-567-57770-2 (hardback)

Typeset by Data Standards Ltd, Frome, Somerset, UK
Printed in Great Britain by the MPG Books Group, Bodmin and King's Lynn

CONTENTS

Chapter Four

ACKNOWLEDGMENTS

This monograph originated as a Ph.D. dissertation written at Baylor University, and so my acknowledgments take into account the larger experience of my doctoral studies. I would like to subvert the conventional order of acknowledgments and express my deepest gratitude first and foremost to my wife and daughters. My daughters, Kelsey Lynne and Emily Grace, are a true source of joy in my life and constant reminders of the goodness and priorities of life. My wife, Sherrie, has been a faithful and steadfast companion on this journey. The words 'appreciation' and 'gratitude' are simply inadequate for conveying what she means to me. She is my life partner and truest friend; our life together is truly a means of grace.

To the New Testament faculty at Baylor University, I would like to express my indebtedness and sincerest appreciation. Dr. Charles Talbert, who was the adviser for my dissertation, provided invaluable insight and direction for this research project; I am blessed to have had the opportunity to study under him. I can only hope that this monograph in some small way honors his scholarship and legacy to New Testament studies. Dr. Mikeal Parsons, who served as second reader for my dissertation, was a constant mentor and model teacher-scholar for me during my studies at Baylor. He was especially influential in my academic development. Dr. Naymond Keathley was very encouraging and provided an essential pastoral presence for me at Baylor. And Dr. Sharyn Dowd contributed much to the ethos of the New Testament area, exemplifying ideally the integration of the heart and head, of faith and scholarship; it is no surprise that she has left the university setting for a ministry position.

I also would like to express my appreciation to Dr. Jeffrey Hamilton, professor of History at Baylor University, who served as my third reader. He provided a most helpful perspective for my dissertation. I would also like to thank Drs. W. H. Bellinger, Jr., and James Kennedy, professors of Old Testament at Baylor, for reading the dissertation and participating in the oral defense. They also contributed much to my graduate studies, having taken graduate seminars with both of them.

There are several others that need to be properly recognized for their support, assistance and help in this writing project as well as my studies at

Baylor in general: Clova Gibson, Academic/Student Support Associate for Graduate Studies in Religion, for her service and 'keeping it all together;' Janet Jasek, Borrower Supervisor for Interlibrary Services at Baylor University's library, for her constant willingness to help in obtaining needed volumes for my research purposes; the congregations of Muldraugh Baptist Church (Muldraugh, KY) and Speegelville Baptist Church (Waco, TX), who blessed me by allowing me to be their pastor and helped me keep a healthy perspective of my scholarly endeavors; and the congregation of Seventh and James Baptist Church (Waco, TX), who provided a spiritual home for my family.

Finally, I would like to thank Dr. Mark Goodacre for accepting this monograph for the Library of New Testament Studies series; and I would like to extend a word of gratitude to Haaris Naqvi of T & T Clark for his support and assistance in the publication process.

ABBREVIATIONS

Note: Abbreviations are taken primarily from *The SBL Handbook of Style: For Ancient Near Eastern, Biblical, and Early Christian Studies.* Edited by Patrick H. Alexander, *et al.* Peabody, Mass.: Hendrickson Publishers, 1999.

Primary Sources

Achilles Tatius, *Leuc. Clit.*	*Leucippe et Clitophon*
Acts Andr.	*Acts of Andrew*
Acts John	*Acts of John*
Acts Pet.	*Acts of Peter*
Acts Thom.	*Acts of Thomas*
Aeschylus, Eum.	Eumenides
Prom.	Prometheus vinctus
Anth. Pal.	*Anthologia Palatina*
Aphthonius, *Progym.*	*Progymnasmata*
Appian, *Bell. civ.*	*Bella civilia*
Hist. rom.	*Historia romana*
Apuleius, *Metam.*	*Metamorphoses*
Aristides, *Orat.*	*Oratio*
Aristodemus, *Schol. Pind. Pyth.*	*Scholia in Pindar Pythionikai*
Aristophanes, *Plut.*	*Plutus*
Arrian, *Anab.*	*Anabasis*
Artemidorus Daldianus, *Onir.*	*Onirocritica*
Athenaeus, *Deipn.*	*Deipnosophistae*
Cassius Dio, *Hist. Rom.*	*Historiae Romanae*
Chariton, *Chaer.*	*De Chaerea et Callirhoe*
Cicero, *Div.*	*De divinatione*
Republ.	*De republica*
Clement of Alexandria, *Protr.*	*Protrepticus*
Diodorus Siculus, *Bib. hist.*	*Bibliotheca historica*
Diogenes Laertius, *Vit. phil.*	*Vitae philosophorum*
Dionysius of Halicarnassus, *Ant. rom.*	*Antiquitates romanae*

Eunapius, *Vit. soph.*	*Vitae sophistarum*
Euripides, *Alc.*	*Alcestis*
Hec.	*Hecuba*
Iph. taur.	*Iphigenia taurica*
Orest.	*Orestes*
Ezek. Trag.	Ezekiel the Tragedian
Galen, *Comm. in Hippocr. de humor.*	*Commentarium in Hippocratis de humoribus*
Heliodorus, *Aeth.*	*Aethiopica*
Herm. *Vis.*	Shepherd of Hermas, *Vision*
Hermogenes, *Progym.*	*Progymnasmata*
Herodotus, *Hist.*	*Historiae*
Hesiod, *Theog.*	*Theogonia*
Hippolytus, *Trad. ap.*	*Traditio apostolica*
Homer, *Il.*	*Ilias*
Od.	*Odyssea*
Irenaeus, *Haer.*	*Adversus haereses*
Isocrates, *Evag.*	*Evagoras (Or. 9)*
John of Sardis, *Comm. in Aphthonii Progym.*	*Commentarium in Aphthonii Progymnasmata*
Jos. Asen.	*Joseph and Aseneth*
Josephus, *A.J.*	*Antiquitates judaicae*
J.W.	*Jewish War*
Jub.	*Jubilees*
Justin, 1 *Apol.*	*Apologia i*
Juvenal, *Sat.*	*Satirae*
L.A.B. (Pseudo-Philo)	*Liber antiquitatum biblicarum*
Lad. Jac.	*Ladder of Jacob*
Livy, *Hist. Rome*	*History of Rome*
Longus, *Daphn.*	*Daphnis and Chloe*
Lucian, *Peregr.*	*De morte Peregrini*
Macrobius, *Comm. in Somn. Scip.*	*Commentarii in Somnium Scipionis*
Nicolaus, *Progym.*	*Progymnasmata*
Pausanias, *Descr.*	*Graeciae description*
Petronius, *Sat.*	*Satyrica*
Philo, *Vit. Mos.*	*De vita Mosis*
Somn.	*De somniis*
Philostratus, *Vit. Apoll.*	*Vita Apollonii*
Plato, *Cri.*	*Crito*
Leg.	*Leges*
Resp.	*Respublica*
Tim.	*Timaeus*
Pliny the Elder, *Nat.*	*Naturalis historia*

Plutarch,	*Ages.*	*Agesilaus*
	Alc.	*Alcibiades*
	Alex.	*Alexander*
	Ant.	*Antonius*
	Arist.	*Aristides*
	Brut.	*Brutus*
	Caes.	*Caesar*
	Cim.	*Cimon*
	Cor.	*Marcius Coriolanus*
	Demetr.	*Demetrius*
	Eum.	*Eumenes*
	Luc.	*Lucullus*
	Pel.	*Pelopidas*
	Per.	*Pericles*
	Quaest. conv.	*Quaestionum convivialum libri IX*
	Rom.	*Romulus*
	Sept. sap. conv.	*Septem sapientium convivium*
	Them.	*Themistocles*
	Thes.	*Theseus*
Quintilian,	*Inst.*	*Institutio oratoria*
Sophocles,	*El.*	*Elektra*
Soranus,	*Vit. Hipp.*	*Vita Hippocratis*
Strabo,	*Geogr.*	*Geographica*
Suetonius,	*Aug.*	*Divus Augustus*
	Cal.	*Gaius Caligula*
	Claud.	*Divus Claudius*
	Dom.	*Domitianus*
	Galb.	*Galba*
	Jul.	*Divus Julius*
	Otho	*Otho*
	Tib.	*Tiberius*
	Vesp.	*Vespasianus*
T. Job		*Testament of Job*
T. Jos.		*Testament of Joseph*
T. Levi		*Testament of Levi*
T. Naph.		*Testament of Naphtali*
Tacitus,	*Ann.*	*Annales*
	Hist.	*Historiae*
Tertullian,	*An.*	*De anima*
	Apol.	*Apologeticus*
	Idol.	*De idololatria*
	Spect.	*De spectaculis*
	Virg.	*De virginibus velandis*
Tg. Ps.-J.		*Targum Pseudo-Jonathan*

Theon, *Progym.*	*Progymnasmata*
Theophrastus, *Char.*	*Characteres*
Virgil, *Aen.*	*Aeneid*
Xenophon, *Apol.*	*Apologia Socratis*
Eq. mag.	*De equitum magistro*
Mem.	*Memorabilia*
Sym.	*Symposium*
Xenophon of Ephesias, *Eph. Tale*	*An Ephesian Tale*
2 Bar.	*2 Baruch (Syriac Apocalypse)*
1 En.	*1 Enoch (Ethiopic Apocalypse)*
2 En.	*2 Enoch (Slavonic Apocalypse)*
2 Macc.	2 Maccabees

Other Abbreviations

ABD	*Anchor Bible Dictionary.* Edited by D. N. Freedman. 6 vols. New York, 1992
ABRL	Anchor Bible Reference Library
ACLS	The American Council of Learned Societies
AGJU	Arbeiten zur Geschichte des antiken Judentums und des Urchristentums
AIPHOS	*Annuaire de l'Institut de philologie et d'histoire orientales et slaves*
AM	*Annales du Midi*
AnBib	Analecta biblica
ANF	*The Ante-Nicene Fathers*
ANRW	*Aufstieg und Niedergang der römischen Welt: Geschichte und Kultur Roms im Spiegel der neueren Forschung.* Edited by H. Temporini and W. Haase. Berlin, 1972–
Anth. Pal.	*Epigrammatum anthologia palatina.* Edited by F. Dübner, and P. Waltz *et al.* Paris, 1864–72, 1928–
AOS	American Oriental Series
BaBesch	*Bulletin antieke Beschavung*
BDAG	Bauer, W., F. W. Danker, W. F. Arndt, and F. W. Gingrich. *Greek-English Lexicon of the New Testament and Other Early Christian Literature.* 3d ed. Chicago, 1999
BeO	*Bibbia e Oriente*
BETL	Bibliotheca Ephemeridum Theologicarum Lovaniensium
Bib	*Biblica*
BibLeb	*Bibel und Leben*
BibOr	Biblica et orientalia
BICS	*Bulletin of the Institute of Classical Studies*
BIS	Biblical Interpretation Series

BKP	Beiträge zur klassischen Philologie
CaJos	*Cahiers de Joséphologie*
CNT	Commentaire du Nouveau Testament
CQ	*Classical Quarterly*
CRINT	Compendia rerum iudaicarum ad Novum Testamentum
DNP	*Der neue Pauly: Enzyklopädie der Antike.* Edited by H. Cancik and H. Schneider. Stuttgart, 1996–
DNTB	*Dictionary of New Testament Background.* Edited by C. A. Evans
GBS	Guides to Biblical Scholarship
HSCP	*Harvard Studies in Classical Philology*
HUCM	Monographs of the Hebrew Union College
HTKNT	Herders theologischer Kommentar zum Neuen Testament
ICC	International Critical Commentary
IDelos	*Inscriptions de Délos.* Edited by F. Durrbach, *et al.* 7 vols. Paris, 1926–
IG	*Inscriptiones graecae.* Editio minor. Berlin, 1924–
IPergamon	*Die Inschriften von Pergamon.* Edited by M. Fränkel and C. Habicht. 3 vols. Berlin, 1890–
IPriene	*Inschriften von Priene.* Edited by H. von Gaertringen. Berlin, 1906
IRT	Issues in Religion and Theology
JAC	*Jahrbuch für Antike und Christentum*
JBL	*Journal of Biblical Literature*
JJS	*Journal of Jewish Studies*
JRS	*Journal of Roman Studies*
JSNT	*Journal for the Study of the New Testament*
JSNTSup	Journal for the Study of the New Testament: Supplement Series
JSOT	*Journal for the Study of the Old Testament*
JSOTSup	Journal for the Study of the Old Testament: Supplement Series
LCL	Loeb Classical Library
NIGTC	New International Greek Testament Commentary
NovT	*Novum Testamentum*
NovTSup	Novum Testamentum Supplements
NRSV	New Revised Standard Version
NTS	*New Testament Studies*
OCD	*The Oxford Classical Dictionary.* Edited by S. Hornblower and A. Spawforth. 3d ed. Oxford, 1996
OECS	The Oxford Early Christian Studies
OTP	*Old Testament Pseudepigrapha.* Edited by J. H. Charlesworth. 2 vols. New York, 1983

PG	Patrologia graeca [= Patrologiae cursus completus: Series graeca]. Edited by J.-P. Migne. 162 vols. Paris, 1857–1886
PGM	*Papyri graecae magicae: Die griechischen Zauberpapyri.* Edited by K. Preisendanz. Berlin, 1928
PRSt	*Perspectives in Religious Studies*
RevQ	*Revue de Qumran*
SBL	Society of Biblical Literature
SBLTT	Society of Biblical Literature Texts and Translations
SBLWAW	Society of Biblical Literature Writings from the Ancient World
SIG	*Sylloge inscriptionum graecarum.* Edited by W. Dittenberger. 4 vols. 3d ed. Leipzig. 1915–1924
SIRIS	*Sylloge inscriptionum religionis Isiacae et Sarapiacae.* Edited by L. Vidmann. Berlin, 1969
SNTSMS	Society for New Testament Studies Monograph Series
SP	Sacra Pagina
TANZ	Texte und Arbeiten zum neutestamentlichen Zeitalter
TAPA	*Transactions of the American Philological Association*
TPAPA	*Transactions and Proceedings of the American Philological Association*
WBC	Word Biblical Commentary
WGRW	Writings from the Greco-Roman World
ZNW	*Zeitschrift für die Neutestamentliche Wissenschaft und die Kunde der älteren Kirche*

Chapter One

INTRODUCTION

In a modern, post-Freud age, dreams are understood as manifestations of an individual's subconscious, a kind of window into the psyche of a person. Dreams in antiquity, however, were understood more generally as a means of how the divine communicates to humanity. This is not to say that the ancients did not recognize that some dreams were insignificant and simply came about because of the 'thoughts of the day,'[1] but this recognition seems to be more of a by-product of when dreams did not prove to be significant. The primary understanding of dreams in antiquity was that dreams represent some objective experience that connected humanity with the will of the divine. Ancients did not have dreams, they were encountered by dreams. In her study on ancient dreams, Patricia Cox Miller states, 'Dreams were autonomous; they were not conceptualized as products of a personal sub- or unconscious but rather as visual images that present themselves to the dreamer.'[2] Thus, ancient dreams had a socio-religious dimension, which in turn influenced the literary representation of dreams in antiquity.

The Gospel of Matthew is the only canonical Gospel that includes dreams in its narrative. There are three dream reports (1.18b-25; 2.13-15, 19-21) and three references to dreams (2.12, 22; 27.19). Given the ancient understanding of dreams and the accompanying literary representation of dreams, how would an ancient audience understand, or 'make sense,' of the Matthean dreams? This volume seeks to answer this question by reading Matthew's dreams as the 'authorial audience.' Before describing the theoretical basis of this approach, however, I will review how Matthew's dreams have been studied by previous scholars, and how this research project seeks to improve upon these studies.

---

1 Herodotus, *Hist.* 7.16.2; cf. Artemidorus, *Onir.* 1.1; Cicero, *Div.* 1.45.

2 Patricia Cox Miller, *Dreams in Late Antiquity: Studies in the Imagination of a Culture* (Princeton: Princeton University Press, 1994), 17.

Previous Scholarship and Present Contribution

Unlike the dreams (and visions) of Acts,[3] those of Matthew lack a full and comprehensive investigation. The dreams of Matthew's Gospel have been addressed only in journal articles or as a part of larger research projects. [4] Earlier analyses addressed the question of sources and the historicity of the dreams in Matthew. W. L. Dulière argues that the infancy narrative of Matthew's Gospel (chs. 1–2) is a distinguishable source based on the 'obsessive preoccupation'[5] with dreams, even referring to the author of this source as *l'Oniriste*.[6] Inferring that Dulière's source critical study denies the authenticity of the Gospel, S. Cavalletti defends the historicity of the dreams in Matthew by appealing to the precedent of the Old Testament, where God often uses dreams for divine communication.[7] Tarcisio Stramare also contends that the Matthean dreams are historical fact, which militates against the designation of 'literary genre' for the presentation of dreams in Matthew.[8] These articles have contributed little to research on the Matthean dreams and reflect more the concerns of

3   For example, John S. Hanson, 'The Dream/Vision Report and Acts 10.1–11.18: A Form-Critical Study' (Ph.D. diss., Harvard University, 1978); and Michael James Day, 'The Function of Post-Pentecost Dream/Vision Reports in Acts,' (Ph.D. diss., The Southern Baptist Theological Seminary, 1994); John B. F. Miller, *'Convinced that God has called us'*: *Dreams, Visions, and the Perception of God's Will in Luke-Acts* (BIS 85; Leiden: Brill, 2007).

4   W. L. Dulière, 'La révélation par songe dans l'Évangile de Matthieu,' *AIPHOS* 13 (1953): 665–9; S. Cavalletti, 'I sogni di San Giuseppe,' *BeO* 2 (1960): 149–51; Dominic M. Crossan, 'Structure & Theology of Mt. 1.18-2.23,' *CaJos* 16 (1968): 119–35; Tarcisio Stramare, 'I sogni di S. Giuseppe,' *CaJos* 19 (1971): 104–22; George M. Soares Prabhu, *The Formula Quotations in the Infancy Narrative of Matthew: An Enquiry into the Tradition History of Mt. 1–2* (AnBib 63; Rome: Biblical Institute Press, 1976), 185–7, 223–5, 234–42; 294–7; Robert Gnuse, 'Dream Genre in the Matthean Infancy Narratives,' *NovT* 32 (1990): 97–120; Raymond E. Brown, *The Birth of the Messiah: A Commentary on the Infancy Narratives in the Gospels of Matthew and Luke* (new updated ed.; ABRL; New York: Doubleday, 1993), 108–17, 129, 194–6; Dale C. Allison, *The New Moses: A Matthean Typology* (Minneapolis: Fortress Press, 1993), 140–65; Janice Capel Anderson, *Matthew's Narrative Web: Over, and Over, and Over Again* (JSNTSup 91; Sheffield: JSOT, 1994), 153–7; Marco Frenschkowski, 'Traum und Traumdeutung im Matthäusevangelium: Einige Beobachtungen,' *JAC* 41 (1998): 5–47; Frances Lynn Flannery-Dailey, 'Standing at the Head of Dreamers: A Study of Dreams in Antiquity' (Ph.D. diss., The University of Iowa, 2000), 402–16; and Derek S. Dodson, 'Dreams, the Ancient Novels, and the Gospel of Matthew: An Intertextual Study,' *PRSt* 29 (2002): 39–52.

5   Dulière, 'La révélation par songe dans l'Évangile de Matthieu,' 665. Dulière's source critical work lacks the sophistication and insight of later redaction critics and therefore is insignificant.

6   Dulière, 'La révélation par songe dans l'Évangile de Matthieu,' 667.

7   Cavalletti, 'I sogni di San Giuseppe,' 149–51, esp. 149.

8   Stramare, 'I sogni di S. Giuseppe,' 122. Interestingly, Stramare differentiates between 'literary genre' (*genere letterario*) and 'literary outline' (*schema letterario*), a feature that he concedes the dreams in Matthew do exhibit.

conservative Christian theology. Moreover, Stramare's denial of an identifiable genre for the narration of dreams is untenable.[9]

The more significant studies of dreams in Matthew's Gospel revolve around the issues of: (1) Moses typology, (2) Matthew's redaction of Mt. 1–2, (3) the literary form of the dreams, and (4) narrative criticism.

Moses Typology and the Dream of Mt. 1.18b-25

Scholarship has convincingly demonstrated that Mt. 1–2, and indeed Matthew as a whole, reflects a Moses typology.[10] Because the various, developing traditions about Moses' birth often include dreams by Pharaoh, Moses' sister, Miriam, and/or Moses' father, Amram, the opening dream narrative of Matthew (1.18b-25) is noted as a contributing feature to the Moses typology in Mt. 1–2. Indeed, Josephus narrates a dream to Amram, which is the closest parallel of dreams in the Moses tradition to Joseph's dream in Mt. 1.1-18.[11]

I do not deny the presence of a Moses typology and the contribution of the first dream-vision report (1.18-25) to that typology. In Chapter Five, however, I will argue that the authorial audience of Matthew's Gospel makes the Mosaic connection with the first dream narrative only *retrospectively* in light of Mt. 2. Giving priority to the Gospel of Matthew's own narrative shape and sequence and its ancient literary context, I will make a case that the authorial audience's initial understanding of the dream of Mt. 1.18b-25 would be in connection with the opening genealogy (1.1-17; note γένεσις in 1.1, 18) and so reflects the pattern and convention of the literary-rhetorical tradition of encomium.

Matthean Dreams and Redaction Criticism

The dreams of Mt. 1–2 also have been the subject of redaction critics, particularly Raymond Brown and George Soares Prabhu.[12] For both Brown and Soares Prabhu, the three dream reports in Mt. 1–2 betray a pre-Matthean dream source that Matthew has used and redacted with other sources in the composition of the infancy narrative of Jesus. Much of their discussion concerns the content and structure of this dream source

9   See John S. Hanson, 'Dreams and Visions in the Graeco-Roman World and Early Christianity,' *ANRW* 23.2: 1395–1427; cp. Gnuse, 'Dream Genre in the Matthean Infancy Narratives,' 97–120.

10   For example, see Crossan, 'Structure & Theology,' 119–35; Brown, *The Birth of the Messiah*, 112–16; and Allison, *The New Moses*, 140–65.

11   Josephus, *A.J.* 2.210-217. It should be noted that this is the only source in which a dream is attributed to Amram.

12   Brown, *The Birth of the Messiah*, 108–17, 129, 194–6; and Soares Prabhu, *Formula Quotations*, 185–7, 223–5, 234–42; 294–7.

before Matthew's redaction of it. Once the source is reconstructed, these scholars proceed to describe Matthew's redactional activity, noting Matthean tendencies, the occurrence of internal tensions or conflicts and the presence of parallels with other material.[13] In the end, the dreams in Matthew are approached by redaction critics diachronically in an effort to reconstruct the compositional history of Mt. 1–2, albeit with the goal of elucidating the theological import of the final form of the text.

The diachronic character of redaction criticism, however, sometimes blurs the reading of the final form. For example, Brown and Soares Prabhu assert that the first dream narrative (1.18-25) has undergone the most redaction. In their effort to reconstruct the pre-Matthean form of the dream report, they actually alter the form of the dream narrative as compared to other Greco-Roman dream reports. The description of Joseph as 'righteous' (1.19) is taken as a Matthean redaction, and so is discussed separately from the dream report. However, Greco-Roman dream reports often include a remark about the dreamer's character.[14] Moreover, these redactional studies do not compare Matthew's dream reports with other literary dreams of the Greco-Roman world, which results in a failure to recognize, and appreciate, Matthew's participation in the literary practices of his time. Thus, the present study interprets the dreams of Matthew in their final form without consideration of Matthew's redaction or possible pre-compositional sources or scenarios.

The Form of Matthew's Dreams

The most comprehensive study of the form of Matthew's dreams is that of Robert Gnuse.[15] Gnuse argues that the dreams in Matthew's infancy narrative share 'deep structural similarities'[16] with the Elohist dreams that are found in Genesis, which indicates the formal dependence of Matthean dreams upon the Elohist dreams. In other words, Matthew has modeled his dreams on the dreams found in Genesis, particularly the dreams in the Elohist tradition. Because Gnuse's study is cited frequently in commentaries and other studies, I will provide a more detailed response to Gnuse in Chapter Five. For now, though, it is sufficient to note that Frances Flannery-Dailey has demonstrated the 'surprisingly standardized' formal pattern of dreams in the literature of the Ancient Near East, Hebrew Bible, Greece and Rome despite the span of time and

13   Brown, *The Birth of the Messiah*, 105–6.
14   Hanson, 'Dreams and Visions,' 1406.
15   Gnuse, 'Dream Genre in the Matthean Infancy Narratives,' 97–120.
16   Gnuse, 'Dream Genre in the Matthean Infancy Narratives,' 107.

cultures.[17] This relatively consistent pattern makes it very difficult to argue for literary mimesis, which Gnuse is ultimately contending in regard to Matthew's use of Genesis.

Flannery-Dailey's analysis of Matthew's dreams is not without problems. She rightly criticizes Gnuse for 'rejecting influence from Jewish dream material contemporary with Matthew,'[18] but in the end she also is too narrow in her comparative material (Jewish texts of Second Temple Judaism) and ignores her own findings (the 'surprisingly standardized' formal pattern of dreams across time and cultures). Flannery-Dailey claims that:

> Like many texts of Second Temple Judaism, Matthew presents dreams as revelations from the divine, with deep connections to prophecy, in a form that is uniquely Jewish. That is, there is an important development that the Matthean dreams make to the biblical traditions that is gleaned from late Second Temple Judaism, namely, *dreams in which an angel appears and imparts a message.*[19]

The Gospel of Matthew is certainly an example of a Jewish text near the end of the first century C.E., and the content of Matthew's dream reports indeed reflects a Jewish tradition and symbolic world view, particularly in having an angel as a dream figure. To assert, however, that the 'form' of Matthew's dreams is 'uniquely Jewish' simply ignores dream reports in other Greco-Roman literature, including the connection to prophecy/ oracles and dream figures imparting messages. This volume will argue that the dreams of Matthew represent a common literary convention and that the authorial audience would have made sense of these dreams in light of the way this literary convention functions in other Greco-Roman, Jewish and Christian texts.

Narrative Critical Approach to Matthew's Dreams

The Matthean dreams have also been analyzed from a narrative critical perspective by Janice Capel Anderson.[20] Anderson investigates the dreams as examples of repetitive literary features that create anticipation and retrospection. On the one hand, Anderson's study is perceptive of the narrative function of Matthew's dreams. She notes that the clustering of dreams in Mt. 1–2 emphasize the divine sanction of the character of Jesus and the beginning of his life. She also observes how the dreams 'provide

---

17 Frances Lynn Flannery-Dailey, 'Standing at the Head of Dreamers: A Study of Dreams in Antiquity' (Ph.D. diss., The University of Iowa, 2000), chs. 1–2.

18 Flannery-Dailey, 'Standing at the Head of Dreamers,' 403.

19 Flannery-Dailey, 'Standing at the Head of Dreamers,' 415 (emphasis original).

20 Janice Capel Anderson, *Matthew's Narrative Web: Over, and Over, and Over Again* (JSNTSup 91; Sheffield: JSOT, 1994), 153–7.

motivation (*divine* motivation) for the chain of events, for the geograph-
ical movements – the arrivals and departures – of characters.'[21]
Anderson's descriptions of anticipation and retrospection in relation to
the dreams, however, are less helpful. Only the first dream of Matthew
(1.18b-25) anticipates a future event. The other dreams are command
dreams that are obeyed by the dreamer, yet Anderson reads these in terms
of anticipation and fulfillment instead of the more obvious terms of
command/obedience. Moreover, Anderson's narrative approach precludes her from seeing how Matthew's dreams share with other ancient
texts a common literary form, which includes the feature of the dreamer
responding to the dream. The obedience of the dreamers in Matthew's
narrative is expected given the literary convention of dreams. Anderson
reads Matthew's dreams in terms of the 'implied reader,'[22] which results in
a 'flat' reading of Matthew's narrative. I intend to read Matthew's dreams
in light of the ancient social and literary contexts of dreams, which – I
believe – results is a more textured or multi-dimensional reading of
Matthew.

Conclusion

This review of previous research concludes with the most notable
examination of dreams in Matthew, that of Marco Frenschkowski.[23]
Though Frenschkowski accepts the form-critical work of Gnuse and
acknowledges the connection of the first Matthean dream narrative with a
Moses typology, he is interested in interpreting the dreams of Matthew's
Gospel in light of ancient dream theories and dream interpretation.
Despite many helpful and insightful observations,[24] Frenschkowski's
conclusions are mainly presented in contrast to this ancient context. First,
Frenschkowski attempts to say something about the Matthean community based on how the dreams in Matthew's Gospel compare to the
ancient social context of dreams. He concludes that: (1) the Matthean
community lacked a professional dream interpreter, given the omission of
symbolic dreams in Matthew; and (2) dreams played no particular,
spiritual importance for the Matthean community, since nothing is
mentioned in the instructions for missionaries (Mt. 10) or in the

---

21   Anderson, *Matthew's Narrative Web*, 157.
22   The 'implied reader' is equivalent to Peter Rabinowitz's 'narrative audience,' which
will be discussed below under *Methodology*.
23   Frenschkowski, 'Traum und Traumdeutung im Matthäusevangelium,' 5–47.
24   Particularly helpful and insightful is his examination of the Matthean dream
terminology – κατ' ὄναρ – in other Greco-Roman literature (14–21) and his specific
comments on the individual dream reports and references, especially the dream of Pilate's
wife (32–34).

ecclesiastical teachings (Mt. 18).[25] Second, Frenschkowski concludes that
the Matthean dreams are in continuity with a main feature of New
Testament theology, the *Disambiguierung des Offenbarungsgeschehens*.[26]
Although these conclusions are incredibly speculative (Matthean community) and over generalized (New Testament theology),
Frenschkowski's investigation of the dreams in Matthew in the larger
context of ancient dream theories and interpretations provides a much-
needed dimension to the study of the Matthean dreams.

My research project will follow Frenschkowski's lead of examining the
dreams of Matthew's Gospel in their ancient context, but I will seek to
avoid a methodological problem inherent in his work. Frenschkowski
does not differentiate between primary sources that address dreams in
terms of theory and technical interpretation and primary sources that
contain dream reports as a part of a larger narrative – e.g., histories,
biographies, and novels. While the two are informed by one another, I will
treat these two types of sources in two different chapters and privilege the
narrative texts in interpreting the dream reports in the Gospel of
Matthew.[27] Moreover, my concern is not a reconstruction of the
Matthean community; it is a reading of Matthew's dreams as the
authorial audience, to which I now turn my attention.

Methodological Considerations

As stated, the theoretical perspective guiding my analysis of the Matthean
dreams is audience criticism with specific interest in what Peter
Rabinowitz calls the 'authorial audience.'[28] Rabinowitz places the
authorial audience on a spectrum in relation to a text. At one end of
the spectrum is the 'actual audience,' the real flesh-and-blood readers of
the text. The actual audience is the only audience 'over which the author
has no guaranteed control.'[29] At the other end of the spectrum is the
hypothetical 'ideal narrative audience.' Rabinowitz is quick to point out
that this audience is ideal 'from the narrator's point of view.'[30] The ideal

---

25 Frenschkowski, 'Traum und Traumdeutung im Matthäusevangelium,' 40–1.

26 Frenschkowski, 'Traum und Traumdeutung im Matthäusevangelium,' 42–3.

27 The essay by Joachim Latacz, 'Funktionen des Traums in der antiken Literatur,' in
Traum und Träumen: Traumanalysen in Wissenschaft, Religion und Kunst (ed. T. Wagner-
Simon und G. Benedetti; Göttingen: Vandenhoeck & Ruprecht, 1984), 10–31, helped me
recognize the importance of this differentiation. Also, his classification of the functions of
dreams in ancient literature provided a basis for the structure of this monograph (see below):
praktischen Zwecken, theoretischen Zwecken, and *künstlerischen Zwecken*.

28 Peter J. Rabinowitz, 'Truth in Fiction: A Reexamination of Audiences,' *Critical
Inquiry* 4 (1977): 126–127.

29 Rabinowitz, 'Truth in Fiction,' 126.

30 Rabinowitz, 'Truth in Fiction,' 134.

narrative audience comes into play only in highly ironic texts, where irony actually creates a differential in relation to the other hypothetical audiences: the authorial audience and the narrative audience. Though both are hypothetical constructs, it is important to distinguish between the authorial audience and the narrative audience. The authorial audience is a hypothetical audience, which is based on the assumed, or presupposed, 'beliefs, knowledge, and familiarity with conventions'[31] that the author has about his or her readers. The authorial audience is constructed on the basis of the text in relation to the literary, social, and cultural contexts with which the author shares with his audience. The narrative audience is also a hypothetical construct, but this audience is constructed on the basis of, even 'extracted from', the text itself, as if the text was a 'closed, autonomous object.'[32] In other words, the narrative audience is constructed only on the basis of the text itself without regard to the larger literary and historical contexts in which the text was written. In contrast to the narrative audience, Rabinowitz further describes the authorial audience:

> The [authorial audience], therefore, is not reducible to textual features but can be determined only by an examination of the interrelation between the text and the context in which the work was produced. The [authorial audience], in other words, is a *contextualized* implied reader, and studies of reading that start here have the potential to open up new questions of history, culture, and ideology.[33]

Thus, reading a text as the authorial audience requires knowledge of the literary, social, and historical contexts in which the text was produced.

This theoretical perspective of audience can be further illustrated by placing it in the context of New Testament studies. Mark Allan Powell provides a helpful categorization and description of how modern biblical scholarship has approached its task of interpreting the Gospels.[34] Powell presents two models. The first model is historical-critical, which is a diachronic approach to the text with the goal of historical reconstruction. The Gospels are used as sources for some larger historical project, such as the historical Jesus, history of traditions, the history of early Christianity,

---

31   Rabinowitz, 'Truth in Fiction,' 126; cf. Rabinowitz, 'Whirl without End: Audience-Oriented Criticism,' in *Contemporary Literary Theory* (ed. G. D. Atkins and L. Morrow; Amherst, Mass.: The University of Massachusetts Press, 1989), 85.

32   Rabinowitz, 'Whirl without End,' 84.

33   Rabinowitz, 'Whirl without End,' 85. For another literary theorist who also attempts to reintroduce a historical perspective to critical literary studies, see Hans Robert Jauss, *Toward an Aesthetic of Reception* (trans. T. Bahti; vol. 2 of *Theory and History of Literature*, ed. W. Godzich and J. Schulte-Sasse; Minneapolis: University of Minnesota Press, 1982), esp. chapter 1, 'Literary History as a Challenge to Literary Theory.'

34   Mark Allan Powell, *What is Narrative Criticism?* (GBS; Minneapolis: Fortress Press, 1990), 6–21.

communities of the evangelists, or even a compositional history of the Gospels themselves. The historical-critical method assumes a referential function of texts. The second model is narrative criticism,[35] which is a synchronic approach to the text with the goal of describing the narrative qualities of the text itself. Rabinowitz's narrative audience is indicative of this model. The Gospels are read only in light of the narratives that they present; the narrative world is the only 'context' in which the text is interpreted. This narrative method assumes a poetic function of texts.

An audience-critical approach, such as Rabinowitz's authorial audience, requires a third category, and it can be placed in the broader umbrella of reception theory (*Rezeptionsgeschichte*).[36] This model is characterized by both reading a text in its final form (synchronic) and understanding the text in light of the audience/readers' historical context (diachronic).[37] The goal of audience criticism is to understand a text in relation to the literary, social, and historical contexts of its readers, and in the case of authorial audience this is the context when the text was first produced. Thus, an audience-critical approach is a contextual reading of the Gospels and assumes a rhetorical function of texts.[38]

It is important that the concept 'authorial audience' is not confused with 'authorial intent' nor seen as a guise for 'authorial intent.' Authorial intent has to do with somehow making the leap from the text to the mind of the author, speculating as to the psychological intentions of the author, which is a dubious claim that has rightly been critiqued.[39] Authorial audience shifts the perspective from author to audience, emphasizing the communicative nature of the text and focusing on the reception of the text. But even here, an authorial audience approach does not presume the ability to know the mental processes of an actual 'flesh-and-blood' audience, nor the concrete circumstances of a text's 'community.' As already stated, the authorial audience is a hypothetical construct, and perhaps it can be better understood in terms of a readership profile. This audience profile is constructed on the basis of a close reading of the text in relation to comparative (literary) material and the larger socio-cultural

---

35   I have adjusted Powell's category here. Powell uses the larger category of literary studies, which he divides into narrative criticism and reader-response criticism.

36   Jauss, *Toward an Aesthetic of Reception*, chapter 1.

37   See Paul de Man's introduction to Jauss, *Toward an Aesthetic of Reception*, xiv, who points out both dimensions of 'synchrony' and 'diachrony' in Jauss's reception theory.

38   For an example of an authorial audience approach to New Testament narratives, see Charles H. Talbert, *Reading Luke-Acts in its Mediterranean Milieu* (NovTSup 107; Leiden: Brill, 2003). See especially Chapter One, 'On Reading Luke and Acts,' in which Talbert also situates audience criticism in the history of New Testament interpretation and describes this approach.

39   W. K. Wimsatt and M. C. Beardsley, 'The Intentional Fallacy,' in *On Literary Intention* (ed. D. Newton-deMolina; Edinburgh: Edinburgh University Press, 1976), 1–13.

milieu. Thus, when I contend that an ancient audience would hear or read Matthew's dreams in one manner or another, I am speaking of a theoretical audience profiled from data drawn from the literary and cultural context of the ancient Mediterranean world. I am not concerned with authorial intent; I am concerned with a contextualized reading of the Matthean dreams.

Therefore, my approach to the dreams in Matthew's Gospel is an audience-critical approach, aiming to read/hear the Matthean dream reports and references in the same manner as Matthew's authorial audience.[40] More simply, I attempt to answer the question, 'How would the authorial audience have heard Matthew's narration of dreams?' This question is answered by: (1) understanding the social and literary contexts of dreams in the Greco-Roman world (the time and culture of the production of Matthew's Gospel), and (2) reading Matthew's dreams against the 'horizon of expectations'[41] that these contexts imply. The assumption is that Matthew writes to be understood, and the larger social and literary conventions of his time provide the commonality with his audience upon which communication takes place.

Overview of this Study

In order to understand the beliefs, values, and expectations that an ancient audience would bring to the dreams in Matthew's Gospel, it is important to describe both the social and literary contexts of ancient dreams. In Chapter Two, I will explore the social context of ancient dreams by examining the ancient practices and theories associated with dreams as dealt with in Greco-Roman, Jewish, and Christian sources. The purpose of this chapter is to describe, in general, the values and beliefs about dreams in antiquity. In Chapters Three and Four, I analyze the literary context of ancient dreams. The purpose of Chapter Three is to demonstrate dreams as a literary convention in ancient literature by considering the form of literary dreams, the rhetoric of dreams and the literary inventiveness of dreams. In Chapter Four, I will analyze the function of specific dream narratives from a sampling of ancient histories, biographies and fiction. Within the social and literary context of dreams in antiquity, Chapter Five will offer a reading of the dream reports and references in Matthew's Gospel, seeking to answer this question: What

40 For an authorial audience approach to Matthew as a whole, see Warren Carter, *Matthew: Storyteller, Interpreter, Evangelist* (Peabody, Massachusetts: Hendrickson Publishers, 1996), esp. 15–118. See also Graham N. Stanton, *A Gospel for a New People: Studies in Matthew* (Louisville: Westminster/John Knox Press, 1993), 71–76.

41 The phrase 'horizon of expectations' comes from Jauss, *Toward an Aesthetic of Reception*, esp. 22–34.

meaning(s) and significance(s) would the authorial audience construct for the dreams in Matthew's narrative? Chapter Six will summarize the results of reading Matthew's dreams as an authorial audience and sketch implications for further research. This monograph also includes an appendix that considers Matthew's transfiguration (17.1-9) as a dream-vision report.

Chapter Two

THE ANCIENT, SOCIAL CONTEXT OF DREAMS

The purpose of this chapter is to describe in general the social context of ancient dreams and the subsequent kinds of values and beliefs an ancient audience would bring to a text that narrates dreams. This description is achieved by: (1) illustrating the ancient practice of dreams; and (2) surveying Greco-Roman theories and classifications of dreams.

The Practice of Dreams

The *practice of dreams* is shorthand for the practical role dreams and their interpretation played in the ancient Mediterranean world. This socio-cultural function of dreams is a feature of that aspect of Greco-Roman religion usually designated 'popular religion' or 'popular piety.'[1] But, as Hans-Josef Klauck advises, 'It is not so easy to demarcate from other religious spheres the phenomena which these concepts are intended to identify.'[2] Thus, he includes in his study of popular piety in the Greco-Roman world such topics as astrology, the healing cult of Asclepius, magic, oracles, and dreams.[3]

Popular religion, however, was not simply about humanity's relation to the divine. The phenomenon of popular religion in antiquity also included aspects that can be considered 'scientific'; that is, ancient religion

---

1   For those who treat this aspect of Greco-Roman religion, see Martin P. Nilsson, *Greek Popular Religion* (ACLS New Series 1; New York: Columbia University Press, 1940), 3–139; André-Jean Festugière, *Personal Religion Among the Greeks* (Berkeley: University of California Press, 1954), 1–142; Luther H. Martin, *Hellenistic Religions: An Introduction* (Oxford: Oxford University Press, 1987), 35–57; Hans-Josef Klauck, *The Religious Context of Early Christianity: A Guide to Graeco-Roman Religions* (Studies of the New Testament and Its World; trans. Brian McNeil; Edinburgh: T & T Clark, 2000), 153–249; Everett Ferguson, *Backgrounds of Early Christianity* (3d ed.; Grand Rapids: Eerdmans, 2003), 213–243. See also the following studies that incorporate Greco-Roman piety in their descriptions of 'paganism': Ramsay MacMullen, *Paganism in the Roman Empire* (New Haven: Yale University Press, 1981), 1–137; and Robin Lane Fox, *Pagans and Christians* (New York: Alfred A. Knopf, 1989), 27–418.

2   Klauck, *The Religious Context of Early Christianity*, 153.

3   Klauck, *The Religious Context of Early Christianity*, 153–249.

informed an understanding of the world and how that world could be manipulated or managed by humans.[4] Popular religion was an expression of humanity's relation both to the divine and to the world, and dreams played an important role in both of these relations. To demonstrate this function of dreams, the following discussion is organized around the topics of: (1) dreams and divination, (2) dreams and ancient magic, (3) dreams and Greco-Roman cults, and (4) professional dream interpreters. It should be carefully noted, however, that these categories are heuristic and that in reality they converge, overlap, and often simply represent a different dimension of the same religious phenomenon.

Dreams and Divination

A central element of Greco-Roman religion was divination (Greek μαντεία or μαντική; Latin *divinatio*). Though Cicero could define divination simply as 'the foresight and knowledge of future events',[5] the assumptions and beliefs underlying divination were that the gods granted this knowledge or insight through various signs. This conviction is articulated by Xenophon in reference to Socrates' respect for the gods:

> Those who believe in divination (μαντικὴν) consult birds and prophetic sayings (φήμαις) and portents (σύμβολα) and sacrifices. For seekers of divination suppose not that the birds or chance encounters know what is advantageous (τὰ συμφέροντα), but that the gods signal (σημαίνειν) for them what is advantageous through them; and Socrates held the same.[6]

Xenophon gives further expression of this sentiment in his *Symposium* through the character Hermogenes:

> Both Greeks and barbarians believe that the gods know everything both present and to come; at any rate, all cities and all races ask the gods, by the diviner's art (διὰ μαντικῆς), for advice as to what to do and what to avoid .... Well, these gods, omniscient and omnipotent, feel so friendly toward me that their watchfulness over me never lets me out of their sight night or day, no matter where I am going or what business I have in view. They know the results also that will follow any act; and so they send to me as messengers omens of sounds (φήμας), dreams (ἐνύπνια), and birds, and thus indicate (σημαίνουσιν) what I ought to do and what I ought not

---

4   Mary Beard, introduction to 'Diviners and Divination at Rome,' by John North, in *Pagan Priests: Religion and Power in the Ancient World* (ed. M. Beard and J. North; London: Duckworth, 1990), 49; and Patricia Cox Miller, *Dreams in Late Antiquity* (Princeton: Princeton University Press, 1994), 6–7.

5   Cicero, *Div.* 1.1 (Falconer, LCL).

6   Xenophon, *Mem.* 1.1.3 (modified trans. of Bonnette; text Smith); see also Xenophon, *Apol.* 11–14.

to do. And when I do their bidding. I never regret it; on the other hand, I
have before now disregarded them and have been punished for it.[7]

As indicated by Xenophon, the various expressions of divination included
dreams. In Plutarch's *The Dinner of the Seven Wise Men*, dreams are
referred to as the 'most ancient and respected form of divination.'[8] This
assessment is mythically portrayed by Aeschylus, who presents
Prometheus as the one who established the 'many ways of divination'
(τρόπους πολλούς μανικῆς), the first of which was the interpretation of
dreams (κἄκρινα πρῶτος ἐξ ὀνειράτων ἃ χρὴ ὕπαρ γενέσθαι).[9]
Euripides credits the goddess Earth (Χθών) with having invented dream
divination in response to Apollo's takeover of the Pythian oracle.[10] This
situation seems to be reflected in the tradition passed on by Pausanias:
'Except those whom they say Apollo inspired of old, none of the seers
(οὐδεὶς μάντεων) uttered oracles, but they were good at explaining
dreams (ὀνείρατα ἐξηγήσασθαι) and interpreting the flights of birds and
the entrails of victims.'[11]
    In addition to these mythical and legendary accounts, the conception of
dreams as a form of divination can be illustrated further by two other
examples. First, the diviner[12] Artemidorus places the production of his
handbook on dream interpretation, *Onirocritica*, in the larger practice of
divination. He states that one of the purposes of writing his *Onirocritica* is
to 'join battle against those who are trying to do away with divination in
general or its various aspects, bringing to bear my own experience and the
proof furnished by the fulfillment of actual dreams, which could prove
capable of holding its ground against all comers.'[13] Artemidorus is acutely

---

7 Xenophon, *Sym.* 4.48 (Todd, LCL); see also Xenophon, *Eq. mag.* 9.9.
8 Plutarch, *Sept. sap. conv.* 159a (Babbitt, LCL). Cf. Tertullian, *An.* 46.11, who states
that Epicharmus and Philochorus the Athenian 'assigned the very highest place among
divinations to dreams' (*ANF* 3.225).
9 Aeschylus, *Prom.* 484–485.
10 Euripides, *Iph. taur.* 1259–68. The story continues, of course, with Apollo gaining
control over dream divination and thus becoming the patron god of divination. Cf. the
magical text of *PGM* I. 327–331 (Betz; text Preisendanz):

> And when [Apollo] comes, ask him what you wish, about the art of prophecy (περὶ
> μαντείας), about divination with epic verses, about the sending dreams (περὶ
> ὀνειροπομπείας), about obtaining revelations in dreams (περὶ ὀνειραιτησίας),
> about interpretation of dreams (περὶ ὀνειροκριτιᾶς), about causing disease, about
> everything that is part of magical knowledge.

11 Pausanias, *Descr.* 1.34.4 (Jones and Ormerod, LCL).
12 Though Artemidorus is known primarily as a professional dream interpreter,
tradition has it that he also wrote another book on the general practice of divination; see
Robert J. White, introduction to *The Interpretation of Dreams* by Artemidorus (trans. Robert
J. White; Noyes Classical Studies; Park Ridge, New Jersey: Noyes Press, 1975), 1.
13 Artemidorus, *Onir.* 1. praef (White).

aware of how divination is being undermined and discredited by less respectable practitioners of divination, such as those who divine by 'dice, from cheese, from sieves, from forms and figures, from palms, from dishes, and from necromancy.'[14] For Artemidorus the only true forms of divination come from 'utterances of sacrificers, bird augurs, astrologers, observers of strange phenomena (τερατοσκόπων), dream interpreters (ὀνειροκριτῶν) and soothsayers who examine livers.'[15] Thus, for Artemidorus, his handbook on dream interpretation represented a true expression of divination and a formidable defense against an increasing criticism of divinatory practices.

The other example that situates the phenomenon of dreams within Greco-Roman divination is Cicero's *De divinatione*.[16] Cicero's interlocutor, Quintus, divides divination into two kinds (*genera*), natural and artificial.[17] Artificial divination refers to those divinatory practices that require the art or skill of interpretation and discernment. These forms of divination include, for example, the inspection of entrails, astrology, augury and the general interpretation of omens. Quintus explains that artificial divination is based on 'conjecture, or on deduction from events previously observed and recorded.'[18] Natural divination, on the other hand, is more immediate and derives from the soul's natural connection with the 'divine soul' that orders the cosmos. In another passage, Quintus describes natural divination in this way: 'Therefore the human soul has an inherent power of presaging or of foreknowing infused into it from without, and made a part of it by the will of God.'[19] It is in natural divination that Quintus places dreams, along with those oracles uttered under divine inspiration or ecstasy.

In demonstrating the divinatory power of dreams, Quintus marshals a

---

14 Artemidorus, *Onir.* 2.69 (White).

15 Artemidorus, *Onir.* 2.69 (White; text Pack).

16 *De divinatione* is structured into two books and presented as a dialogue or debate between himself and his brother Quintus. Book 1 represents Quintus's argument for divination, which in essence is a Stoic position. Book 2 is Cicero's response, which is a critique and rejection of divination; this critique will be considered in the second part of this chapter, 'Dream Classifications and Theories.'

It is interesting to note that scholars are beginning to question whether Cicero's position is an outright rejection of divination; see Mary Beard, 'Cicero and Divination: The Formation of a Latin Discourse,' *JRS* 76 (1986): 33–46; Malcolm Schofield, 'Cicero for and against Divination,' *JRS* 76 (1986): 47–65; and Susanne William Rasmussen, 'Cicero's Stand on Prodigies: A Non-existent Dilemma?' in *Divination and Portents in the Roman World* (ed. R. L. Wildfang and J. Isager; Odense University Classical Studies 21; Odense University Press, 2000), 9–24.

17 Cicero, *Div.* 1.11-12; cf. 1.70-72.

18 Cicero, *Div.* 1.72 (Falconer, LCL).

19 Cicero, *Div.* 1.66 (Falconer, LCL).

variety of examples from literature, history, and personal experience.[20] The following provides a sampling of his illustrations. First, Quintus recounts the legend about the Sicilian tyrant Phalaris.[21] It is said that Phalaris' mother dreamed that the statue of Mercury in her house poured blood from a bowl in its right hand, and the blood completely covered the floor of the house. Quintus confirms the consensus that the dream of Phalaris' mother rightly portended the extreme cruelty of her son. Another illustration of dream divination comes from the military campaign of Hannibal.[22] After his occupation of the city of Lacinium, Hannibal wanted to take with him one of the golden columns of the temple of Juno. On the night before leaving, the goddess Juno appeared to Hannibal in a dream and warned him against taking the golden column, threatening in turn to take away the vision of his good eye. Hannibal heeded the dream and did not carry off the temple column. Finally, Quintus relates his own dream concerning Cicero.[23] While serving as the proconsul of Asia, Quintus dreamed that Cicero was riding a horse toward a large river. Suddenly, Cicero and the horse plunged into the river disappearing from sight. A moment later, however, Cicero re-emerges still on the horse and reaches the opposite side of the river 'with a cheerful countenance.'[24] As the meaning of the dream was not readily apparent, Quintus consulted expert dream interpreters, who accurately predicted Cicero's subsequent banishment from Rome and his eventual return.[25]

In light of these examples, a couple of brief observations about dream divination are offered. First, not all divinatory dreams are about foretelling the future. Hannibal's dream represents a direct command or warning by the deity. Much of the inscriptional evidence of dreams in the ancient Mediterranean world reflects this dimension of dream divination.[26] Second, despite Quintus' sharp delineation between natural and artificial divination, dream divination blurs this distinction. Quintus argues that dreams are a type of natural divination, but some dreams – like his own of Cicero – require the help of expert diviners who practice the art of dream interpretation.[27] Artemidorus' *Onirocritica* demonstrates fully this artificial quality of dream divination. In an empirical, scientific-

---

20   Cicero, *Div.* 1.39-71.
21   Cicero, *Div.* 1.46.
22   Cicero, *Div.* 1.48-49.
23   Cicero, *Div.* 1.58.
24   Cicero, *Div.* 1.58 (Falconer, LCL).
25   See Falconer's note (LCL), p. 288, n. 2.
26   See Gil H. Renberg. ' "Commanded By the Gods": An Epigraphical Study of Dreams and Visions in Greek and Roman Religious Life' (Ph.D. diss., Duke University, 2003).
27   In another example of dream divination, Quintus relates how the mother of Dionysius, the tyrant of Sicily, consulted professional diviners in Sicily called the 'Galeotae' about the meaning of her dream; Cicero, *Div.* 1.39.

like manner, Artemidorus carefully builds upon the respected works of former dream interpreters, incorporates the many insights of contemporary interpreters whom he has personally interviewed, and relies upon his own experiences.[28] It is a deductive endeavor with the purpose of perfecting the skill of dream interpretation. Thus, whether knowledge about the future or about the will of the gods, it was believed that dreams were one means of divine communication, and this form of divination may or may not require the art of interpretation.

The Jewish scriptures reflect this divinatory understanding of dreams and present dreams as an accepted form of divination in Israel's religious heritage.[29] In the stories of the ancestors, God often communicates, guides, and protects through dreams: Abimelech's dream (Gen. 20.3-7), Jacob's dreams (Gen. 28.10-22; 31.10-13), Laban's dream (Gen. 31.24), and Joseph, who not only receives dreams but also interprets them (Gen. 37.5-10; 40–42). In Numbers 12.6-8, it is explained that God communicates to prophets through visions and dreams, though these usual forms of communication are not necessary with Moses, to whom God speaks face to face. The prophet-judge Samuel hears God calling in a dream at Shiloh (1 Sam. 3.1-21). After Samuel dies, king Saul inquires of the Lord before a battle, 'but the Lord did not answer him, not by dreams, or by Urim, or prophets' (1 Sam. 28.6; NRSV). The text assumes that these are customary forms of divine communication, but when they prove ineffective, which is probably intended to underscore God's rejection of Saul,[30] Saul then seeks forms of divination that are prohibited.[31] Gideon, on the other hand, receives divine counsel through a dream before his battle with the Midianites and consequently defeats his enemy (Judg. 7.9-16). The prophet Joel foretells of a renewed community that will experience again God's presence through prophecy, dreams, and visions (2.28). Daniel's ability to interpret dreams and visions is a gift from God (1.17); he also is the recipient of divine dreams and visions (chs. 7–12). In general, the Jewish scriptures present dreams as a legitimate form of divine communication.

The Jewish scriptures are critical of dream divination, however, when the practice compromises Israel's monotheistic faith. Prophecy and

---

28 Artemidorus, *Onir.* 1. praef. See also Claes Blum, *Studies in the Dream-Book of Artemidorus* (Uppsala: Almqvist & Wiksells, 1939), 1–52; White, introduction to *The Interpretation of Dreams*, 6–10; and S. R. F. Price, 'The Future of Dreams: From Freud to Artemidorus,' *Past and Present* 113 (1986): 24–28.

29 For a discussion of divination and ancient Israel, see Frederick H. Cryer, *Divination in Ancient Israel and its Near Eastern Environment: A Socio-Historical Investigation* (JSOTSup 142; Sheffield: JSOT Press, 1994), 229–305.

30 Cryer, *Divination in Ancient Israel*, 265.

31 Cf. Deut. 18.9-14, where an extended list of forbidden forms of divination is given, but it does not include dream divination.

dreams are paired in Deuteronomy 13.1-5, but the passage warns against heeding the counsel of 'prophets or those who divine by dreams' if their message leads the people to serve other gods. Jeremiah speaks against prophets whose dreams 'make my people forget my name' (23.23-32; cf. 29.8-9) and so includes dreams in the list of forbidden forms of divination (27.9). Zechariah criticizes the leaders of Judah because they have allowed the teraphim, diviners, and dreamers to practice their divination in isolation from the Lord (10.1-3). These negative assessments of dream divination are related to a violation of monotheism. Their critique is leveled against those who misuse dream divination, not against dreams *per se* but as a means of divine communication.[32]

This section has attempted to demonstrate in general terms the ancient understanding that dreams and their interpretation were one form of divination. The various practices of dreams described in the following sections assume this basic belief about dreams. Moreover, the Jewish and Christian traditions follow the precedent of their scriptures: dreams are accepted as a legitimate form of divine communication, but suspicion and criticism may arise when dream divination is practiced in a pagan or heterodox context. Examples of such criticisms, where applicable, will be offered in the following sections.

Dreams and Ancient Magic

As a particular expression of religion in the Greco-Roman world and as a specific aspect of divination,[33] ancient magic was also associated with the practice of dreams. This association is exhibited most clearly in the *Greek Magical Papyri*, which contain two types of dream rituals or spells: (1) the dream-request ritual (ὀνειραιτητά) and (2) the dream-sending ritual (ὀνειροπομπός, ὀνειροπομπία). In the former ritual, the practitioner conjures revelatory dreams for him or herself; in the latter one, the

---

32   Scott Noegel, 'Dreams and Dream Interpreters in Mesopotamia and in the Hebrew Bible [Old Testament],' in *Dreams: A Reader on Religious, Cultural, and Psychological Dimensions of Dreaming* (ed. K. Bulkeley; New York: Palgrave, 2001), 59–60.

33   Unlike scholarship in the nineteenth and early twentieth centuries, modern scholarship recognizes that magic in its ancient context is not antithetical to religion but represents one end of a spectrum of religious practices. See Naomi Janowitz, *Magic in the Roman World: Pagans, Jews and Christians* (Religion in the First Christian Centuries; London: Routledge, 2001), 1–8; Marvin Meyer and Richard Smith, eds., *Ancient Christian Magic: Coptic Texts of Ritual Power* (San Francisco: HarperSanFrancisco, 1994), 1–9; Klauck, *The Religious Context of Early Christianity*, 215–18; Hans Dieter Betz, 'Magic and Mystery in the Greek Magical Papyri,' in *Magika Hiera: Ancient Greek Magic and Religion* (ed. C. A. Faraone and D. Obbink; Oxford: Oxford University Press, 1991), 244–259; Robert L. Fowler, 'Greek Magic, Greek Religion,' in *Oxford Readings in Greek Religion* (ed. R. Buxton; New York: Oxford University Press, 2000), 317–343; David E. Aune, 'Magic in Early Christianity,' *ANRW* 23.1.1510-1516.

practitioner invokes dreams to appear to another person for some specified task. Though a few magical rituals are general spells and claim the ability to do both,[34] dream rituals are for the most part specifically designed for either requesting a dream or sending a dream.

The primary purpose of dream-request rituals is the revelation of some knowledge, information, or advice. Consider the following example:

> Request for a dream oracle (ὀνειραιτητά), a request which is always used. Formula to be spoken to the day lamp: 'NAIENCHRĒ NAIENCHRĒ, mother of fire and water, you are the one who rises before, ARCHENTECHTHA; reveal to me concerning the NN matter. If yes, show me a plant and water, but if not, fire and iron, immediately, immediately.'[35]

The practitioner of this magical ritual presumably would need advice or information that is easily answered by 'yes' or 'no.' It is not certain whether the practitioner would receive his or her answer through a symbolic dream, in which the symbols of 'yes' (plant/water) or 'no' (fire/iron) would somehow be played out, or by the appearance of the goddess ('mother of fire and water'), whereby she appears in a form corresponding to the appropriate answer.[36]

Most of the dream-request rituals are much more elaborate and do not restrict the requested information to a simple 'yes' or 'no' but leave it open-ended with the formulaic 'reveal to me concerning the NN matter.'[37] The magical ritual entitled 'Dream-Request from Besas' is a case in point.[38] The ritual first calls for the practitioner to draw a picture of the god Besa, which is found 'in the beginning of the book.'[39] The figure is to be drawn presumably on the hand[40] with ink made from the 'blood of a white dove, likewise of a crow, also sap of the mulberry, juice of single-

---

34 For example, *PGM* IV. 2442–2621 (Betz): 'It inflicts sickness excellently and destroys powerfully, sends dreams beautifully, accomplishes dream revelations marvelously and in its many demonstrations has been marveled at for having no failure in these matters' (lines 2443–6). See also, *PGM* IV. 2006–2125 (lines 2076–81).

35 *PGM* VII. 250–254 (Betz).

36 Cf. also *PGM* XXIIb. 27–31 (Betz): '[If] the petition I have made is appropriate, [show] me water and a grove; if otherwise, show me water and a stone'; and XXIIb. 32–35 (Betz): 'If this matter has been granted to me, show me a courtesan; otherwise, a soldier.'

37 See *PGM* IV. 2501–2505; IV. 3172–3208 (line 3207); VII. 222–249 (line 247); VII. 359–369 (line 369); VII. 478–490 (line 479); VII. 703–726 (line 714); VII. 740–755 (line 744); VII. 795–854 (line 36; cf. 841); VII. 1009–1016 (line 1015); XII. 144–152 (line 152).

38 *PGM* VII. 222–249. Cf. the parallel dream-request ritual VIII. 64–110.

39 Line 249 (Betz). The picture is missing from the papyri, but the parallel spell VIII. 64–110 provides a description of the Besa figure to be drawn: 'a naked man, standing, having a diadem on his head, and in his right hand a sword that by means of a bent [arm] rests on his neck, and in the left hand a wand' (lines 105–109 [Betz]).

40 Once again, based on *PGM* VIII. 64–110.

stemmed wormwood, cinnabar, and rainwater.'[41] After the drawing of
Besa, the practitioner then wraps his or her hand with a black cloth of Isis.
The prayer-formula, which is quite lengthy, is to be spoken to a lamp and
ends with a petition, where the specific request is to be inserted: 'Come,
lord, reveal to me concerning the NN matter, without deceit, without
treachery, immediately, immediately; quickly, quickly.'[42]

The deities petitioned by the dream-request rituals vary greatly. We find
Hermes – the classical Homeric dream-sender – and the Greco-Egyptian
oracle god Besa addressed in some rituals,[43] but for the most part these
dream-request rituals follow the magical custom of addressing the divine
with many names, particularly in the manner of the *voces magicae*. For
example, the spoken prayer-formula of *PGM* VII. 359–369 states:

> SACHNOUNE PAĒMALIGOTĒRĒĒNCH, the one who shakes, who thunders,
> who has swallowed the serpent, surrounds the moon, and hour by hour
> raises the disk of the sun, 'CHTHETHŌNI' is your name. I ask you, lords of
> the gods, SĒTH CHRĒPS: reveal to me concerning the things I wish.[44]

It should also be noted that dream-request rituals are sometimes
connected with necromancy, as in the case of *PGM* IV. 2006–2125.

Although the dream-request rituals may vary in their divine addressees,
specific instructions and ceremonial materials, there are some recurring
features found in these magical spells. First, many of the dream-request
rituals include the use of a lamp; in most cases, the prayer-formula is to be
spoken to a lamp.[45] The prayer-formula may be recited seven times,[46] or
in one case it is simply repeated 'until [the lamp] is extinguished.'[47] In
another dream-request ritual, the prayer-formula is written on papyrus
and then placed under the lamp. The most detailed dream-request ritual
utilizing a lamp is *PGM* IV. 3172–3208.[48] The lamp cannot be painted red
and is to be filled with pure olive oil. While the lamp is facing east, the
practitioner recites the prescribed prayer seven times. Before going to
sleep, the practitioner places the lamp on a tripod made of reeds, which
has undergone its own ritualistic construction.[49] The use of lamp magic is

---

41   Lines 223–5 (Betz).
42   Lines 247–8 (Betz).
43   For Hermes, see *PGM* V. 370–446; VII. 664–685; XVIIb. 1–23. For Bes (or Besa,
Besas), see *PGM* VII. 222–49; VIII. 64–110. Cf. also the graffito inscription that describes Bes
as the 'wholly truthful dream-giver and oracle-giver' (Renberg, Test. No. 21).
44   Lines 365–9 (Betz).
45   *PGM* IV. 3172–3208; VII. 222–249; VII. 250–254; VII. 359–569; VII. 664–685; XXIIb.
27–31; and XXIIb. 32–35.
46   *PGM* IV. 3172–3208; VII. 359–369; VII. 664–685.
47   *PGM* XXIIb. 27–31 (Betz).
48   Cf. the use of the lamp in the dream-sending ritual *PGM* XII. 121–143.
49   Lines 3173–3186, 3196–3197.

not unique to dream-request rituals, but its prominent use in these spells is no doubt related to the shared nocturnal existence of dreams and lamps.[50]

A second frequent element found in the dream-request rituals is the placing of an item on or beside the head of the practitioner as he or she sleeps. The most common item is some type of branch as in *PGM* IV. 3172–3208, which simply directs, 'let the head of the practitioner be crowned with olive branches.'[51] Sometimes the request or the divine names are written on the leaves of the branch[52] or a strip of linen, which is then wrapped around the branch.[53] One dream-request ritual places the prayer-formula, which has been written on tin, under the pillow of the practitioner.[54] An explanation of this association of the dream-request ritual and the head is the ancient understanding that the dream figure often stands beside or above the head of the dreamer.[55] This concept is ritually acted out in *PGM* V. 370–446; in this magical ritual, a doll-like figure of Hermes is to be fashioned out of the prescribed ingredients.[56] The practitioner is then to 'let it rest beside your head, and go to sleep after saying the spell without giving an answer to anyone.'[57]

A third common feature of the dream-request rituals is the directive for purity. In several of these magical spells, the practitioner is instructed to be in a state of purity before he or she goes to sleep, such as, 'when you are about to go to sleep, being pure in every respect' (καθάρος ἀπὸ παντός)[58] and 'go to sleep in a pure condition' (ἀγνὸς ὢν κοιμῶ).[59] One ritual calls for the practitioner to be in a state of purity for three days before the sleep of the dream revelation,[60] while another text commands that both the practitioner and the place of sleeping be pure.[61] How this purity is attained is not specified, though one dream-request ritual calls for the

---

50 Samson Eitrem, 'Dreams and Divination in Magical Ritual,' in *Magika Hiera: Ancient Greek Magic and Religion* (ed. C. A. Faraone and D. Obbink; New York: Oxford University Press, 1991), 176.

51 Line 3198 (Betz).

52 *PGM* VII. 1009–1016 (lines 1015–16); VII. 795–845 (lines 801–4, 823–7, 843–5).

53 *PGM* VII. 664–85 (lines 664–6).

54 PGM VII. 740–55. Cf. also *PGM* VII. 478–490, which calls for a strip of tin that has the names of the deities to be placed around the neck of the practitioner.

55 See John S. Hanson, 'Dreams and Visions in the Graeco-Roman World and Early Christianity,' *ANRW* 23.2: 1410. Consider also the title of Frances Flannery-Dailey's study of dreams in antiquity: ' "Standing at the Head of Dreamers": A Study of Dreams in Antiquity' (Ph.D. diss., The University of Iowa, 2000).

56 Cf. the dream-sending rituals *PGM* IV. 1716–1870 and VII. 862–918, which also contain the use of dolls.

57 Lines 498–9.

58 *PGM* VII. 359–369 (line 363) (Betz; text Preisendanz).

59 *PGM* VII. 703–726 (line 725) (Betz; text Preisendanz).

60 *PGM* VII. 740–755 (line 749).

61 *PGM* VII. 795–845 (lines 843–4).

practitioner to cover him or herself with olive oil before sleeping[62] and
another prescribes the burning of incense before lying down.[63] This
concern and custom of purity reflected in dream-request rituals parallels,
and is most likely influenced by, the incubation rites of various Greco-
Roman cults. For example, in his ancient travelogue[64] *Description of
Greece*, Pausanias relates the tradition about incubation at the temple of
Amphairaus in Oropus:

> One who has come to consult Amphairaus is wont first to purify himself
> (καθήρασθαι). The mode of purification (καθάρσιον) is to sacrifice to the
> god, and they sacrifice not only to him but also to all those whose names
> are on the altar.[65]

Lastly, the prayer-formulas of a couple of the dream-request rituals
stipulate or insist that the information or revelation given through the
dream be truthful and comprehensible. We have already quoted the
prayer-formula ending of *PGM* VII. 222–249, which seeks a revelation
'without deceit, without treachery' (αψευστως, ασκανδαλίστως).[66] The
prayer-formula of *PGM* VII. 795–845 emphasizes this concern with
repetitive petitions: 'Hence I call upon you all that you may come quickly
in this night, and reveal to me clearly (σαφῶς) and firmly (βεβαίως),
concerning those matters I desire';[67] and, 'Hence, I call upon you in this
night, and you may reveal all things to me through dreams with accuracy
(κατὰ τοὺς ὕπνους ἐπ' ἀκριβείας).'[68] Corresponding to these ritual texts
is a magical amulet, used no doubt in a dream-request ritual, that has the
inscription, 'counsel me this night in truth [and] with memory' (ἐπ'
ἀληθεία μετὰ μνήμης).[69] These concerns for truthfulness and recollection
reflect some ancient, customary problems with dream divination. First,
dreams could prove to be deceptive or simply insignificant. A passage
from Herodotus provides a helpful illustration.[70] The Persian king,
Xerxes, has a dream that advises him to make war against the Greeks.
Xerxes' counsellor, Artabanus, cautions the king that some dreams are
simply products of the day's thoughts and concerns (i.e., insignificant,

62 *PGM* XII. 190–192.
63 *PGM* V. 370–446.
64 The travelogue was actually a type of ancient literature known as periegetic literature.
For comments and bibliography, see Antony J. S. Spawforth, 'tourism,' *OCD* 1535.
65 Pausanias, *Descr.* 1.34.5 (Jones and Ormerod, LCL). Cf. also the account of
incubation given by Aristophanes, *Plut.* 653–747, which includes, 'we first led him down to
the sea to purify him.' The practice of incubation will be discussed below in connection with
dreams and Greco-Roman cults.
66 Line 246 (Betz; text Preisendanz).
67 Lines 834–6 (Betz; text Preisendanz).
68 Lines 841–2 (Betz; text Preisendanz).
69 *IG* XIV 2413, 16 (text Renberg, Test. No. 30).
70 Herodotus, *Hist.* 7.12.

non-divinatory). Artabanus, however, has the same dream and is therefore convinced of its divine origin. Xerxes leads a campaign against the Greeks only to be defeated. The dream proves to be deceptive, an instance reminiscent of the 'lying dream' of Agamemnon in the *Iliad*.[71] Secondly, the common experience of dreams attests that one can awaken from sleep knowing or sensing that he or she experienced a dream, but the dream is vague or simply cannot be remembered. This common occurrence is actually used by Cicero in his argument against dream divination.[72] These dream-request rituals seek to prevent such potential impediments with the added petitionary qualifiers.

Whereas the purpose of dream-request rituals is limited to revelation, the functions of dream-sending rituals include revelation, imprecation and erotic attraction. The dream-sending ritual entitled 'Zminis of Tentyra's spell for sending dreams'[73] is an example of sending a dream for the purpose of revelation. In this spell the many-named deity is petitioned 'to go to him, NN, this very hour, this very night, and to tell him in a dream such-and-such.'[74] The magical ritual *PGM* IV. 2622–2707 is an example of an imprecatory spell, which is intended to cause harm or injury to another person whether physically or psychologically. One means of this harmful activity is dreams,[75] although the exact manner of how dreams effect the harm is uncertain – nightmares, menacing omens, or the appearance and retributive action of the deity? Interestingly, the ritual also includes a protective charm for the practitioner, so that he or she will be guarded 'from every daimon of the air on the earth and under the earth, and from every angel and phantom and ghostly visitation and enchantment.'[76] Thus, this protective charm ironically guards against the very kind of imprecatory magic being administered by the spell.[77]

The most common purpose for dream-sending rituals is to attract a lover.[78] The love-attracting ritual *PGM* IV. 1716–1870, for example, includes as an addendum the procedure for using an Eros doll that will serve as an 'assistant and supporter and sender of dreams.'[79] The Eros

---

71   Homer, *Il.* 1.1-41.
72   Cicero, *Div.* 2.124.
73   *PGM* XII. 121–143.
74   Lines 139–40 (Betz); cf. lines 131–2, 135–7.
75   Lines 2624–5.
76   Lines 2699–2701.
77   If we include this protective charm as a function of dream magic, then dreams are associated with each of the functional types of magic set forth by Theodor Hopfner: protective, imprecatory, erotic, and revelatory. *Griechisch-ägyptischer Offenbarungszauber* (2 vols.; reprint of Leipzig: H. Haessel, 1921; Amsterdam: A. M. Hakkert, 1974).
78   *PGM* IV. 1716–1870; VII. 407–410; VII. 862–918.
79   Line 1850 (Betz). Cf. the dream-request ritual *PGM* VII. 478–490, where Eros is called upon for general revelation.

doll will send dreams that will accomplish the plan of the practitioner: 'Turn the "soul" of her NN to me NN, so that she may love me, so that she may feel passion for me, so that she may give me what is in her power.'[80] In *PGM* VII. 862–918, the sending of dreams is intended to bring the desired lover to the practitioner's bedroom that very night; it does not matter whether her coming is prompted by a frightful dream or an erotic dream.[81] One dream-sending ritual, which presumably functions for erotic attraction, allows the practitioner to send himself in a dream: 'If you wish to appear to someone at night in dreams (ὀνείροις), say ... : "CHEIAMŌPSEI ERPEBŌTH," let her, NN, whom NN bore, see me in her dreams (ὕπνοις), immediately, immediately; quickly, quickly.'[82]

Dream-sending rituals are less represented in the *Greek Magical Papyri* than dream-request rituals, therefore it is more difficult to identify common elements among the dream-sending rituals. Their lack of common elements, however, are more likely related to their multiplicity of functions – revelation, imprecation, and erotic attraction. The dream-sending rituals do share some elements with dream-request rituals, and I have identified those commonalities in footnotes.

There is one other feature of dream magic that has not been noted: necromancy. There are two magical rituals in the *Greek Magical Papyri* that utilize dreams and necromancy, though both spells are attraction spells and are associated with a certain Pitys;[83] and so they may simply represent parallel versions of the same spell. *PGM* IV. 1928–2005 is a general spell of attraction that conjures a dead spirit to serve 'as helper and avenger for whatever business I crave from him.'[84] In the prayer-formula, the practitioner requests the deity to send the dead spirit at night so that the dead spirit may, 'tell me whatever my mind designs'[85] and, 'reveal to me the what and whence, whereby he now can render me his service.'[86] Thus, the initial encounter between the practitioner and dead spirit takes place via a dream, though the means of the dead spirit's service is unspecified.

Having considered dream magic as expressed in the *Greek Magical Papyri*, we now turn to consider whether there is evidence of Jewish and

---

80   Lines 1807–9 (Betz).
81   Lines 887–9 (Betz). For more discussion of the relationship between eroticism, dreams, and magic, see John J. Winkler, 'The Constraints of Eros,' in *Magika Hiera: Ancient Greek Magic and Religion* (ed. C. A. Faraone and D. Obbink; New York: Oxford University Press, 1991), 214–243, esp. 224–230.
82   *PGM* VII. 407–410 (Betz; text Preisendanz).
83   *PGM* IV. 1928–2005; IV. 2006–2125.
84   Line 1954 (Betz).
85   Line 1971 (Betz).
86   Lines 1977–8 (Betz).

Christian dream magic.[87] The *Greek Magical Papyri* finds something of a counterpart in the Jewish magic book *Sepher Ha-Razim*. The cosmological structure of the book dates from the late third to early fourth century CE, but the magical rituals that are arranged in this structure represent earlier material and are similar in style and content to *PGM* spells.[88] There is only one ritual that is connected with dreams, however, and it has a revelatory function.[89] Unlike the *PGM* rituals that seek a revelation via dreams, this ritual is designed to obtain a revelation for the purpose of interpreting the dreams of others. The spell prescribes rites of purity, such as wearing a new cloak, fasting and burning incense of myrrh and frankincense. The purity rites are followed by a prayer-formula that addresses the forty four angels who are 'in charge of dreaming' and includes the request, 'make known to me what is in the heart of N son of N and what is his desire, and what is the interpretation of his dream and what is his thought.'[90] On the third night, the requested revelation is made know by a vision of a pillar of fire and a cloud in the image of a man. Thus, this revelatory ritual, though not conjuring or sending a dream, petitions angels as dream messengers for the purpose of interpreting dreams.

The magic ritual *PGM* VII. 1009–1016 also addresses traditionally Jewish angels and assumes their function as dream messengers. The spell is entitled 'Dream-divination' and includes the following prayer-formula:

> I call upon [you], Sabaoth, Michael, Raphael and you, [powerful archangel] Gabriel, do not [simply] pass by me [as you bring visions], but let one of you enter and reveal [to me] concerning the NN matter, AIAI ACHĒNĒ IAŌ.

It should be carefully noted that *Greek Magical Papyri* represent the highly syncretistic character of Greco-Roman Egypt, and so it is remains uncertain whether or not this ritual originated in a Jewish context.[91] But this ritual does have affinities with the *Sepher Ha-Razim* spell in that both

---

87   Despite the strong objection to magic in the biblical tradition and patristic literature, Jewish and Christian religious practices included elements that are considered magical. For helpful discussions and bibliographies, see Paul S. Alexander, 'Incantations and Books of Magic,' in *The History of the Jewish People in the Age of Jesus Christ*, by Emil Schürer (rev. and ed. G. Vermes, F. Millar, and M. Goodman; 3 vols.; Edinburgh: T&T Clark, 1986), 3.342-79; and David E. Aune, 'Magic in Early Christianity,' *ANRW* 23.1.1507-1557.

88   Michael A. Morgan, introduction to *Sepher Ha-Razim: The Book of the Mysteries* (trans. Michael A. Morgan; SBLTT 25; Chico, Calif.: Scholars Press, 1983), 8–11.

89   *Sepher Ha-Razim* 2.209-240 (Morgan, 40–42).

90   *Sepher Ha-Razim* 2.229-30 (Morgan, 42).

91   Hans Dieter Betz, 'Introduction to the Greek Magical Papyri,' in *The Greek Magical Papyri in Translation, Including the Demotic Spells* (ed. Hans Dieter Betz; 2d ed.; Chicago: University of Chicago Press, 1992), xliv–xlviii.

are elaborate magical spells that presume the association of traditional Jewish angels with dreams.[92]

The Dead Sea scroll 4Q560 should be mentioned also, though it is badly fragmented and its significance for dream magic is based on emendation.[93] The text is an incantation formula intended to ward off various demons or evil spirits, particularly in relation to childbirth, sickness, sleep, and possibly the security of possessions. The line associated with dream magic is as follows: '. . . and forbidden to disturb by night in dreams or by day in sleep, the male Shrine-spirit and the female Shrine-spirit, breacher-demons of.'[94] Though the term 'sleep' is intact, Penney and Wise emend the text to include dreams. Their emendation is convincingly based on third- to sixth-century Aramaic (Babylonian) incantation bowls and amulets that contain parallels to 4Q560 including charms against the visitation of demons in dreams. The emendation also is informed by the widespread belief, both Ancient Near Eastern and Greco-Roman, that dreams were a means of demonic harm.[95] As Penney and Wise state, '4Q560 is therefore an important witness to the development of magical traditions in the Greco-Roman world generally, and among Second Temple Jews specifically.'[96]

In addition to these Jewish magical texts, there are some instances in Jewish literature where revelatory dreams and visions are obtained as a result of prayer and/or fasting and so can be considered an expression of dream magic. Daniel is the recipient of dreams and visions,[97] some of which were acquired through 'prayer and supplication with fasting and sackcloth and ashes.'[98] The dreams and visions described in *4 Ezra* are often accompanied by prayer and/or fasting.[99] The third dream-vision of *4 Ezra* is especially interesting in that an angel gives Ezra instructions as to how to receive the next vision:

> But if you will let seven days more pass – do not fast during them,
> however; but go into a field of flowers where no house has been built,

92 For a discussion of dreams and angels, see Miller, *Dreams in Late Antiquity*, 59–65.

93 This discussion of 4Q560 is based on Douglas L. Penney and Michael O. Wise, 'By the Power of Beelzebub: An Aramaic Incantation Formula from Qumran (4Q560),' *JBL* 113 (1994): 627–650.

94 4Q560 I, 5 (Penney and Wise, 'By the Power of Beelzebub,' 632).

95 See above discussion of *PGM* IV. 2622–2707. See also references listed in Penney and Wise, 'By the Power of Beelzebub,' 642, nn. 65 and 67.

96 Penney and Wise, 'By the Power of Beelzebub,' 649.

97 Though the discussion thus far has concentrated on dreams, it should be noted that in antiquity dreams and waking visions were understood as substantially the same: one could receive a vision while asleep or awake. The similarity of dreams and visions, at least their literary represenation, will be further discussed in the appendix.

98 Dan 9.3 (NRSV); cf. also 10.2-3.

99 *4 Ezra* 3.1-3ff; 5.20-22ff; and 6.35-37ff.

and eat only of the flowers of the field, and taste no meat and drink no
wine, but eat only flowers, and pray to the Most High continually – then
I will come and talk to you.[100]

The dream-visions of Enoch are preceded by his recitation of the
Watcher's memorial prayer and petitions.[101] Though these texts lack the
elaborate rituals associated with the dream magic of the *Greek Magical
Papyri*, they do present an association of religious acts (prayer and
fasting) with the reception of dreams, which in the broader Greco-Roman
context can be considered an aspect of dream magic.

The widespread practice of dream magic in the Greco-Roman world is
also attested, and sharply criticized, in Christian apologetics and polemics.
As a part of his argument for the immortality of the soul and resurrection,
Justin Martyr asks his pagan readers to consider the various practices of
divination including 'sent-dreams and [daemon]-attendants that are
summoned by the *magoi*' (οἱ λεγόμενοι παρὰ τοῖς μάγοις
ὀνειροπομποὶ καὶ πάρεδροι).[102] Tertullian characterizes pagan diviners
as magicians who practice necromancy, perform deceptive miracles and
'put dreams into people's minds by the power of the angels and demons
whose aid they have invited.'[103] Irenaeus describes the practices of certain
heresies in terms of magic. The followers of Simon Magus are said to
practice the magical arts of exorcisms, incantations, love-charms, spells,
attendants (*paredri*), and sent-dreams (*oniropompi*).[104] Carpocrates are
described in similar terms; they perform incantations, love-charms,
attendants (*paredri*), and sent-dreams (*oniropompi*).[105] As the *Greek
Magical Papyri* demonstrate, a common feature of Greco-Roman magic
includes sent-dreams which can utilize attendants and facilitate love
charms.

Eitrem states that such disparaging comments betray the fact 'that there
were Christians who believed in mantic dreams without reservation.'[106]
Two observations are needed in order to qualify such a categorical
statement. First, one must take into account the rhetoric of magic. The
accusation of magic was typical of ancient polemic and often included

---

100   *4 Ezra* 9.23-25 (Metzger, *OTP*). For a fascinating review of the association of
narcotic flowers, sleep, and dreams in antiquity, see Flannery-Dailey, 'Standing at the Heads
of Dreamers,' 217–18.

101   *1 En.* 13.7-8.

102   Justin, 1 *Apol.* 18.3 (text Marcovich). For the role of daemon-attendants in dream
magic, see Eitrem, 'Dreams and Divination in Magical Ritual,' 180–1.

103   Tertullian, *Apol.* 23 (*ANF* 3.37).

104   Irenaeus, *Haer.* 1.23.4.

105   Irenaeus, *Haer.* 1.25.3.

106   Eitrem, 'Dreams and Divination in Magical Ritual,' 182.

stereotypical language.[107] Thus, the descriptions of heretical practices in terms of magic cannot be taken at face value. Second, in terms of dream magic, the descriptions are consistently sent-dreams; there is no accusation of requested-dreams. Sent-dreams may simply be part of the rhetoric of magic, but the absence of requested-dreams could suggest the acceptance of this form of dream magic. In the *Shepherd of Hermas*, a revelation is requested through prayer and fasting and is granted in a dream.[108] The martyr Perpetua is asked by her brother to request a vision from God so that it may be known whether she will be released or martyred. Perpetua consents and prays to God for a vision, which is granted in the form of a dream.[109] Following the Jewish tradition, these revelatory dreams are obtained through the ritualistic activities of prayer and/or fasting, which in the Greco-Roman context can be considered magical.[110] Once again, within the context of paganism and heresy dream magic is routinely condemned by Christian writers, but within the context of proto-orthodoxy aspects of dream magic may have existed.

As stated in the beginning of our discussion of the practice of dreams, it is important to recognize the vague distinction between magic, divination and cultic practices in the Greco-Roman world. What is condemned as magic by one group is simply the religious practices of another group.[111] The elements of dream divination and magic as discussed find expression in the cultic activities of the Greco-Roman world.

Dreams and Greco-Roman Cults

In his *Laws*, Plato bemoans the situation of his time in which cults, temples and altars were easily established by anyone at any place and any time; and he specifically mentions dreams (ὄνειροι) and visions (φάσματα) as the cause of this unchecked escalation of assorted cults and their accompanying dedicatory gifts.[112] Plato's description of this association of dreams and visions with cultic activity is illustrated and supported by an abundance of inscriptions as well as literary accounts. We will begin this study of dreams and cults by reviewing accounts of how certain cults were established or introduced based on a dream.

---

107   See Janowitz, *Magic in the Roman World*, 9–26; and Mihwa Choi, 'Chrisitanity, Magic, and Difference: Name-Calling and Resistance between the Lines in *Contra Celsum*,' *Semeia* 79 (1997): 75–92.

108   Herm. *Vis.* 3.1.1-2; also cf. 2.2.1.

109   *Passion of Perpetua and Felicitas*, 4.1-2, 10.

110   See Fox, *Pagans and Christians*, 335–6.

111   Janowitz, *Magic in the Roman World*, 16–17; see also Alan F. Segal, 'Hellenistic Magic: Some Questions,' in *Studies in Gnosticism and Hellenistic Religions* (ed. R. Van Den Brock and M. J. Vermaseren; Leiden: E. J. Brill, 1981), 349–75.

112   Plato, *Leg.* 909E-910A.

Dating from the fourth or third century B.C.E., an inscription from the city of Priene relates how a certain Philios was commanded in a dream to establish the cult of Naulochos, a local hero:

> While sleeping, Philios, a Cypriot from Salamis and son of Ariston, saw a dream (ὄναρ): Naulochos and the Thesmophoroi, chaste mistresses in white apparel. And in threefold visions (ὄψεσι) they commanded him to worship Naulochos as patron hero of the city and pointed out the place for his shrine. Because of this, Philios established the cult of Naulochos.[113]

Such an establishment of a hero cult is reminiscent of the interpretative comments of Artemidorus. He states that if one sees in a dream a hero or heroine who is 'downcast, unattractive, and small,' the dream signifies the need to honor that hero 'through the institution of a cult.'[114]

Another quite lengthy inscription from the late second or early first century B.C.E at Philadelphia narrates the establishment and regulations of a private – or associational – cult.[115] According to the inscription, Zeus gave the cultic regulations (παραγγέλματα) to a certain Dionysius in his sleep (καθ' ὕπνον). These regulations included, 'the performance of the purifications, the cleansings, and the mysteries, in accordance with both the ancestral customs and what has now been written.'[116] In addition to Zeus, the shrine also included a number of altars dedicated to traditional deities and divinized abstractions (e.g., Arete, Hygieia, Agathe Tyche, Agathos Daimon, and others). Barton and Horsley contend that the inscription moves beyond a simple reconstitution of previous cultic activity: 'it bears witness to the establishment of what is substantially a new cult,' and, 'the dream provides the sanction for these alterations.'[117]

Found within the precincts of the Sarapis sanctuary at Thessalonika, an inscription dating from the first or second century C.E. recounts how the

---

113   *IPriene* 196 (text Renberg, Cat. No. 387; modified translation from F. T. van Straten, 'Daikrates' Dream: A Votive Relief from Kos, and some other kat'onar Dedications,' *BaBesch* 51 (1976): 15).

114   Artemidorus, *Onir.* 2.69 (White). The inscription and Artemidorus' comments do have differences. The inscription recounts a command, while Artemidorus' comments only deal with symbolic dreams. We will discuss these different categories of dreams and Artemidorus' particular concerns in Part 2 of this chapter.

115   *SIG*³ 985. Text, translation, and discussion of this inscription is provided by S. C. Barton and G. H. R. Horsley, 'A Hellenistic Cult Group and the New Testament Churches,' *JAC* 24 (1981): 7–41.

116   *SIG*³ 985, lines 12–14 (modified trans. of Barton and Horsley).

117   Barton and Horsley, 'A Hellenistic Cult Group and the New Testament Churches,' 12.

cult of Sarapis was introduced to the Lokrian city of Opous.[118] Like the
Asclepius cult, the cult of Sarapis provided divine counsel and healing
through the practice of incubation; that is, the supplicant would sleep in a
designated space within the temple precinct in order to receive divine help
through a dream. In the inscription, a man named Xenainetos comes to
the Sarapis shrine at Thessalonika for some unspecified counsel. As he
sleeps, Sarapis appears to him and instructs him that when he returns to
Opous he is 'to report to Eurynomos the son of Timasitheos that he
should receive him [i.e., the god] and his sister Isis; and to give to
Eurynomos the letter which was under his pillow.'[119] Xenainetos awakens
and is perplexed by the dream (ὄνειρον) because of the political enmity
(ἀντιπολειτείαν) that exists between him and Eurynomos. Xenainetos
falls asleep again and has the same dream. When he awakens, he finds a
letter under his pillow, just as it was indicated in the dream. When he
returns to Opous, Xenainetos relates his experience to Eurynomos and
gives him the letter, which describes the event exactly as Xenainetos had
reported it. Eurynomos then acknowledges Sarapis and Isis and appoints
a woman named Sosinike to perform the proper sacrifices in her house
along with her other household gods. The Sarapis cult becomes more
public after Sosinike's death, when her granddaughter 'transmitted the
(cult) and administered the mysteries of the gods among those who also
were non-participants in the rites.'[120] Horsley suggests that the inscription
functioned as a 'piece of religious propaganda' for the Sarapis/Isis cult in
Opous.[121] The propaganda, however, most likely serves the Sarapis cult of
Thessalonike, since the inscription was displayed there. It perhaps
heightened the status of Thessalonike as a center of Sarapis/Isis worship
and its propagation.

There are also several literary accounts that associate dreams and the
establishment of a cult. First, Pausanias relates the tradition about the
founding of the temple of Thetis, a sea-nymph and mother of Achilles, in
the city of Laconia. After being taken to Laconia as a prisoner of war, a
priestess of Thetis named Cleo establishes the cult in that city 'because of
a vision in a dream' (κατὰ ὄψιν ὀνείρατος).[122]

Plutarch gives an account of an incident in the life of Themistocles, in
which 'the Mother of the Gods appeared to him in a dream' (τὴν μητέρα

---

118 *IG* X.2, 1, 255. Text, translation, and discussion of this inscription is provided by G.
H. R. Horsley, *New Documents Illustrating Early Christianity: A Review of the Greek
Inscriptions and Papyri published in 1976* (North Ryde, Australia: Macquarie University,
1981), 29–32.

119 *IG* X.2, 1, 255, lines 5–7 (Horsley).

120 *IG* X.2, 1, 255, lines 20–23 (Horsley).

121 Horsley, *New Documents Illustrating Early Christianity*, 20.

122 Pausanias, *Descr.* 3.14.4 (Jones and Ormerod, LCL).

τῶν θεῶν ὄναρ φανεῖσαν).[123] Pisidian mercenaries were waiting in a village called the Lion's Head to assassinate Themistocles. In something of a riddle, the goddess in the dream warned Themistocles to 'shun a head of lions, so that you may not encounter a lion.' The dream ended with the goddess demanding that Themistocles' daughter be given as the goddess' servant. Themistocles bypassed the village, and through a series of events occasioned by his detour, Themistocles was auspiciously saved from the assassins' plot. As Plutarch writes, 'Thus Themistocles escaped the peril, and because he was amazed at the epiphany (ἐπιφάνειαν) of the goddess, he built a temple in Magnesia in honour of Dindymené, and made his daughter Mnesiptolema her priestess.'[124] The selection of Themistocles' daughter as a priestess based on a dream illustrates another cultic function of dreams: the appointment of cultic personnel via a dream.[125]

In addition to the establishment of a cult on the basis of a dream, a number of inscriptions bear witness to the dedication of a temple or setting up an altar because someone was commanded or signified to do so in a dream. In Pergamum from the imperial period, a woman named Tyllias sets up a temple in accordance with a dream: 'In accordance with a dream Tyllias d[edicated] the temple to — for a certain divine act' (Τυλλίας κατ' ὄναρ Δ[—] τῶι θείωι τὸν ναὸν ἱ[δρύσατο]).[126] The cultic location of where this inscription was displayed is unknown; and the inscription is broken presumably where the deity for whom the temple is dedicated is specified. Also in Pergamum, an adherent of Demeter named Leucios Castricios Paulos set up two altars in the sanctuary of Demeter in response to dreams. One altar was set up for Arete ('Virtue') and Sophrosune ('Temperance') and has the inscription, 'To Arete and Sophrosune. Leucios Castricios Paulos, a devotee, [set up this altar] in accordance with a dream' (Ἀρετῇ καὶ Σωφροσύνῃ Λεύκιος Καστρίκιος Παῦλος μύστης κατ' ὄναρ). The other altar was dedicated to Pistis ('Faith') and Homonia ('Concord') and reads, 'To Pistis and Homonia. Leucios Castricios Paulos, a devotee, [set up this altar] in accordance with a dream (Πίστει καὶ Ὁμο νοίᾳ Λεύκιος Καστρίκιος Παῦλος μύστης κατ' ὄναρ).[127]

In the Asclepius sanctuary at Epidauros, a temple and statue were set

---

123 Plutarch, *Them.* 30.1 (Perrin, LCL).
124 Plutarch, *Them.* 30.3 (Perrin, LCL).
125 For other examples, see van Straten, 'Daikrates' Dream,' 16 n. 240.
126 *IPergamon* VII.2, 295 (text Renberg, Cat. No. 356).
127 Renberg, Cat. No. 352 and 353. Renberg cites the publication of these inscriptions as Hugo Hepding, 'Die Arbeiten zu Pergamon 1908–1909, II: Die Inschriften,' *AM* 35 (1910), 359–360.

up for the god Telesphorus[128] by a certain Phaboullos because of a dream:
'To Savior Telesphorus. Because of a dream Phaboullos [set up] the
temple and the statue' (Τελεσφόρωι Σωτῆρι Φάβουλλος ἐξ ὀνείρατος
τὸν ναὸν καὶ τὸ ἄγαλμα).[129] The Asclepieion at Epidauros also housed a
couple of altars that were set up based on the experience of a dream. The
inscription on one altar reads, 'in accordance with a dream Hierokles [set
up this] altar of Mercy' ('Ελέου βωμὸν| εροκλῆς κατ' ὄναρ).[130] Another
altar has the inscription, 'in accordance with a dream Spondos, son of
Diopeithes, [set up this altar] of Remembrance of Auxesia in his twenty
fifth year of bearing the sacrificial fire' (Μνείας Αὐξησιας [Σπ]όνδος
Διοπείθους πυροφορήσας [τὸ] κε' ἔτος κατ' ὄναρ).[131]

As a means of divine communication, dreams were not only the
inspiration for establishing cults and setting up altars and temples, they
were also the *modus operandi* of divination for some Greco-Roman cults,
including the cults of Asclepius, Sarapis/Isis, Amphiaraus and various
local heroes.[132] Individuals would visit these cults and undergo the ritual
of incubation in order to obtain a dream. The actual procedure of
incubation is not described in any inscriptions; only a few literary sources
depict the ritual.[133] Once again, Pausanias' description of the Temple of
Amphiaraus in Oropus illustrates the ritual of incubation:

> One who has come to consult Amphairaus is wont first to purify
> himself. The mode of purification is to sacrifice to the god, and they
> sacrifice not only to him but also to all those whose names are on the
> altar. And when all these things have been first done, they sacrifice a
> ram, and, spreading the skin under them, go to sleep and await
> enlightenment in a dream (ἀναμένοντες δήλωσίν ὀνείρατος).[134]

The overall structure of incubation can be discerned when comparing
Pausanias' account with the other sources. As already indicated with some
of the magical dream rituals, the supplicant first undergoes purification
rites, whether by sacrificing, bathing and/or making an offering.[135] Then
the supplicant enters a sacred sleep-room, where he or she would

128   As the offspring of Asclepius, Telesphorus was a healing deity that was worshipped
alongside of Asclepius and Hygieia.
129   *IG* IV² 1, 561 (text Renberg, Cat. No. 44).
130   *IG* IV² 1, 513 (text Renberg, Cat. No. 51).
131   *IG* IV² 1, 386 (text Renberg, Cat. No. 46). Auxesia was the goddess of growth.
132   Renberg, '"Commanded By the Gods,"' 256–259.
133   Pausanias, *Descr.* 1.34.5 (Amphairaus at Oropus) and 9.39.5-14 (Trophonius at
Lebadeia); Strabo, *Geogr.* 6.3.9 (Calchas at Daunia); and Aristophanes, *Plut.* 653–747
(Asclepius at Athens). For a discussion and bibliography on incubation, see Fritz Graf,
'Inkubation,' *DNP* 5.1006-7.
134   Pausanias, *Descr.* 1.34.5 (Jones and Ormerod, LCL).
135   Aristophanes, *Plut.* 653–747; Pausanias, *Descr.* 9.39.5-14.

sleep upon the skin of a sacrificed animal[136] or a straw mattress[137] and receive a dream. Though not described in the literary accounts, the inscriptions indicate that the supplicant would be expected to pay a fee or offer a dedicatory gift the following morning.[138]

As evidenced by the abundance of inscriptional testimonies, the purpose of seeking a dream at a temple was primarily for the purpose of healing, especially at the temples of Asclepius and Amphairaus.[139] As shown by Klauck, the inscriptions generally follow a certain pattern: (1) the name of the supplicant, (2) the nature of the illness, (3) the manner of healing by means of a dream, and (4) a demonstration of the healing.[140] The following samples illustrate this pattern, but more importantly for our purposes they demonstrate the ancient cultic practice of dreams and healing.

> Cleinatas of Thebes with the lice. He came with a great number of lice on his body, slept in the Temple, and sees a vision (ὄψιν). It seemed (ἐδόκει) to him that the god stripped him and made him stand upright, named and with a broom brushed the lice from off his body. When day came he left the Temple well.[141]

> Timon ... wounded by a spear under his eye. While sleeping in the Temple he saw a dream (ἐνύπνιον). It seemed (ἐδόκει) to him that the god rubbed down a herb and poured it into his eye. And he became well.[142]

> Nicasibula of Messene for offspring slept in the Temple and saw a dream (ἐνύπνιον). It seemed (ἐδόκει) to her that the god approached her with a snake which was creeping behind him; and with that snake had intercourse. Within a year she had two sons.[143]

These testimonies come from the large columns of the Asclepius Temple in Epidaurus, and so they no doubt serve as propaganda for the cult and as hopeful encouragement to those who sought healing.[144] The ancient belief

---

136 Strabo, *Geogr.* 6.3.9.

137 Aristophanes, *Plut.* 653–747.

138 For example, see *IG* IV² 1, 121–22.22 (Edelstein, T. 423.22).

139 For the most convenient and copious, though not exhaustive, collection and translation of the Asclepius testimonies, see Emma J. Edelstein and Ludwig Edelstein, eds., *Asclepius: Collection and Interpretation of the Testimonies* (with new introduction by Gary B. Ferngren; Baltimore: Johns Hopkins University Press, 1998).

140 Klauck, *The Religious Context of Early Christianity*, 162–163.

141 *IG* IV² 1, 121–22.28 (Edelstein, T. 423.28).

142 *IG* IV² 1, 121–22.40 (Edelstein, T. 423.40).

143 *IG* IV² 1, 121–22.42 (Edelstein, T. 423.42).

144 Klauck, *The Religious Context of Early Christianity*, 166. Klauck also states that the 'massive collection of accounts of healing, with its universalizing effect attained through mentioning the names and places of origin of those who sought help, diverts the attention from the unfavorable statistics concerning healings' (166).

and experience of incubation for the purpose of healing, however, is widely attested in various and diverse sources[145] and proves to be an important aspect of the ancient belief about dreams.

Although cultic incubation was largely for purposes of healing, individuals would also undergo this dream ritual in order to obtain an oracle. For example, dating from the imperial period, there is graffiti scribbled on the wall of the *Memnonion* in Abydos (Egypt), presumably by someone going to the temple for incubation: 'I Achilles am coming so that a vision will appear to me and give a sign about the things I am praying.' (ἐγὼ Ἀχιλλεὺς ἔ < ρ > χομαι θεάσασθαι ὄνιρον σημένοντά μοι περὶ ὧν εὔχομαι).[146] Even the Asclepius cult entertained requests other than those of healing.[147] One of the inscriptional testimonies[148] recounts how a boy dove into the sea and came up into an enclosure surrounded by rocks and could not get out. When the boy did not return home, the boy's father entreated Asclepius through incubation. In a dream (ἐνύπνιον), the god showed the father the exact location of the boy. When the father left the Temple, he found the boy just as the dream had directed. Renberg notes that despite the lack of epigraphical evidence, 'there must have been numerous other shrines and sanctuaries where ancient worshippers could consult the resident divinity and receive a dream-oracle.'[149] Like the dream-request rituals in the magical texts, dreams were sought in some cultic settings for revelatory purposes.

Turning to the Jewish and Christian tradition of dreams and cults, one finds several accounts in the Jewish scriptures that associate dreams and cultic activity. In Genesis 28.10-22, Jacob has a dream in which he sees a ladder that reaches to heaven and hears God speaking. He responds to the dream by setting up a sacred pillar, pouring oil on it, and making a vow. He calls the place Bethel, which becomes an important sanctuary in ancient Israel. Something similar takes place with Isaac and the sanctuary of Beer-sheba (Gen. 26.23-25). The Lord appears to Isaac at night and reiterates the promise first made to Abraham; Isaac responds by building an altar. Though Jacob and Isaac are not commanded in the dream to establish the respective cults of Bethel and Beer-sheba, the dream

---

145   Once again, these sources can be consulted in Edelstein and Edelstein, *Asclepius*, 1.179-342.

146   Renberg, Test. No. 21. Renberg cites the publication of this inscription as Perdrizet-Lefebre, *Memnonion*, No. 238.

147   See *IG* II² 4355 (Renberg, Cat. No. 9) and *IG* II² 4358 (Renberg, Cat. No. 10), dedicatory gifts offered to Asclepius for receiving counsel or advice (ὑποθήκαις and ὑποθημοσ [ύναις] respectively) presumably through a dream.

148   *IG* IV² 1, 121–22.24 (Edelstein, T. 423.24).

149   Renberg, ' "Commanded By the Gods," ' 258.

traditions and their responses function to legitimatize the sanctuaries.[150] Moreover, the stories would be customary to a Greco-Roman audience, whose religious context associates dreams, the establishments of cults and the setting up of altars.[151]

The Jewish scriptures also contain stories that can be considered incubations. In 1 Kings 3.1-15, Solomon goes to the 'high place' at Gibeon, where he offers sacrifices and incenses and receives a dream. In the dream Solomon requests wisdom in order to lead rightly the people; God grants his request. Less certain as to incubation is the story of the boy Samuel (1 Sam. 3).[152] Though there is no sacrifice or request, Samuel is sleeping 'in the temple of the LORD, where the ark of God was' (1 Sam. 3.3; NRSV), when the Lord speaks to him. Though specific incubation features are missing, the cultic servant Samuel (v. 1) receives a dream while sleeping in the temple. For a Greco-Roman reader, the cultic setting for the dream oracle would be familiar and perhaps suggestive of an incubation experience.

The association of dreams and cultic matters are also described in post-biblical literary texts. In *Jubilees* 32.1-2, Levi spends the night at Bethel, the place of his father's dream, and has his own dream, which signifies his appointment as priest. The priestly office of Levi based on a dream is further expressed in the *Testament of Levi*. Levi visits Bethel and has a dream in which he is installed and ordained as priest in an elaborate ceremony.[153] In *2 Enoch* 69.4-6, Methusalam, the son of Enoch, at the request of the people, comes to the altar of the Lord to pray that the Lord would raise up a priest for them. He then sleeps at the altar; the Lord appears to him in a dream and commands him to take on the function of priest. The circumstances of visiting the altar, making a request and sleeping indicate the intention of incubation. Another example of incubation is found in *2 Baruch* 34.1–43.3. On behalf of the people, Baruch goes to the Holy of Holies to pray. After he prays, he 'fell asleep at that place and saw a vision in the night.'[154] Finally, Josephus recounts an instance of incubation.[155] On hearing of Alexander the Great's approaching army, the high priest Jaddus enters the temple, makes prayers and

---

150 Robert Gnuse, *The Dream Theophany of Samuel: Its Structure in Relation to Ancient Near Eastern Dreams and Its Theological Significance* (Lanham, Md.: University Press of America, 1984), 67–68; and Shaul Bar, *A Letter That Has Not Been Read: Dreams in the Hebrew Bible* (HUCM 25; Cincinnati: Hebrew Union College Press, 2001), 183–90.

151 See Gen 35.6-15 where Jacob returns to the place of his dream and sets up an altar.

152 For those who argue the story as incubation, see references in Bar, *A Letter That Has Not Been Read*, 180 n. 154. Against an example of incubation, see Gnuse, *The Dream Theophany of Samuel*, 150–52.

153 *T. Levi* 8.1-19.

154 *2 Bar.* 36.1 (Klijn. *OTP*).

155 Josephus, *A.J.* 11.326-328.

sacrifices, and then sleeps at the place of the altar. God tells him in a dream to welcome the army with the appropriate gestures and the people will be protected. Given the literary character of these texts and the lack of archaeological evidence for Jewish incubation, the practice of incubation in Judaism remains uncertain. It is not a customary practice of Judaism, though occasionally it may have been performed. It is interesting to note, however, that Strabo recounts a tradition of Jewish incubation as part of his description of the Jews. He states that Moses taught that 'people who have good dreams (τοὺς εὐονείρους) should sleep in the sanctuary, not only themselves on their own behalf, but also others for the rest of the people.'[156]

The association of dreams and cults in Christianity seems to be a late development emerging with the cults of the martyrs. Though cautiously because of their popularity, Canon 83 of the council of Carthage seeks to check the unauthorized establishment of altars and shrines for martyrs, particularly those altars that have been set up because of dreams. The shrines of martyrs also became places of incubation. The most famous of these was the cult of St. Thecla, where healing, revelation and guidance were often granted through dreams.[157]

Dreams functioned in Greco-Roman cults in a variety of ways: establishing cults, setting up altars, appointing cultic personnel and incubation. This cultic function of dreams further illustrates the divinatory nature of dreams in the ancient Mediterranean world.

Dream Interpreters

An understanding of the practice of dreams in the Greco-Roman world is not complete without properly recognizing the mediating role of dream interpreters. This role was referred to in the above discussion of dreams and divination, where dream interpreters and their art were shown to be firmly established within the larger practice of ancient divination. Given the common experience of dreams, one can reasonably imagine that dream interpreters were regularly consulted. This perception is back-handedly supported by Theophrastus, who in his critique of superstition (δ|εσιδαιμονία) scoffs at a population that 'never has a dream but rushes to dream interpreters (ὀνειροκρίτας), diviners (μάντεις), or even bird-diviners (ὀρηιτηοσκόπους) to ask what god or goddess must be honored.'[158] Theophratus' comment provides a structure to the following

---

156 Strabo, *Geog.* 16.2.35 (Jones, LCL).

157 See Stephen J. Davis, *The Cult of Saint Thecla: A Tradition of Women's Piety in Late Antiquity* (OECS; Oxford: Oxford University Press, 2001), 48, 58, 60, and 126; Polymnia Athanassiadi, 'Dreams, Theurgy and Freelance Divination: The Testimony of Iamblichus,' *JRSt* 83 (1993): 125; and Miller, *Dreams in Late Antiquity*, 117.

158 Theophrastus, *Char.* 16.11 (modified trans. from Edmonds, LCL).

investigation of dream interpreters: (1) the mediating role of dream interpreters in the cultic honoring of deities; and (2) dream interpreters as a profession among diviners. Thus, the following investigation of dream interpreters will first consider dream interpreters in relation to Greco-Roman cults and then the profession of dream interpretation in more general terms.

In the discussion of dreams and Greco-Roman cults, we noted that temples and altars were often set up in accordance with a dream. It remains uncertain, however, whether these dedications – along with other numerous inscriptional dedications based on a dream – were the result of a direct, immediate appearance of the deity in a dream, or whether the dream was a symbolic dream that needed interpretation. Renberg states the problem as follows:

> It must be remembered that *viso/iusso* dedications represent the end of a process, whereas the dream or vision was the beginning of that process: the final appearance of an inscription recording a dream or vision may not always have been the immediate and direct result of divine communication. One of the many problems associated with *viso/iusso* dedications is the question of whether the individuals who commissioned them did so following consultation with a religious authority, instead of interpreting the dreams themselves. The potential involvement of such interpreters in the process culminating in the erection of *viso/iusso* dedications, not given due attention by those who have studied this phenomenon, is significant because reliance on an expert interpreter would suggest that a dream was more likely to have featured obscure symbols, human messengers, or mute divinities rather than a god clearly expressing his wishes.[159]

Despite this terminational character of the inscriptions, which has the effect of concealing the possible role of dream interpreters, there is evidence that indicates that dream interpreters at times played a mediating role in the cultic honoring of deities.

In addition to Theophratus' remark, that connects dream interpreters and other diviners with cultic honoring of deities, there are several inscriptions that actually state the role of a dream interpreter in their being set up. At the Sarapis/Isis cult at Delos dating from the early first century BCE, two identical inscriptions were dedicated, 'according to a command through the dream-interpreter Menodoros' (κατὰ πρόσταγμα διὰ ὀνειροκρίτου Μηνοδώρου).[160] In addition to naming the dream interpreter (Menodoros), the inscriptions also specify the priest who was officiating at the time of the dedication, a certain Leonos. Another Delos

159 Renberg, ' "Commanded By the Gods," ' 249–250.

160 *IDelos* 2105 and 2106 (text Renberg, Cat. No. 142 and 143). Cp. also the badly damaged *IDelos* 2110 (text Renberg, Cat. No. 148).

inscription indicates that an unnamed dream interpreter (προσσαναφέροντες τῶι ὀνειροκρίτηι) was instrumental in the setting up of the dedication; it also includes the presiding priest, a certain Aristion.[161] The probable scenario of these inscriptions is that the one offering the dedicatory gift first consulted a dream interpreter. The interpreter discerned the dream as a command to honor the god and the appropriate dedication was then made before the priest. What is uncertain, however, is the exact nature of the relationship between the dream interpreters and the cults: are the dream interpreters official personnel of the cult or are they independent professionals?

An archaeological artifact found near the temple of Sarapis in Sakkara (Memphis) offers one possible answer to this question. On a limestone stele dated around 200 BCE, the following inscription is found: 'I interpret dreams by the command of the god. To good success! A Cretan is the one who interprets here' ('Ενύπνια κρίνω τοῦ θεοῦ πρόστιγμα ἔχων· τυχἀγαθᾶι· Κρής ἐστιν ὁ κρίνων τάδε).[162] Noting two holes in the top of the stele, Étienne Bernand proposes that it was a suspended sign outside the dream interpreter's place of residence, which was located along the commercially crowded road that led to the temple.[163] The purpose of this sign, of course, was to attract patrons as they approached the temple of Sarapis. Bernand's interpretation is plausible based on a comment by Plutarch about a certain Lysimachus, the grandson of Aristides. Plutarch states that Lysimachus 'made his own living by means of a sort of dream-interpreting tablet (πινακίου ὀνειροκριτικοῦ), his seat being near the so-called Iaccheium [i.e., Temple of Bacchus].'[164] Bernand believes that the Cretan dream interpreter was a private individual who was authorized by the temple officials.[165] This sort of arrangement, of course, would be economically beneficial both to the Cretan as well as to the Sarapis cult. Although Lysimachus makes his living by the temple, Plutarch refers to him as 'a very poor man' (μάλα πένητα),[166] which suggests a less formal or official connection to the temple personnel. Thus, whether authorized or not, these two examples suggest that in some cases dream interpreters strategically stationed themselves near temples in order

161   *IDelos* 2151 (text Renberg, Cat. No. 150).
162   Étienne Bernand, *Inscriptions métriques de l'Égypte gréco-romaine: recherches sur la poésie épigrammatique des grecs en Égypte* (Annales littéraires de l'Université de Besançon 98; Paris: Belles Lettres, 1969), 436. A picture of the stele is provided on plate LXXIX. See also, Frenschkowski, 'Traum und Traumdeutung im Matthäusevangelium,' 12, who offers a verbal description of the stele.
163   Bernand, *Inscriptions métriques de l'Égypte gréco-romaine*, 436–8.
164   Plutarch, *Arist.* 27.3 (Perrin, LCL).
165   Bernand, *Inscriptions métriques de l'Égypte gréco-romaine*, 438.
166   Plutarch, *Arist.* 27.3 (Perrin, LCL).

to provide a service for those coming to the temple, a service that most likely resulted in a dedicatory gift.

The relationship between dream interpreters and various cults is further complicated by the fact that some inscriptions include dream interpreters with a list of temple personnel. An inscription from the Sarapis sanctuary in Athens was dedicated, 'according to a command, during the priesthood of Menander, son of Artemon, of Alopeke, when Asopokles of Phyla was *kleidouchos* ['keeper of the keys'], Sosikrates of Laodikeia was *zakoros* ['temple attendant'], and Dionysos of Antioch was judging dreams (κρίνοντος τὰ ὁράματα Διονυσίου Ἀντιοχέως).'[167] It is most probable that the dream interpreter Dionysos played a role in the setting up of this dedicatory inscription, but his place among the cult personnel remains ambiguous.[168] Is he a cult official, or is he a dream interpreter, like the Cretan or Lysimachus, who practices his art in close proximity to the temple?

Another Athenian inscription, this time connected with the cult of Aphrodite, was dedicated by a woman, 'who is both [Aphrodite's] torch-bearer and a dream-interpreter' (οὖσα καὶ λυχνάπτρια αὐτῆς καὶ ὀνειροκρίτις).[169] The inscription then concludes by identifying certain cultic officials: Aimilios, the keeper of the sacred vestments; Dionysos, the minister of the Bacchus festival; and Eukarpos, temple-attendant of sacred vessels. Once again, uncertainty surrounds the precise situation. Does the woman's role as dream interpreter have any relation to her role as torch bearer of the Aphrodite cult? In any case, dream interpreters were associated with various cults, although the exact nature of that association remains unclear.

What is most certain, however, is the widespread existence of dream interpreters in the Greco-Roman world.[170] Tertullian attests to the established tradition of dream interpretation by listing esteemed dream interpreters: Artemon, Antiphon, Strato, Philochorus, Epicharmus, Serapion, Cratippus, and Dionysius of Rhodes and Hermippus.[171] Throughout his *Onirocritica*, Artemidorus refers to numerous professional dream interpreters and their handbooks on dream interpretation: Antiphon of Athens, Aristander of Telmessus, Demetrius of Phalerum, Antipater, Alexander of Myndus, Panyasis of Halicarnassus, Nicostratus

---

167 *SIRIS*, No. 5 [late 2nd cent. BCE] (text Renberg, Cat. No. 25; translation Renberg, 255).

168 Cf. Renberg, '"Commanded By the Gods,"' 255.

169 *IG* II² 4771 (text Leuci, p. 246).

170 For a collection of primary sources of dream interpreters, see Darius Del Corno, ed., *Graecorum de re onirocritica scriptorum reliquiae* (Milan: Istituto Editoriale Cisalpino, 1969).

171 Tertullian, *An.* 46.10.

of Ephesus, Apollonuis of Attalia, Apollodorus of Telmessus and Geminus of Tyre.[172]

Dream interpreters were often considered diviners who practiced other divinatory arts as well. A case in point is Aristander of Telmessus, the legendary diviner of Alexander the Great. Artemidorus refers to him as 'the best dream interpreter,'[173] and his interpretation of dreams in relation to the life of Alexander are chronicled by Alexander's biographers.[174] But the diviner Aristander also discerned the significance of a sweating statute,[175] divination by sacrifice,[176] interpreting portending behaviors of birds,[177] and perceived the auspicious significance of chance circumstances.[178]

The interpretation of dreams was not only practiced by esteemed diviners, but it was performed by those who eked out a living in the marketplaces. Artemidorus not only draws upon the dream-books of respected dream interpreters but he has also consulted dream interpreters considered less respectable:

> I, on the other hand, have not only taken special pains to procure every book on the interpretation of dreams, but have consorted for many years with the much-despised diviners of the marketplace. People who assume a holier-than-thou countenance and who arch their eyebrows in a superior way dismiss them as beggars, charlatans, and buffoons, but I have ignored their disparagement.[179]

This critical attitude of marketplace diviners referred to by Artemidorus is confirmed by Cicero, who quotes such sentiments from a certain Appius and Ennius.[180] Thus, there existed a spectrum of dream interpreters in the ancient world along the lines of cultic and 'secular', professional and freelance, respected and disreputable.

For Jews and Christians, the biblical tradition presented Joseph and Daniel as dream interpreters *par excellence*. Interestingly, both Joseph and Daniel practice the art of dream interpretation in the service of foreign kings, Pharaoh and Nebuchadnezzar respectively, whose own diviners are

---

172   Cp. Artemidorus' references to such dream interpreters: *Onir*. 2.14 (Antiphon of Athens); 1.31 (Aristander of Telmessus); 2.44 (Demetrius of Phalerum); 4.65 (Antipater); 1.67, 2.9, 2.66 (Alexander of Myndus); 1.2, 1.64, 2.34 (Panyasis of Halicarnassus); 1.2 (Nicostratus of Ephesus); 1.32, 3.28 (Apollonuis of Attalia); 1.79 (Apollodorus of Telmessus); and 2.44 (Geminus of Tyre).

173   Artemidorus, *Onir*. 4.23 (White).

174   Plutarch, *Alex*. 2.4; Arrian, *Anab*. 2.18.1.

175   Plutarch, *Alex*. 14.8 (par. Arrian, *Anab*. 1.11.2).

176   Plutarch, *Alex*. 25.1-4.

177   Arrian, *Anab*. 1.25.6-8; 2.26.4.

178   Arrian, *Anab*. 3.2.1-2; 3.7.6.

179   Artemidorus, *Onir*. 1.praef. (White).

180   Cicero, *Div*. 1.132.

not able to interpret their dreams.[181] Also noteworthy is that both Joseph
and Daniel credit God for their ability to interpret dreams, because God is
the source of their interpretation. Joseph asks rhetorically, 'Do not
interpretations belong to God' (Gen. 40.8 NRSV); and Daniel receives the
meaning of Nebuchadnezzar's dream in a dream of his own (Dan. 2.19).
Moreover, Daniel's dream-visions in chapters 7–12 are accompanied by
interpretations given by angels.

The existence of Jewish dream interpreters is evident in 'Middle
Judaism'[182] and even seems to be characteristic of Jewish divination.
Josephus reports about a symbolic dream of the tetrarch Archelaus. When
other dream interpreters – presumably Jewish – disagreed as to its
meaning, an Essene named Simon correctly interpreted the dream, which
came to pass five days later.[183] Josephus considered himself a dream
interpreter; writing in the third person, Josephus states: 'He was an
interpreter of dreams (κρίσεις ὀνείρων) and skilled in divining the
meaning of ambiguous utterances of the Deity; a priest himself and of
priestly descent, he was not ignorant of the prophecies in the sacred
books.'[184] The juxtaposition in his statement of being a dream interpreter
and a priest has been taken by several scholars to mean that 'dream
interpretation in this era was a priestly function.'[185] Like those of the
larger Greco-Roman world, Jewish dream interpreters could also be
found among the 'marketplace' diviners. Though cast in the genre and
style of satire, Juvenal refers to a 'palsied' Jewish woman who begs and
seeks gain by dream interpretation:

> She is an interpreter of the laws of Jerusalem, a high priestess of the tree,
> a trusty go-between of the highest heaven. She, too, fills her palm, but
> more sparingly, for Jews will tell you dreams of any kind you please for
> the minutest coins.[186]

---

181   Gen. 41.8 and Dan. 2.2-11.
182   The term 'Middle Judaism' is take from Gabriele Boccaccini, *Middle Judaism: Jewish
Thought, 300 B.C.E to 200 C.E.* (Minneapolis: Fortress Press, 1991), who attempts to provide a
more neutral term to the time-period that is sometimes referred to as 'Second Temple
Judaism.'
183   Josephus, *A.J.* 17.345-348.
184   Josephus, *J.W.* 3.352 (Thackeray, LCL).
185   Robert Gnuse, *Dreams and the Dream Reports in the Writings of Josephus: A Tradio-
Historical Analysis* (AGJU 36; Leiden: E.J. Brill, 1996), 137 (see n. 27 for secondary
literature).
186   Juvenal, *Sat.* 6.542-547 (Ramsay, LCL).

The Talmud also attests to a strong tradition of dream interpreters in ancient Judaism,[187] even containing what are most certainly excerpts from a Jewish dream book.[188]

The evidence is very slim for dream interpreters in early Christianity. Once again, within a Gentile context, Christianity is critical of dream interpreters because of their connection with paganism. Thus, the *Apostolic Traditions* as transmitted by Hippolytus prohibits the occupation of dream interpretation for Christians, but dream interpretation is included with other professions such as magicians, astrologers, diviners and snake charmers.[189] Clement of Alexandria counts dream interpreters as instruments of demons.[190] Yet, Christians seem to have interpreted dreams. The martyr Perpetua is able to interpret her dreams in a manner consistent with the larger Greco-Roman tradition of dream interpretation.[191] A particular Christian approach to dream interpretation is the reciprocal relationship of dreams and scriptural interpretation. Patricia Miller argues that in patristic literature symbolic dreams often become 'the place where Scripture is interpreted.'[192] In other words, the images and visions of dreams are not necessarily the object of interpretation but 'function both in the formal and material ways as the principle as well as the substance of interpretation.'[193] To interpret dreams is to interpret scripture.

Having described the practice of dreams in the Greco-Roman world, I now turn to ancient dream classifications and theories.

The Classifications and Theories of Dreams[194]

As described above, dreams had a religious function in the Greco-Roman world and were considered one form of divination. The phenomenon of dreams, however, demonstrated that not every dream was divinatory. Some dreams, perhaps most, simply passed with no significance. What was the nature of dreams, and from where do dreams come? This

---

187 Brigitte Stemberger, 'Der Traum in der rabbinischen Literatur,' *Kairos* 18 (1976): 1–42; Ernst L. Ehrlich, 'Der Traum in Talmud,' *ZNW* 47 (1956): 133–45; Bar, *A Letter That Has Not Been Read*, 101–7; and Monford Harris, *Studies in Jewish Dream Interpretation* (Northvale, New Jersey: Jason Aronson Inc., 1994), 3–24.

188 *b. Berakot* 55a-57b. See Bar, *A Letter That Has Not Been Read*, 107.

189 Hippolytus, *Trad. ap.* 15.

190 Clement of Alexandria, *Protr.* 1.3.2 and 2.11.2-3.

191 Miller, *Dreams in Late Antiquity*, 148–83.

192 Patricia Cox Miller, 'Dreams in Patristic Literature: Divine Sense or Pagan Nonsense?' *Studia Patristica* 18, 2 (1989): 186.

193 Miller, 'Dreams in Patristic Literature,' 187.

194 For this section, I have used material from my article 'Philo's *De somniis* in the Context of Ancient Dream Theories and Classifications,' *PRSt* 30 (2003): 299–312.

predicament of the human experience in antiquity gave rise to an intellectual tradition about the theory and classification of dreams. The following is a survey of this tradition.

In reviewing dream theory in antiquity, Patricia Miller states that there were two general ways of conceptualizing dreams in antiquity: 'One was psychobiological and attempted to naturalize the phenomena of sleep and its attendant phantasms; the other was theological and connected the dreaming soul with an invisible but very real realm of spiritual beings – angels, daemons, gods.'[195] Cicero and Aristotle are representative of the psychobiological theory of dreams. Cicero even uses Aristotle to argue against the divinatory function of dreams. Against his Stoic interlocutor, Cicero states:

> Since you deny that God made [both true and false dreams] you must admit that nature made them all. By 'nature,' in this connexion, I mean that force because of which the soul can never be stationary and free from motion and activity. And when, because of the weariness of the body, the soul can use neither the limbs nor the senses, it lapses into varied and untrustworthy visions, which emanate from what Aristotle terms 'the clinging remnants of the soul's waking acts and thoughts.' These 'remnants,' when aroused, sometimes produce strange types of dreams.[196]

The polemical context of Cicero's statements, however, should not obscure the fact that a psychobiological theory of dreams did not necessarily preclude the possibility of meaningful dreams. For example, the medical writer Galen (2nd cent.) held to a psychobiological theory of dreams,[197] but he believed that some dreams could help in the diagnosis of his patients and even reveal surgical procedures:

> Some people scorn dreams, omens, and portents. But I know that I have often made a diagnosis from dreams and, guided by two very clear dreams, I once made an incision into the artery between the thumb and the index finger of the right hand, and allowed the blood to flow until it ceased flowing on its own, as the dream had instructed. I have saved many people by applying a cure prescribed in a dream.[198]

---

195 Miller, *Dreams in Late Antiquity*, 42.
196 Cicero, *Div.* 2.128 (Falconer, LCL).
197 'In sleep the soul seems to sink into the depths of the body, withdrawing from external sense-objects, and so becomes aware of the bodily condition' (περὶ τῆς ἐξ ἐνυπνίων διαγνώσεως, VI.843 Kühn); quoted and translated in E. R. Dodds, *The Greeks and the Irrational* (Berkeley: University of California Press, 1966), 133 n. 104.
198 Galen, *Comm. in Hippocr. de humor.* 2.2. Quoted and translated in Miller, *Dreams in Late Antiquity*, 46. For a discussion of Galen's views on dreams, see A. H. M. Kessels, 'Ancient Systems of Dream-Classification,' *Mnemosyne* 22 (1969): 422–4.

The psychobiological theory of dreams represented the minority view in antiquity. The predominant view, as demonstrated above, was the theological theory: dreams were one of the ways in which the divine communicates to men and women. The explication of ancient dream theories as psychobiological and theological is a modern attempt to comprehend better the multifaceted idea of dreams in antiquity. In antiquity, however, these various beliefs about dreams were not mutually exclusive but sometimes held together in accordance with differing motivations and purposes. Consequently, there developed in antiquity the practice of classifying dreams.

The classification of dreams is already given its mythical expression in Homer's *Odyssey*, where Penelope describes to the disguised Odysseus two classes of dreams:

> For two are the gates of shadowy dreams (ἀμενηνῶν ὀνείρων), and one is fashioned of horn and one of ivory. Those dreams that pass through the gate of sawn ivory deceive men, bringing words that find no fulfillment. But those that come forth through the gate of polished horn bring true issues to pass, when any mortal sees them.[199]

This basic distinction between true (divinatory) and false (non-divinatory) dreams became the basis upon which subsequent classifications developed. Plato seems to reflect this fundamental, two-fold category of dreams based on the state of the soul. In the *Republic*, Plato comments on how the immoral soul manifests its beastly and savage nature in corresponding dreams.[200] But when the soul is virtuous and guided by reason, that person 'is most likely to apprehend truth, and the visions of his dreams (αἱ ὄψεις φαντάζονται τῶν ἐνυπνίων) are least likely to be lawless.'[201] It should be noted, however, that Plato does not present a formal classification of dreams.[202] Thus, this survey of formal classifications of dreams will begin with the classification of Herophilus, which reflects this basic distinction between significant and insignificant dreams.

The classification of the medical writer Herophilus (c.330–260 B.C.E) is found in Plutarch's *De placita philosophorum* 5.1.2 and Galen's *Historia*

---

199   Homer, *Od.* 19.562-7 (Murray, LCL).
200   Plato, *Resp.* 571c.
201   Plato, *Resp.* 572b. Cf. Plato, *Tim.* 71e–72b and Artemidorus, *Onir.* 4.praef.
202   *Contra* Behr, *Aelius Aristides and the Sacred Tales*, 173, who states, 'Plato is the first known authority who systematized the arguments and arrangements of this [two-fold] classification.' Plato's idea about dreams can only be demonstrated from several, unrelated comments found throughout his works. See David Gallop, 'Dreaming and Waking in Plato,' *Essays in Ancient Greek Philosophy* (ed. by J. P. Anton with G. L. Kustas; Albany: State University of New York Press, 1971), 187–90; and Kessels, 'Ancient Systems of Dream-Classification,' 392–3.

philosophiae 106.²⁰³ Herophilus identifies three classes of dreams: (1) the god-sent dreams (θεοπέμπτους), (2) natural (φυσικούς) dreams that are reflecting images of the soul (εἰδωλοποιουμένης ψυξῆς), and (3) a 'combination' (συγκριματικούς) type of dream that proceeds from 'what we wish we would see.' The first two classes of dreams seem to be set in opposition to one another. Herophilus' φυσικός dream-type corresponds to Cicero's psychobiological description of the dream phenomenon, and thus it possesses no predictive quality. The θεοπέμπτος class, then, represents those dreams that are predictive and function as divination. Therefore, in the language of Homer, θεοπέμπτοι dreams come through the gate of horn (true), and φυσικοί dreams come through the gate of ivory (false). The meaning of Herophilus' third class, 'combination' dreams is ambiguous.²⁰⁴ It seems to be a combination of the θεοπέμπτος and the φυσικός dreams, insofar as the dream has an anthropological origin but it still comes to pass. Thus, the dream-classification of Herophilus represents a basic system of predictive and non-predictive dreams.

The dream classification of Artemidorus also emphasizes this two-fold distinction between significant and insignificant dreams, but his classification also reflects a five-class system. His classification of dreams begins with a distinction between ἐνύπνιον and ὄνειρος.²⁰⁵ As Artemidorus succinctly summarizes in the preface of Book 4:

> A dream that has no meaning (ἀσήμαντον) and predicts nothing (οὐδενὸς προαγορευτικὸν), one that is active only while one sleeps and that has arisen from an irrational desire, an extraordinary fear, or from a surfeit or lack of food is called an *enhypnion* (ἐνύπνιον). But a dream that operates after sleep and that comes true (ἀποβάλλοντος) either for good or bad is called an *oneiros* (ὄνειρος).²⁰⁶

Ὄνειρος is further divided on the basis of its signifying function. Dreams that correspond directly to the predicted event are called theorematic (θεωρημάτικοι). Artemidorus' example is this: 'A man who was at sea dreamt that he suffered shipwreck, and it actually came true in the way

---

203 Herophilus' text is quoted and discussed, but not translated, in Kessels, 'Ancient Systems of Dream-Classification,' 414; see also Dodd, *The Greeks and the Irrational*, 124 n. 28. The text in Galen reads: Ἡρόφιλος τῶν ὀνείρων τοὺς μὲν θεοπέμπτους κατ' ἀνάγκην γίνεσθαι, τοὺς δὲ φυσικοὺς εἰδωλοποιουμένης τῆς ψυξῆς τὸ συμφέρον αὐτῇ καὶ τὸ πάντως ἐσόμενον· τοὺς δὲ συγκριματικοὺς [Plutarch, συγκραματικοὺς] αὐτομάτως κατ' εἰδώλων πρόσπτωσιν ὅταν ἃ βουλόμεθα βλέπωμεν· φιλούτων γίγνεται τὰς ἐρωμένας ἐρωντων ἐν ὕπνοις.

204 For a discussion of this third class, see Kessels, 'Ancient Systems of Dream-Classification,' 417–22.

205 Artemidorus, *Onir.* 1.1.

206 Artemidorus, *Onir.* 4.praef. (White; text Pack).

that it had been presented in sleep.'[207] On the other hand, allegorical dreams (ἀλληγορικοὶ ὄνειροι) 'signify one thing by means of another.'[208] Allegorical dreams require interpretation and so the purpose of Artemidorus' *Onirocritica* is to set forth the meaning and significance of allegorical dreams.[209]

As stated above, Artemidorus knows a five-class schema of dreams, but he does not find it helpful for his purposes. To the insignificant ἐνύπνιον he adds the φάντασμα ('apparition'); and with the significant ὄνειρος he includes the ὅραμα ('vision') and χρηματισμός ('oracle').[210] According to Artemidorus, the ὅραμα and χρηματισμός are self-evident (theorematic), and therefore they require no elaboration or discussion.[211]

This non-elaboration is perhaps explained by Macrobius in his *Commentary on the Dream of Scipio* (4th C.E.), which contains an explication of this five-dream classification. Macrobius summarizes the five types of dreams as follows:

> There is the enigmatic dream, in Greek *oneiros*, in Latin *somnium*; second, there is the prophetic vision, in Greek *horama*, in Latin *visio*; third, there is the oracular dream, in Greek *chrematismos*, in Latin *oraculum*; fourth, there is the nightmare, in Greek *enypnion*, in Latin *insomnium*; and last, the apparition, in Greek *phantasma*, which Cicero, when he has the occasion to use the word, calls *visum*.[212]

Like Artemidorus, Macrobius notes that the nightmare (ἐνύπνιον/ *insomnium*) and apparition (φάντασμα/*visum*) are non-predictive and insignificant.[213] The other three types of dreams, however, are discussed on the basis of their significance. The χρηματισμός/*oraculum* is a dream 'in which a parent, or a pious or revered man, or a priest, or even a god clearly reveals what will or will not transpire, and what action to take or to avoid.'[214] The ὅραμα/*visio* is a 'prophetic vision' of what actually will take place.[215] This type of dream corresponds to Artemidorus' theorematic dream of a shipwreck. The ὄνειρος/*somnium* 'conceals with strange

---

207   Artemidorus, *Onir.* 1.2 (White).
208   Artemidorus, *Onir.* 1.2 (White).
209   Artemidorus also discusses theorematic and allegorical dreams in 4.1. For helpful studies on Artemidorus' dream theory, see Luther H. Martin, 'Artemidorus: Dream Theory in Late Antiquity,' *The Second Century* 8 (1991): 100–2; and Blum, *Studies in the Dream-Book of Artemidorus*, 52–91.
210   Artemidorus, *Onir.* 1.2.
211   Artemidorus, *Onir.* 1.2.
212   Macrobius, *Comm. in Somn. Scip.* 3.2 (Stahl).
213   Macrobius, *Comm. in Somn. Scip.* 3.3.
214   Macrobius, *Comm. in Somn. Scip.* 3.8 (Stahl).
215   Macrobius, *Comm. in Somn. Scip.* 3.9.

shapes and veils with ambiguity the true meaning of the information being offered, and requires an interpretation for its understanding.'[216]

Given Macrobius' comments on the five-dream classification, Artemidorus' treatment – or non-treatment – of the various dream types can now be explained. As already stated, the ἐνύπνιον and φάντασμα are non-predictive and signify nothing. The ὅραμα and χρηματισμός, on the other hand, are predictive and significant, but they are theorematic; that is, their meanings are straightforward and do not need interpretation. Only the ὄνειρος, being allegorical, requires interpretation, which is the focus of Artemidorus' *Onirocritica*. Thus, Artemidorus' dream classification is influenced by practical concerns and can be presented as follows:

ἐνύπνιοι – non-predictive/insignificant dreams
  ἐνύπνιον
  φάντασμα
ὄνειροι – predictive/significant dreams
  ὅραμα – theorematic
  χρηματισμός – theorematic
  ὄνειρος – allegorical

In addition to the two- and five-class classification of dreams, there also existed a three-class system. The Stoic philosopher Posidonius put forward a three-class system of dreams, which was preserved by Cicero:

> Now Posidonius holds the view that there are three ways in which men dream as the result of divine impulse (*deorum appulsu*): first, the soul (*animus*) is clairvoyant of itself because of its kinship with the gods; second, the air is full of immortal souls (*immortalium animorum*), already clearly stamped, as it were, with the marks of truth (*veritatis*); and third, the gods in person converse with men when they are asleep.[217]

Several features of Posidonius' three-dream classification are to be noted. First, all three dream types are categorized under the designation *deorum appulsu*; therefore, all three dreams are predictive. There does, however, seem to be an increasing degree of immediacy with the divine: (1) the soul's own divine nature, (2) the soul's contact with other intermediary souls and (3) the divine presence. Second, Posidonius' classification lacks specific labels or terms for each type of dream, which suggests an intention different from the technical concerns of Artemidorus and Macrobius. Third, it is uncertain whether or not Posidonius included a category of non-predictive dreams.

Although there have been attempts to reconcile Posidonius' classifica-

---

216 Macrobius, *Comm. in Somn. Scip.* 3.10 (Stahl).
217 Cicero, *Div.* 1.64 (Falconer, LCL).

tion with the one of Artemidorus/Macrobius,[218] the two classifications do represent different approaches to dreams. Kessels contends that the two systems are answering two fundamentally different questions.[219] The five-class system of Artemidorus/Macrobius answers a practical question: Is a particular dream predictive or not; and if it is, does it require an interpretation (allegorical/enigmatic) or is it straightforward (theorematic)? The classification of Posidonius answers the question: 'How is it possible that human beings (with the aid of God) are able to get a certain knowledge of the future in their dreams?'[220] Although Kessels seems correct in arguing for a distinction between the two dream classifications, it should be noted that at the theoretical level there is some commonality.

The three-class system of dreams is also attested by the Jewish philosopher Philo. At the beginning of both books 1 and 2 of his *De somniis,* Philo comments, and reviews, that his subject matter is God-sent dreams (θεοπέμπτοι ὄνειροι), of which there are three classes. His description of the three classes of θεοπέμπτοι ὄνειροι is as follows:

> *First class* – 'The treatise before this one embraced that first class of heaven-sent dreams (θεοπέμπτων ὀνείρων), in which, as we said, the Deity (τὸ θεῖον) of His own motion sends to us the visions (τὰς φαντασίας) which are presented to us in sleep.'[221] 'The first kind [of dreams] we saw to be those in which God originates the movement and invisibly suggests this obscure to us but patent to Himself.'[222] '[T]he Sacred Guide [i.e., Moses] gave a perfectly clear and lucid interpretation of the appearances (φαντασίας) which come under the first description, in as much as the intimations given by God through these dreams (ὀνείρων) were of the nature of plain oracles (χρησμοῖς).'[223]

> *Second class* – 'The second class [of dreams] is that in which our own mind (νοῦς), moving out of itself together with the Mind of the Universe, seems to be possessed and God-inspired (θεοφορεῖσθαι), and so capable of receiving some foretaste and foreknowledge of things to come.'[224] 'The second kind consisted [of dreams] in which our understanding (διανοίας) moves in concert with the soul of the Universe and becomes filled with divinely induced madness (θεοφορήτου μανίας), which is permitted to foretell many coming events.'[225]

218   For example, Blum, *Studies in the Dream-Book of Artemidorus,* 67–71.
219   Kessels, 'Ancient Systems of Dream-Classification,' 399–400.
220   Kessels, 'Ancient Systems of Dream-Classification,' 400.
221   Philo, *Somn.* 1.1 (Colson, LCL).
222   Philo, *Somn.* 2.2 (Colson, LCL; brackets added).
223   Philo, *Somn.* 2.3 (Colson, LCL).
224   Philo, *Somn.* 1.2 (Colson, LCL; brackets added).
225   Philo, *Somn.* 2.2 (Colson, LCL; brackets added).

Third class – 'This third kind [of dream] arises whenever the soul in sleep, setting itself in motion and agitation of its own accord, becomes frenzied, and with the prescient power due to such inspiration foretells the future.'[226] 'The appearances (φαντασίαι) of the third kind being more obscure than the former, owing to the deep and impenetrable nature of the riddle (αἴνιγμα) involved in them, demanded a scientific skill in discerning the meaning of the dreams (τῆς ὀνειροκριτικῆς ἐπιστήμης).'[227]

Philo's overarching category for the dreams found in Genesis is θεόπεμπτοι, which seems to be a semi-technical term used in the dream literature of antiquity. We have already seen this term used in Herophilus' dream classification, where it has the general sense of predictive dreams. It also seems to be synonymous with Posidonius' *deorum appulsu*. Artemidorus uses the term θεόπεμπτα to describe predictive dreams as opposed to 'anxiety-dreams and petitionary dreams,' which belong to the ἐνύπνιον class.[228] Interestingly, he quickly qualifies his comments by stating:

> I do not, like Aristotle, inquire as to whether the cause of our dreaming is outside of us and comes from the gods or whether it is motivated by something within, which disposes the soul in a certain way and causes a natural event to happen to it. Rather, I use the word in the same way that we customarily call all unforeseen things god-sent (θεόπεμπτα).[229]

Thus, Philo's use of the term θεόπεμπτοι is another indicator that his *De somniis* functions within the dream literature of the Greco-Roman world. As such, the term θεόπεμπτοι should not be interpreted in an overly Jewish, theological sense. It simply means predictive dreams, which can originate either from the divine or from the soul itself.

Philo's dream classification has been shown to share a common tradition with Posidonius' classification. Philo's particular expression of these dream classes, however, requires comment. The term χρησμός may be one term that Philo uses distinctively in relation to dreams, although it is used only once in reference to dreams; all other occurrences of χρησμός in *De somniis* are in reference to Scripture, usually a quotation.[230] In *De somniis* 2.3, Philo further describes the first class of dreams:

> The Sacred Guide [i.e., Moses] gave a perfectly clear and lucid interpretation of the appearances (φαντασίας) which come under the

226 Philo, *Somn.* 2.1 (Colson, LCL; brackets added).
227 Philo, *Somn.* 2.4 (Colson, LCL).
228 Artemidorus, *Onir.* 1.6 (White).
229 Artemidorus, *Onir.* 1.6 (White; text Pack).
230 Philo, *Somn.* 1.159; 1.172; 1.177; 1.207 (no quotation); 1.247; 2.142; 2.221; 2.297.

first description, inasmuch as the intimations given by God through these dreams (ὀνείρων) were of the nature of plain oracles (χρησμοῖς).

Two inferences can be drawn from this characterization of the first class of dreams. First, Philo's χρησμός seems to correspond to the χρηματισμός of Artemidorus/Macrobius, 'in which a parent, or a pious or revered man, or a priest, or even a god clearly reveals what will or will not transpire, and what action to take or to avoid.'[231] If the dreams of Abimelech (Gen. 20.3-7) and Laban (Gen. 31.24) were indeed the dreams treated in the lost work, Philo's χρησμός would correspond well to God's 'speaking' in those dreams. As such, and this is our second inference, Philo's first class of dreams would be considered theorematic; that is, a dream that needs no interpretation.

The subject of interpretation leads to another observation about Philo's dream categories. It is only with the third category of dreams that Philo connects the skill of dream interpretation. In *De somniis* 2.4, he characterizes this class of dreams as an enigma and states that they require 'scientific dream interpretation' (τῆς ὀνειροκριτικῆς ἐπιστήμης). When interpreting the dream of Joseph (Gen. 37.9), which is a third class dream, Philo again is concerned with 'how the rules of dream-interpretation (ὀνειροκριτικῇ τέξνῃ) explain it.'[232] This dream class parallels the enigmatic dream (ὄνειρος/*somnium*) of Artemidorus/Macrobius, which 'conceals with strange shapes and veils with ambiguity the true meaning of the information being offered, and requires an interpretation for its understanding.'[233] Therefore, Philo's third class is allegorical.

What about Philo's second class of dreams? In *De somniis* 2.3, he states that they are enigmatic (αἰνιγματώδης), 'but the riddle was not in very high degree concealed from the quick-sighted.' For Philo, the virtuous soul is able to perceive the truth, or meaning, in these dreams that originate from the soul's interaction with the divine intermediary, whether angels,[234] the archangel,[235] or the Logos.[236] Thus, the virtuous dreamer needs no aid in interpretation for the second class of dreams, for they are theorematic.

Philo's classification of dreams, then, can be compared to Artemidorus' functional design:

---

231   Macrobius, *Comm. in Somn. Scip.* 3.8 (Stahl).
232   Philo, *Somn.* 2.110 (Colson, LCL).
233   Macrobius, *Comm. in Somn. Scip.* 3.10 (Stahl).
234   Philo, *Somn.* 1.148.
235   Philo, *Somn.* 1.157.
236   Philo, *Somn.* 1.190; 1.230.

Artemidorus	*Philo*
ὄνειροι – predictive dreams	θεοπέμπτοι ὄνειροι – predictive dreams
ὅραμα – theorematic	First class – theorematic
χρηματισμός – theorematic	Second class – theorematic
ὄνειρος – allegorical	Third class – allegorical

Thus, Philo's dream classification has a practical correlation with the dream theory of Artemidorus/Macrobious and a formal one with the dream classification of Posidonius.[237]

The three-class system of dreams is also attested by the Christian writer Tertullian in his *De anima*, yet reflecting a Christian apologetic perspective.[238] Tertullian's classification of dreams emphasizes their origin. The first category of dreams has their origin in daemons. Tertullian has in view here the common, prevalent understanding and experience of pagan dream divination. Though these dreams sometimes prove true and helpful,[239] their ultimate purpose is to deceive and harm because they distract attention from the recognition of the one true God.[240] Christians are not immune to dream devices of the daemonic. Tertullian's second class of dreams originates from God. These dreams are 'honest, holy, prophetic, inspired, instructive, and inviting to virtue';[241] and can be received by non-Christians alike. Based on other writings, Tertullian is particularly interested in how God-sent dreams function in a disciplinary or admonishing way for Christians.[242] For example, in his treatise *De idololatria*, Tertullian gives example of how a Christian was chastised in a dream because his servants had adorned the gates of his house, a gesture of honoring 'entrance' gods.[243] Although not stated explicitly, Tertullian's interpretive guide for distinguishing daemonic dreams from God-sent dreams seems to be something like the rule of faith. The third class of dreams has a naturalistic origin in the activity of the soul.[244] When the body is at sleep, the soul remains active because of its connection with the power of *ecstasis*. Even though the experiences of anxiety, joy, and sorrow are experienced in these dreams, they are illusions and insignificant.

The various classifications and theories of dreams were attempts to explain the origin and phenomena of significant and insignificant dreams. Significant dreams were primarily of two kinds: (1) a message dream, in

---

237 It should be noted that Philo seems to refer to insignificant dreams in 2.105; 2.133; 2.162.

238 J. H. Waszink, *Tertulliani De Animia* (Amsterdam: J. M. Meulenhoff, 1947), 502.

239 Tertullian, *An.* 47.1.

240 Tertullian, *An.* 46.12.

241 Tertullian, *An.* 47.2 (*ANF* 3.225-6).

242 Miller, *Dreams in Late Antiquity*, 66–7.

243 Tertullian, *Idol.* 15; for other punitive dreams see also *Spect.* 26 and *Virg.* 17.

244 Tertullian, *An.* 45.1-6; 47.3.

which a god, divine being, or authoritative person communicated a message to the dreamer; and (2) a symbolic dream that needed interpreting, whether from a professional dream interpreter or by oneself. Non-significant dreams are attributed to the activity of the soul in response to the circumstances of one's life.

Conclusion

This chapter has attempted to demonstrate that dreams and their interpretation were a fixture of Greco-Roman religion and functioned in its various aspects: divination, magic, and cults. So established were dreams in the context of religion that an intellectual tradition developed in order to explain and understand the phenomenon as a part of the human experience. Given this social context of dreams, an ancient reader would read a narrative that contained dream reports with a world view that accepted and valued dreams as a mode of divine communication. Indeed, this social context of dreams no doubt had an effect on the literary tradition of the Greco-Roman world. It is this literary tradition of dreams that I now in turn investigate.

Chapter Three

THE ANCIENT, LITERARY CONTEXT OF DREAMS, PART I:
THE SCRIPT OF DREAMS

Whereas the previous chapter described the social construction of dreams in the Greco-Roman world, in the present chapter, and the following one, I will analyze dreams as a literary convention in Greco-Roman literature. No doubt the social and literary contexts of dreams are intrinsically related to and inform one another; for the social construction of dreams provides the *realia* from which literary dreams initiate their meaning and value. E. R. Dodds makes a similar observation in his cultural description of dreams in ancient Greece, though his concerns move in the opposite direction to establish the 'cultural-pattern' of dreams:

> In light of this evidence we must, I think, recognise that the stylisation of the 'divine dream' or *chrematismos* is not purely literary; it ... belongs to the religious experience of the people, though poets from Homer downwards have adapted it to their literary purposes by using it as a literary motif.[1]

Dodds' characterization of dreams as a literary motif adapted to the literary purposes of ancient poets reflects the consensus of modern scholarship. Modern scholarship has appropriately recognized the literary dimension of dreams, particularly in the study of Greco-Roman epic and dramatic poetry.[2] Already in the early twentieth century, the classicist William Stuart Messer emphasized the literary quality of dreams in his study of Homer and the Greek tragedies. Messer showed how the

---

1 E. R. Dodds, *The Greeks and the Irrational* (Berkeley: University of California Press, 1966), 108. Cf. also Dario Del Corno, 'Dreams and their Interpretation in Ancient Greece,' *BICS* 29 (1982): 57, who recognizes the literary character of dreams in Homer yet notes their obvious, even necessary, correlation with the public experience of dreams.

2 William Stuart Messer, *The Dream in Homer and Greek Tragedy* (Columbia University Studies in Classical Philology; New York: Columbia University Press, 1918), 1–102; Kenneth J. Reckford, 'Catharsis and Dream-Interpretation in Aristophane's *Wasps*,' *TAPA* 107 (1977): 283–312; A. H. M. Kessels, 'Dreams in Apollonius' *Argonautica*,' in *Actus: Studies in Honour of H. L. W. Nelson* (ed. H. L. W. Nelson, J. den Boeft, and A. H. M. Kessels; Utrecht: Instituut vor Klassieke Talen, 1982), 155–173; James F. Morris, '"Dream Scenes" in Homer: A Study in Variation,' *TAPA* 113 (1983): 39–54; Joachim Latacz, 'Funktionen des Traums in der antiken Literatur,' in *Traum und Träumen: Traumanalysen in Wissenschaft,*

Homeric dream is an 'artistic literary device' that advances the narrative plot at critical moments and provides a means of divine action.[3] He further states that dreams in the Greek tragedies, though adapted to the dramatic form, are 'an imitation, more or less direct, of the dreams used by Homer.'[4] Serving as a kind of bookend to Messer's study, Christine Walde has more recently analyzed dreams as a literary motif in Greek and Latin poetry, from Homer to Lucan. Walde recognizes, on the one hand, that dreams display a set of formal features that characterize the literary dream as conventional; but on the other hand, literary dreams of ancient poetry have a narrative versatility that allows authors to employ dreams for a multiplicity of literary strategies and to adapt them to the specific narrative of each author.[5]

The present analysis of dreams as a literary convention will focus on Greco-Roman prose literature, which no doubt was influenced by the poetic tradition.[6] My understanding of literary convention is informed by Robert Alter, who in his influential book, *The Art of Biblical Narrative* (1981), introduced to biblical (Old Testament) studies the concept of literary convention as employed by modern literary critics. Alter explains that a literary convention is a 'tacit agreement between the artist and audience about the ordering of the art work.'[7] This 'tacit agreement' generates a set of expectations about structure, sequence and the organization of motifs along a range of literary levels, from the macro-level of a text's genre[8] to the micro-level of structural phrases and word-plays. These expectations, of course, can be variously satisfied or even subverted, depending on how the author utilizes literary conventions. But

---

Religion und Kunst (ed. T. Wagner-Simon und G. Benedetti; Göttingen: Vandenhoeck & Ruprecht, 1984), 20–27; Christine Walde, *Die Traumdarstellungen in der griechisch-römischen Dichtung* (Leipzig: K. G. Saur München, 2001), 1–433.

3 Messer, *The Dream in Homer and Greek Tragedy*, vii and 47–52.

4 Messer, *The Dream in Homer and Greek Tragedy*, 57.

5 Walde, *Die Traumdarstellungen in der griechisch-römischen Dichtung*, esp. 3–4 and 417–420. The following statement is representative: 'Von der Warte des antiken Dichters aus zeichnet den Traum als literarisches Motiv sowohl hohe Individualität als auch hohe Anpassungsfähigkeit, sowohl Schlichtheit als auch höchste Komplexität aus. Das Motiv erfüllt also gleichzeitig die Kriterien ‚Nicht austauschbar' und ‚vielfältig verwendbar'. Was den Traum so leicht handhabbar macht, führt allerdings dazu, daß ihn die Interpreten der literarischen Kunstwerke oft übersehen oder als konventionell abstempeln' (417–418).

6 Walde, *Die Traumdarstellungen in der griechisch-römischen Dichtung*, 4. See also Peter Frisch, *Die Träume bei Herodot* (BKP 27; Meisenheim am Glan: Verlag Anton Hain, 1968), 49–52.

7 Robert Alter, *The Art of Biblical Narrative* (New York: Basic Books, 1981), 4. See also Alter's 'How Convention Helps Us Read: The Case of the Bible's Annunciation Type-Scene,' *Prooftexts* 3 (1983): 115–119.

8 For a discussion of convention and expectation for the issue of genre, see Richard A. Burridge, *What Are the Gospels? A Comparison with Graeco-Roman Biography* (2d ed.; Grand Rapids: Eerdmans, 2004), 32–36.

in the end, the effect of a literary convention is determined by the shared, inherited literary praxis of both the author and audience. For modern readers of ancient literature, the ability to identify these literary conventions is paramount to reading these texts as an ancient audience would have.[9] In demonstrating dreams as a literary convention, this chapter will advance by investigating what I call the *script of dreams*, while the following chapter will illustrate the various literary functions of dreams.

The phrase *script of dreams* intends to convey several meanings in relation to dreams as a literary convention. First, it emphasizes the written, literary representation of dreams. Having described the social function of dreams in Chapter Two, it is important to underscore that dreams also had a literary dimension and that this literary quality of dreams was recognized in antiquity. Second, the *script of dreams* expresses the fact that literary dreams follow a conventional form or pattern; there is something of a 'script' to how one narrates or reports dreams in ancient literature. Finally, though the literary representation of dreams exhibits a formal pattern, dreams as a literary unit could be adapted, or 'scripted,' for a range of literary functions. While Chapter Four will illustrate the specific functions of literary dreams, the present chapter will include a section that explores this creative aspect of scripting dreams. The script of dreams, as nuanced by these comments, will be examined more fully by analyzing (1) the literary form of dreams, (2) the rhetoric of dreams, and (3) the literary inventiveness of dreams.

The Literary Form of Dreams

As stated above, Robert Alter brought to Old Testament studies the modern literary concept of convention. It is interesting to note that his comments concerning literary convention actually served as a prelude to his discussion and analysis of one particular literary convention: the 'type-scene.'[10] As noted by Alter, 'type-scene' is a term first used by Walter Arend in Homeric studies and refers to a literary unit that displays 'certain

---

9 Alter's characterization of this necessity is helpful: 'Reading any body of literature involves a specialized mode of perception in which every culture trains its members from childhood. As modern readers of the Bible, we need to relearn something of *this mode of perception that was second nature to the original audiences.* Instead of relegating every perceived recurrence in the text to the limbo of duplicated sources or fixed folkloric archetypes, we may begin to see that the resurgence of certain pronounced patterns at certain narrative junctures was *conventionally anticipated, even counted on, and that against that ground of anticipation the biblical authors set words, motifs, themes, personages, and actions into an elaborate dance of significant innovation.*' (*The Art of Biblical Narrative*, 62 [emphasis added]).

10 Alter, *The Art of Biblical Narrative*, ch. 3.

prominent elements of a repetitive compositional pattern.'[11] One of the type–scenes identified by Arend, but not discussed by Alter, was the 'dream scene.'[12] Subsequent scholarship[13] has refined Arend's analysis and has identified the elements of the Homeric dream scene as follows, illustrated by the dream of Penelope in the *Odyssey* (4.786–5.2):

Reference to night and retirement of the dreamer: 'evening' came and Penelope 'lay there in her upper chamber' (4.789).

Description of the dreamer's mental state: Penelope did not eat or drink, 'pondering whether her peerless son would escape death' (4.789-90).

Sending and arrival of the dream figure: '[Athena] sent [the phantom] to the house of diving Odysseus. . . . So into the chamber it passed by the thong of the bolt' (4.795-802).

Likeness of the dream figure: '[Athena] made a phantom, and likened it in form to a woman, Iphthime, daughter of great-hearted Icarius' (4.796-798).

Position of the dream figure: '. . . and [the phantom] stood above her head' (4.803).

Message of the dream figure (which may include a dialogue with the dreamer): 'and [the phantom] said, "Sleepest thou, Penelope, thy heart sore stricken? Nay, the gods that live at ease suffer thee not to weep or be distressed, seeing that thy son is yet to return; for in no wise is he a sinner in the eyes of the gods"' (4.804-837).

Departure of the dream figure: 'So saying the phantom glided away by the bolt of the door into the breath of the winds' (4.838-839a).

Reaction of the dreamer: 'And [Penelope] started up from sleep, and her heart was warmed with comfort, that so clear a vision had sped to her in the darkness of night' (4.839b-841).

This bare listing of formal features obscures Homer's highly stylized language and the elaboration of some features. These repetitive compositional elements, however, are consistently present, and for Homeric scholars the dream scene represents a discernible literary convention in the *Odyssey* and *Iliad*.[14]

---

11   Alter, *The Art of Biblical Narrative*, 50.

12   Walter Arend, *Die typischen Scenen bei Homer* (Berlin: Weidmann, 1933), 61–63.

13   See David M. Gunn, 'Thematic Composition and Homeric Authorship,' *HSCP* 75 (1971): 15–17; and Morris, '"Dream Scenes" in Homer,' 39–54.

14   For the significance of type-scenes in Homer, see Mark W. Edwards, 'Homer and Oral Tradition: the Type-Scene,' *Oral Tradition* 7 (1992): 283–330.

The epics of Homer, however, are not the only literary works that represent dreams according to a formal pattern. If the study of literary dreams were broadened beyond Homer, it would be observed that dreams are found throughout the varied literary genres of the Greco-Roman period; and yet, the formal features of the dream narrative are fairly consistent and comparable to Homeric dreams.[15] This consistent pattern of dreams in the various literature of the Greco-Roman world has been aptly demonstrated by John Hanson.[16] For now, it is sufficient to summarize Hanson's conclusions; his form-critical work will be employed in our analysis of literary dreams in the following chapter. Hanson identifies four formal features of the dream narrative: (1) scene-setting, (2) dream-vision terminology, (3) dream-vision proper, and (4) reaction and/ or response.[17] Hanson uses the term 'dream-vision' because it more precisely communicates the fact that the literary forms of dreams and waking visions are practically indistinguishable. Moreover, dreams and waking visions constitute a similar phenomenon; but this terminology is cumbersome, and so I will simply use the term 'dream.'

The dream narrative begins with (1) the *scene-setting*, which can include: (a) the identification of the dreamer, along with a sketch of his or her character; (b) the place where the dream occurs; (c) the time in which the dream occurs; (d) the mental state of the dreamer; and/or (e) the activity of sleeping. As Hanson states, 'the degree of detail in this section can vary considerably, depending on numerous possible factors, including the literary context, general purpose of the report, or the particular interest of the narrator.'[18]

After the scene-setting, the dream narrative usually signifies the dream phenomena by some (2) *dream terminology*.[19] While ὄναρ, ὄνειρος, and ἐνύπνιον are the most common terms for dreams, other synonyms are

---

15 Cf. Frances Flannery-Daily, who, in her ambitious study of dreams in Ancient Near Eastern, Greek, Roman and Hellenistic Jewish literature, adopts the form-critical work of Leo Oppenheim and discovers a 'surprisingly standardized [pattern] across many cultures for millennia' ('Standing at the Head of Dreamers: A Study of Dreams in Antiquity' [Ph.D. diss., The University of Iowa, 2000], 1, see chs. 1–2); and John S. Hanson, 'Dreams and Visions in the Graeco-Roman World and Early Christianity,' *ANRW* 23.2.1396: 'Especially in formal, literary ways, the fundamental character of dream-vision reports does not significantly change from the Homeric poets to the end of late antiquity. Further, there are striking parallels between dream-vision materials of the Hellenistic and Roman periods and those of earlier cultures such as Assyria, Egypt, and Israel.'

16 Hanson, 'Dreams and Visions,' 1395–1427.

17 Hanson, 'Dreams and Visions,' 1400–1413.

18 Hanson, 'Dreams and Visions,' 1405.

19 Hanson notes that the dream-vision term may also be found in other parts of the dream scene; Hanson, 'Dreams and Visions,' 1407, n. 49.

employed, such as ὅραμα, ὄψις, φάσμα, φάντασμα, φαντασία, ἀποκάλυψις, ἐπιφάνεια, εἰκών and ὀπτασία.[20] In addition to the dream terminology, the dream proper is often introduced by δοκέω (ἐδόκει/ἔδοξε). The five sample texts that Hanson uses to demonstrate the form of the dream narrative employ the following terms/phrases: ἐγένετο ὄναρ τοιόνδε· ἐδόκει ('this kind of dream happened: it seemed'; Philostratus, *Vit. Apoll.* 4, 34); ἔδοξε καθ᾽ ὕπ < ν > ον ('it seemed during sleep'; *IG* X, 2, fasc. 1, no. 255); κατακοιμηθεὶς δὲ νύκτωρ ἐδόκει ('and having fallen asleep at night it seemed'; Plutarch, *Luc.* 12, 1); ὄψιν εἶδεν ἀλλόκοτον. ἐδόκει... ('he saw a strange vision/apparition. It seemed...'; Plutarch, *Eum.* 6, 4); and ὅραμα διὰ νυκτὸς ('a vision during the night'; Acts 16.9).

Hanson divides (3) the *dream proper* into three types: audio-visual dreams, auditory dreams, and visual dreams. The audio-visual dream has both the appearance of a dream figure and what the dream figure says or indicates. Formal features associated with the dream figure are (a) the identification of the dream figure, (b) the description of the dream figure, and/or (c) the position of the dream figure in relation to the dreamer (e.g., 'at the head of,' 'standing over,' or 'standing by' the dreamer). After (d) the message is given, sometimes (e) the departure of the dream figure is noted. I will refer to this type of dream as a visitant dream, because the dream figure visits the dreamer to impart some message. The auditory dream is a dream-vision in which something is only heard. One could argue that the auditory dream is simply a condensed version of the visitant dream, since the voice of the dream figure is usually identified.[21] The visual dream is commonly identified as an allegorical or symbolic dream, which calls for an interpretation. In this type of dream a scene or set of occurrences is described; if there are dream figures, they are simply part of the scene being described. For the most part, this classification of dreams holds true; but in certain cases a blurring of the lines can occur.

The dream narrative concludes with a description of the dreamer's (4) *reaction* and/or *response*. The dreamer's reaction can include waking, amazement, perplexity, fear, etc. The dreamer's reaction may also include some process of interpretation. The dreamer's response is 'simply the direct action that the dreamer is depicted as taking in consequence of the dream-vision proper.'[22] Thus, the form of the dream narrative can be outlined as follows:

---

20 Hanson, 'Dreams and Visions,' 1407–8.

21 Even if the dream figure is not identified, a dream figure seems to be assumed. This assumption stands behind R. G. A. van Lieshout's statement that there is 'not one example of an exclusively auditive dream-experience in classical Greek references to dreaming' (*Greeks on Dreams* [Utrecht: HES Publishers, 1980], 24).

22 Hanson, 'Dreams and Visions,' 1413.

1. *Scene-setting*
    a. identification of dreamer, along with a sketch of his or her character
    b. place
    c. time
    d. mental state of dreamer
    e. sleep
2. *Dream Terminology*
3. *Dream proper* (three types) - often introduced by δοκεῖν
    a. Visitant dream – dream figure visits to deliver message
        i.   identification of dream figure
        ii. description of dream figure
        iii. position of dream figure
        iv. message
        v.   departure of dream figure
    b. Auditory dream – dream message only heard
    c. Symbolic dream – scene or event described; interpretation required
4. *Reaction* and/or *Response* of dreamer

In summary, dreams in Greco-Roman literature are narrated or reported according to a formal pattern, which includes scene-setting, dream terminology, the dream proper and reaction/response. Though all the sub-features of these major elements may not appear in every dream representation, the dream narrative clearly represents a compositional pattern that ancient audiences would recognize and expect. Thus, the literary form of dreams contributes to our understanding of dreams as a literary convention.

The Rhetoric of Dreams

The literary quality of dreams can also be explored by considering dreams in the Greco-Roman rhetorical tradition. Before analyzing dreams in Greco-Roman rhetoric, however, it is important to clarify the relationship between Greco-Roman rhetoric and literature and answer a fundamental methodological question: How does the study of Greco-Roman rhetoric contribute to the analysis of ancient literary praxis? This issue is best addressed by considering the sources of the rhetorical tradition: the Greek *progymnasmata* and the rhetorical handbooks.

The Greek *progymnasmata* are preliminary, rhetorical exercises for children in antiquity before they received formal education in rhetoric. More than just preparation for an education in rhetoric, however, the *progymnasmata* set forth a curriculum for prose composition: prescribing writing exercises for basic literary forms such as the fable, narrative, comparison, *chreia*, speech in character and encomium, to mention a few.

This education in prose composition bears upon the wider literary activity of antiquity, as stated by the author of the earliest extant *progymnasmata*, Theon:

> Now I have included these remarks, not thinking that all are useful to all beginners, but in order that we may know that training in exercises is absolutely useful not only to those who are going to practice rhetoric but also if one wishes to undertake the function of poets or historians or any other writers. These things are, as it were, the foundation of every kind of discourse ... .[23]

Moreover, the Greek *progymnasmata* are not only prescriptive in the sense of setting forth exercises, but they are also descriptive in terms of depicting how classical authors employed the various compositional forms. As such, the *progymnasmata* represent a form of ancient literary criticism, analyzing classical literature in light of the compositional exercises. This descriptive character of the *progymnasmata* also reveals the traditional nature of these literary-rhetorical exercises: the *progymnasmata* are not innovative but illustrative of time-honored rhetorical-literary practices. Thus, the Greek *progymnasmata* provide an essential resource for studying the literary-rhetorical conventions and values of antiquity.

The rhetorical handbooks are to be used more cautiously. Their primary purpose is training for public speeches, especially in the courtroom. But even here, one can find numerous references and quotations from ancient authors used as examples of what the rhetoricians seek to illustrate. Attention should always be given to the context and purpose of a statement in the handbooks.

In the Greco-Roman rhetorical traditions, specific references to dreams are found in discussions of encomium and style. This section will proceed by looking at dreams in relation to these two subjects.

Dreams and Encomiastic Rhetoric

Encomium is treated by the rhetors as both a speech, along with judicial and deliberative speeches, and a compositional exercise of the *progymnasmata*. It is characterized variously as the exposition of the virtues and greatness of persons, animals or inanimate objects, though persons are the more common subject. In the encomium of a person, one begins with certain *topoi*, such as origin and birth. Given their divinatory nature, dreams are sometimes recommended for developing the birth *topos*.

---

23 Theon, *Progym.* 70 (Kennedy, 13). Cf. also George A. Kennedy's remarks that the progymnasmata presented an 'understanding of conventional literary forms for those who entered on literature as a career or as an elegant pastime' (Introduction to *Progymnasmata: Greek Textbooks of Prose Composition and Rhetoric* [ed. and trans. George A. Kennedy; WGRW 10; Atlanta: Society of Biblical Literature, 2003], ix).

So, Hermogenes instructs, 'you will mention also any marvelous (θαύματος) occurrences at birth, for example from dreams (ὀνειράτων) or signs (συμβόλων) or things like that.'[24] Nicolaus mentions specific examples of dreams in relation to the birth *topos*:

> After these remarks about origin we shall come to the circumstances of his birth; for example, if there is something we can say about him at the time of his mother's birth pains, as it is said of the mother of Pericles, Agariste, that a god told her in a dream that she would give birth to a lion, or the tradition about the mother of Cyrus about the vine and the flood of water in a dream. Many such stories have been passed down to us; for example, about Evagoras, the king of Cyprus, and others.[25]

In his treatise on the imperial encomium speech, Menander the Rhetor refers to dreams in a similar fashion:

> After country and family, then, let the third heading, as we have said, be 'birth', and if any divine sign (σύμβολον) occurred at the time of his birth, either on land or in the heavens or on the sea, compare the circumstances with those of Romulus, Cyrus, and similar stories, since in these cases also there were miraculous happenings (τινὰ θυαμάσια) connected with their births – the dream of Cyrus' mother, the suckling of Romulus by the she-wolf. If there is anything like this in connection with the emperor, work it up (ἐξέργασαι); if it is possible to invent (πλάσαι), and to do this convincingly, do not hesitate; the subject (ὑπόθεσις) permits this, because the audience has no choice but to accept the encomium without examination.[26]

These rhetoricians present dreams as an illustration of how the birth *topos* of an encomium can be expressed. In the case of Nicolaus, dreams are the only examples offered to demonstrate the birth *topos*. It should be noted that the traditions of these notable dreams are for the most part found in literary works. The dream concerning Cyrus' mother, for example, is reported by Herodotus in his *Histories* (1.107.2) as a part of an introduction to the story of Cyrus. The dream of Pericles' mother is included at the beginning of Plutarch's biography of Pericles (3.2), a beginning that is clearly reflective of the encomium tradition.[27] Thus, as a motif of the birth *topos* dreams contribute to the rhetoric of encomium, in both prose literature and speeches, by signifying the future greatness of an individual.

---

24   Hermogenes, *Progym.* 7.22-24 [15] (trans. Kennedy, 82; text Rabe).
25   Nicolaus, *Progym.* 8 [51–52] (Kennedy, 157).
26   Menander, Περὶ ἐπιδεικτιῶν 2.371 (Russell and Wilson, 80–83).
27   Before noting the dream of Pericles' mother, Plutarch tells about Pericles' homeland and ancestry, which are consistent elements of the origin *topos* (Plutarch, *Per.* 3.1).

Dreams and Rhetorical Style

Dreams are also offered as examples in discussions of rhetorical style. As part of his treatise on the imperial encomium, Menander the Rhetor deals with an informal type of speech called the 'talk' (λαλιά). The 'talk', being informal, is characterized by its disregard for any technical rules of order and its 'charming' (ἡδονή) and 'sweet' (γλυκυτής) style.[28] In contrast to a more sophisticated style that uses periods and enthymemes, this 'sweet' style is 'simpler and plainer' (ἁπλουστέρα καὶ ἀφελεστέρα) like Xenophon, Philostratus and Herodotus, which are 'full of pleasant narratives' (γλυκέων διηγημάτων).[29] Dream reports reflect this 'sweet' style, and so Menander instructs that 'one also ought to invent dreams' (χρὴ δὲ καὶ ὀνείρατα πλάττειν) when composing the 'talk'.[30]

The significance of Menander's comments for our study is two-fold. First, Menander clearly contributes to our analysis of the script of dreams by providing an ancient perspective on their literary character: the reporting of dreams is associated with a style that is characteristic of the prose narrative of Xenophon and Herodotus. Second, Menander encourages the invention of dreams for an informal type of speech that has been regarded as 'essentially "literature." '[31] Russell and Wilson continue by stating, 'The practice of the *lalia* certainly made it possible for writers to handle a wide variety of topics in an imaginable and untrammelled [*sic.*] way.'[32] Along with inventing fables,[33] quoting the poets, and using the stories, apophthegms and proverbs of Plutarch's *Lives*,[34] the invention of dreams also contributes to this 'imaginable' quality of the 'talk'.

A discussion of dreams and style is also given by John of Sardis in his *Commentary on the Progymnasmata of Aphthonius*.[35] In elaborating on

---

28   Menander, Περὶ ἐπιδεικτικῶν 2.389 (Russell and Wilson, 116).

29   Menander, Περὶ ἐπιδεικτικῶν 2.389 (Russell and Wilson, 116–117).

30   Menander, Περὶ ἐπιδεικτικῶν 2.390 (modified trans. of Russell and Wilson, 116–117).

31   D. A. Russell and N. G. Wilson, *Menander Rhetor* (Oxford: Oxford University Press, 1981), 121.

32   Russell and Wilson, *Menander Rhetor*, 121.

33   Menander, Περὶ ἐπιδεικτικῶν 2.390 (Russell and Wilson, 118–119).

34   Menander, Περὶ ἐπιδεικτικῶν 2.392-3 (Russell and Wilson, 122–123).

35   This work attributed to John of Sardis dates from the ninth century, a time-frame which raises questions about its use for a study of Hellenistic literature. The commentary, however, is in actuality a compilation of previous commentaries (see Kennedy, *Progymnasmata*, xii). More importantly, though, Ronald Hock has made the case that John of Sardis is a valuable resource for those studying the *progymnasmata*, because it provides an ancient explanation of why Aphthonius 'defined, classified, and illustrated as he did' (Ronald Hock, 'Why We Should Read the Commentaries on Aphthonius' Progymnasmata' [paper presented at the annual meeting of the Society of Biblical Literature, Philadelphia, Pa., 19 November 2005]). John of Sardis, then, also provides an ancient perspective on the literary nature of dreams.

Aphthonius' statement that the compositional form *ekphrasis* should have a 'relaxed' (ἀνειμένως) style, John of Sardis states in language similar to Menander that the style should be 'sweet (ἡδύς) and relaxed, without periods and enthymemes.'[36] After demonstrating this relaxed style with examples from Thucydides, Xenophon, and Herodotus, he concludes by stating,

> This simple style also invites poetic license (αὐτονομίαν ποιητικήν), such as describing the gods descending from heaven and ascending and engaging in dialogue – the source of Herodotus' description of the gods as kings of Egypt – and inventing dreams and oracles (ὀνείρους τε πλάττεται καὶ χρησμούς).[37]

The comments of John of Sardis are suggestive in several ways. First, like Menander, he mentions dreams in the discussion of a style that is characteristic of prose, narrative literature. The association of dreams with this kind of literary analysis of Thucydides, Xenophon and Herodotus draws attention to the literary aspect of dreams. Second, John of Sardis states that this style permits literary creativity (ποιητικός) and specifically mentions the invention of dreams. This feature will be discussed further in the next section.

Summary

In summary, a study of dreams in the Greco-Roman rhetorical tradition demonstrates that dreams were occasionally part of discussions that focused on literary-rhetorical issues. This context of literary-rhetorical analysis highlights the literary character of dreams and suggests that ancient auditors also understood that dreams have a literary dimension and reflect certain literary-rhetorical practices. Thus, this survey of dreams and Greco-Roman rhetoric supports my proposal concerning the script of dreams; that is, the literary dimension of dreams was recognized by ancient authors. The rhetoricians also make several references to the invention of dreams, and it is to this subject that I now turn.

The Inventiveness of Dreams

The investigation into the rhetoric of dreams revealed several references to the invention of dreams; that is, the report or narration of a dream is the creative invention of the author. Two remarks suggest that the invention of dreams was quite widespread. First, in his encomium of Evagoras,

---

36   John of Sardis, *Comm. in Aphthonii Progym.* 37, 21 [223] (Kennedy, 218; text Rabe).
37   John of Sardis, *Comm. in Aphthonii Progym.* 37, 21 [224] (modified trans. of Kennedy, 219; text Rabe).

Isocrates offers a convoluted statement as to why he has decided not to comment on the birth of Evagoras, though he believes there is much to say:

> I prefer to say nothing of the portents, the oracles, the visions that come in sleep (τὰς μὲν φήμας καὶ τὰς μαντείας καὶ τὰς ὄψεις τὰς ἐν τοῖς ὕπνοις γενομένας), from which the impression might be gained that he was of superhuman birth, not because I disbelieve the reports, but that I may make it clear to all that I am so far from resorting to invention (πλασάμενος) in speaking of his deeds that even of those matters which are in fact true I dismiss such as are known only to the few and of which not all the citizens are cognizant.[38]

Isocrates seems to be reacting to the fact that, not only are dreams a conventional motif for encomium, but the invention of dreams – as well as other forms of divination – are common as well. The hesitancy of Isocrates to develop the birth *topos* is based on the anticipated reaction of his audience: the mentioning of dreams may ring hollow with his audience because of the regular practice of inventing dreams. This sentiment is explicitly mentioned by Quintilian, who in his discussion of the *narratio* states that 'dreams and superstitions have long since lost their value, owing to the very ease with which they can be invented.'[39]

These statements, along with the comments from the previous section on the rhetoric of dreams, indicate that the invention of dreams was a common practice in Greco-Roman rhetoric, which in turn may reflect a similar practice in Greco-Roman literature. Cicero already recognized the inventiveness of dreams in poetic literature, acknowledging that the dreams found in Greek and Roman poetry are fictional (*ficta a poëta*; 'a fiction of the poet') and belong to the world of fable or myth (*somina fabularum*; 'dreams of fables').[40] This section, in turn, will tentatively explore the inventiveness of dreams in prose narratives as a way to demonstrate further the script of dreams. The inventiveness of dreams does not negate the reporting of actual dreams or the transmitting of traditions about notable dreams, but it does highlight the creative venue that dreams attract and thus their literary representation.[41] This exploration will proceed by considering: (1) literary imitation of dreams, (2)

---

38   Isocrates, *Evag.* 9.21 (modified trans. of Norlin, LCL).
39   Quintilian, *Inst.* 4.2.94 (Butler, LCL).
40   Cicero, *Div.* 1.40-43.
41   Hanson's assessment is instructive here: 'Whether or not these literary reports have a historical basis is in most cases an irresolvable question. The accepted mode of narrating a dream or vision determines the memory or imagination of dreamers and literati alike. As a result, it is difficult to move from the literary level to actual experience, even if some of the dream-vision reports correspond to some reality' ('Dreams and Visions,' 1400–1401).

Homeric quotations and allusions in dreams, (3) the double-dream report, and (4) dreams and 'Rewritten Bible.'

Literary Imitation of Dreams

Given the formal, conventional pattern of dream reports, it is difficult to demonstrate a dream narrative as an imitation of another literary dream.[42] This difficulty notwithstanding, I want to survey two dream narratives that have been considered literary imitations.

The first illustration of literary imitation comes from Herodotus' narration of the dreams of Xerxes (*Hist.* 7). It is widely held that Herodotus has modeled this account on the dream of Agamemnon in book two of the *Iliad*.[43] In both accounts, a warrior-king has a dream that compels him to enter into a military campaign, which ends in disastrous consequences. Having already decided not to wage war against the Greeks, the Persian king, Xerxes, dreams that a 'tall and handsome man stood over [him]' (7.12) and counseled him to invade the Greeks 'at once' (7.14). To emphasize this decision as the will of the divine, Herodotus narrates two more dream scenes that have the same dream figure repeating the same instruction, again to Xerxes and once to his uncle Artabanus (7.14, 17).[44] The Persians, however, fail in their campaign against the Greeks. The *Iliad* presents Zeus sending 'a destructive dream' (οὖλος ὄνειρος)[45] to the Achaean king, Agamemnon, with the counsel to

---

42 Recognizing the difficulty of identifying imitation in specific texts, Dennis R. MacDonald has created six criteria for determining the presence of literary imitation: accessibility, analogy, density, sequencing of motifs, distinctive traits, and interpretability. MacDonald applies these criteria to show how the New Testament authors (Mark and Luke) imitated Homer. Many of MacDonald's conclusions, however, fail to convince, primarily because he does not satisfy his own criteria or in the end some criteria are simply too subjective. See his two major works: *The Homeric Epics and the Gospel of Mark* (New Haven: Yale University Press, 2000) and *Does the New Testament Imitate Homer?: Four Cases from the Acts of the Apostles* (New Haven: Yale University Press, 2003). For a critique of MacDonald's reading of the New Testament, see Karl Olav Sandnes, '*Imitatio Homeri?*: An Appraisal of Dennis R. MacDonald's "Mimesis Criticism," ' *JBL* 124 (2005): 715–732.

43 E.g., see Deborah Boedeker, 'Epic Heritage and Mythical Patterns in Herodotus,' in *Brill's Companion to Herodotus* (ed. E. J. Bakker, I. J. F. de Jong, and H. van Wees; Leiden: Brill, 2002), 103; Detlev Fehling, *Herodotus and his 'Sources': Citation, Invention, and Narrative Art* (trans. J. G. Howie; Leeds, Great Britain: Francis Cairns, 1990), 204; Thomas Harrison, *Divinity and History: The Religion of Herodotus* (Oxford Classical Monograph; New York: Clarendon Press, 2000), 132, 136–137; and MacDonald, *Does the New Testament Imitate Homer?*, 37–43. For those who question this assertion, see Henry R. Immerwahr, 'Historical Action in Herodotus,' *TPAPA* 85 (1954): 34–36; and Stephanie West, 'And it came to pass that Pharaoh dreamed: Notes on Herodotus 1.139, 141,' *CQ* 37 (1987): 264–265.

44 This series of dreams will be considered more fully in the next chapter.

45 Homer, *Il.* 2.8.

attack the city of Troy 'with all haste' (πανσυδίη).[46] The dream 'stood above his head, in the likeness of the son of Neleus, Nestor, whom above all the elders Agamemnon held in honor'[47] and persuaded Agamemnon that Troy was ready for the taking 'now' (νῦν).[48] The result, however, is a prolonged military engagement with many Greeks dying.

Several factors suggest that Herodotus is imitating the *Iliad*. First, the function of these two dreams, to mislead, is unusual. As the following chapter will show, literary dreams are quite consistent in portending the future. Dreams predict events that may be fortunate or unfortunate, or dreams can even be misinterpreted; but in almost every instance dreams prove to be accurate and are fulfilled. A deceitful dream, like that experienced by Xerxes, is not the norm and most certainly recalls the highly familiar dream of Agamemnon.[49] Second, the deceitful dreams of both Xerxes and Agamemnon are presented as acts of divine retribution. The failed expedition of Xerxes, which the dream initiates, is a consequence of divine envy (φθόνος) against the hubris of the Persians (7.10).[50] In the *Iliad*, Zeus sends the deceitful dream in order to punish Agamemnon, who has dishonored Achilles (1.505). Third, in both Homer and Herodotus the dream figures command that the ill-fated campaigns begin immediately (πανσυδίη, *Il.* 2.29; αὐτίκα, *Hist.* 7.14). Fourth, of the fourteen dreams that Herodotus narrates it is only in the dream of Xerxes that he describes the dream figure departing ('vanish away'; ἀποπέτομαι). Dream narratives in Homer almost always include the dream figure departing,[51] and when Agamemnon relates the dream to the council of elders he uses the term ἀποπέτομαι ('vanish away') to describe the dream figure's departure (2.71).[52] Thus, it seems that Herodotus has shaped the dream narrative of Xerxes according to the Homeric dream of Agamemnon.

Another example of possible literary imitation is the dream of Archelaus in Josephus (*War* 2.112-113/*Ant.* 17.345-348).[53] Some have suggested that Josephus has based his narration of Archelaus' dream on

---

46 Homer, *Il.* 2.12; cf. 2.29.

47 Homer, *Il.* 2.20-21 (Murray, LCL).

48 Homer, *Il.* 2.29.

49 For a discussion of the ubiquity of Agamemnon's dream in antiquity, see MacDonald, *Does the New Testament Imitate Homer?*, 26–28.

50 Nick Fisher, 'Popular Morality in Herodotus,' in *Brill's Companion to Herodotus* (ed. E. J. Bakker, I. J. F. de Jong, and H. van Wees; Leiden: Brill, 2002), 220–224.

51 *Il.* 2.35; 23.100-101; 24.692-694; *Od.* 4.838-839; 6.41-47; 15.43; 20.55.

52 The term used in the dream report itself is ἀποβαίνω ('depart'; 2.35).

53 The subtle but interesting differences between the accounts of Archelaus' dream in *War* and *Antiquities* will be explored more fully in Chapter Four.

the oneiric tales of Joseph in the biblical book of Genesis.[54] Archelaus has a symbolic dream in which 'he saw nine full, large ears of corn being devoured by oxen.'[55] He then summons 'diviners (μάντεις) and certain ones of the Chaldeans' to interpret for him the meaning of the dream. When their interpretations conflict with one another, a certain Simon the Essene comes forward and provides an interpretation that will prove to be accurate: the number of ears of corn represents years and the devouring oxen signify change; the dream indicates the number of years of Archelaus' rule. In Genesis 41, Pharaoh has two symbolic dreams. In the first dream, he sees 'seven sleek and fat cows' eaten by seven 'ugly and thin cows.'[56] In the second dream, Pharaoh sees 'seven ears of grain, plump and good,' swallowed by 'seven ears, thin and blighted.'[57] To determine the meaning of the dreams, Pharaoh summons 'all the magicians of Egypt and all its wise men,'[58] but no one was able to interpret the dream. As one who has the reputation of interpreting dreams, Joseph is then brought to Pharaoh to offer an explanation of the dreams. Joseph discerns that both dreams signify the same future: seven years of abundance followed by seven years of famine.

The parallels of Archelaus' dream with the Joseph tales are centered on a shared motif, and similarities in the content of the dreams. In both accounts, a ruler has a symbolic dream and calls upon his pagan, professional diviners to interpret the dream. When the professional diviners cannot interpret the dream, a Hebrew/Jewish person comes forward and properly reveals the meaning of the dream. This shared motif lends the most persuasive case for literary imitation. In addition to this motif, however, it should be noted that both dreams have agricultural images in which the number of ears of grain/corn is interpreted as years. Though not as evident as Herodotus' imitation of the *Iliad*, it can be argued that Josephus has at least been inspired by the biblical story of Joseph in his narrating the dream of Archelaus.

These instances of literary imitation illustrate one aspect of the invention of dreams. As stated above, the conventional and formal nature of dream reports makes the detection of literary mimesis quite

54   See discussion and bibliographic references in Robert K. Gnuse, *Dreams and Dream Reports in the Writings of Josephus: A Traditio-Historical Analysis* (AGJU 36; Leiden: E. J. Brill, 1996), 132–33 and 245–255. These discussions also include comparisons with Daniel, but Daniel also seems to be an imitation of the Joseph stories (Gnuse, *Dreams and Dream Reports in the Writings of Josephus*, 246).

55   Josephus, *J.W.* 2.112.

56   Gen 41.2-4 (NRSV).

57   Gen 41.5-7 (NRSV).

58   Gen 41.8 (NRSV).

precarious. But given the practice of literary imitation in antiquity[59] and the literary tradition of dreams, it should not be surprising if some dreams evoke a particular literary precursor. Herodotus and Josephus seem to be participating in this literary practice in narrating their respective dreams and so demonstrate one facet of the invention of dreams.

Homeric Quotations and Echoes[60]

The inventiveness of dreams may also be exemplified by the presence of Homeric quotations or echoes in a dream report. Plutarch narrates two dreams that include a quotation or echo of Homer. In reporting the dream of Alexander that inspires the founding of Alexandria, Plutarch presents the dream figure as Homer[61] who quotes from his *Odyssey:*

> Then, in the night as he was sleeping, he saw a marvelous vision (ὄψιν εἶδε θαυμαστήν): A man with very gray hair and an honorable appearance seemed to be standing by him and speaking these words:
> '*Now there is a certain island in the much-dashing sea,*
> *in front of Egypt; And they call it Pharos.*'[62]

This fashioning of the dream in relation to Homer is most certainly related to the legendary library at Alexandria. The other example is found in Plutarch's *Lucullus*. On a military campaign, Lucullus has a dream:

> Having fallen asleep in the night it seemed that he saw the goddess [i.e., Aphrodite] standing over him and saying:
> 'Why do you sleep, great-hearted lion?
> The fawns are near for you.'[63]

The dream message is an allusion to the *Odyssey*, in which Menelaus likens Odysseus' eventual revenge upon the suitors of Penelope to a lion that brings destruction to fawns:

> Just as when in the thicket lair of a powerful lion a doe has laid to sleep her new born suckling fawns, and roams over the mountain slopes and grassy vales seeking pasture, and then the lion comes to his lair and upon her two fawns lets loose a cruel doom, so will Odysseus let loose a cruel doom upon these men.[64]

---

59   See the collection of essays in Dennis R. MacDonald, ed., *Mimesis and Intertextuality in Antiquity and Christianity* (Studies in Antiquity and Christianity; Harrisburg, Pa.: Trinity Press International, 2001).

60   Much of this material is taken from my article 'Dreams, the Ancient Novels, and the Gospel of Matthew: An Intertextual Study,' *PRSt* 29 (2002): 45.

61   J. R. Hamilton, *Plutarch: Alexander* (2d ed.; London: Bristol Classical Press, 1999), 67.

62   Plutarch, *Alex.* 26.3 (modified trans. of Perrin, LCL), quoting *Od.* 4.354-355.

63   Plutarch, *Luc.* 12.1 (modified trans. of Perrin, LCL).

64   Homer, *Od.* 4.335-339 (Murray, LCL).

Plutarch creatively uses the Homeric echo as the dream message, which results in Lucullus capturing his enemy.

One other example of a dream report including a Homeric quotation is found in Plato's *Crito*. Socrates relates to Crito a dream that, according to Socrates, portends his death:

> It seemed to me that a certain beautiful and fair woman, who had a white garment came and called me and said, 'O Socrates, *on the third day you will come to fertile Phthia* (ἤματί κεν τριτάτῳ Φθίην ἐρίβωλον ἵκοιο).'[65]

The dream message is a quotation from a speech of Achilles, in which he speaks of going home: 'On the third day I will come to fertile Phthia (ἤματί κε τριτάτῳ Φθίην ἐπίβωλον ἱκοίμην).'[66] Plato imaginatively employs the Homeric quotation to interpret the death of Socrates as a kind of going home.

The final examples of Homeric quotations and echoes in dream narratives come from the Greek novels. Though the Greek novels are fiction, and so leave no doubt as to the inventiveness of their dreams, the very fact that this practice of intertextuality also shows up in the novels may highlight the inventive character of the previous dreams of Plutarch and Plato. The dream narrative in Chariton's *Chaereas and Callirhoe* 2.9.6 includes a quotation from the Homeric dream of Achilles in the *Iliad*:

> A vision of Chaereas stood over her, *like him in every way, in stature and fair eyes and voice, and wearing just such clothes* (πάντα αὐτῷ ὁμοία μέγεθός τε καὶ ὄμματα κάλ᾽ ἐϊκυῖα, καὶ φωνήν, καὶ τοῖα περὶ χροῒ εἵματα ἕστο >).[67]

> Then there came to him the spirit of hapless Patroclus, *in all things like his very self, in stature and fair eyes and voice, wearing just such clothes* (πάντ᾽ αὐτῷ μέγεθός τε καὶ ὄμματα κάλ᾽ ἐϊκυῖα, καὶ φωνήν, καὶ τοῖα περὶ χροῒ εἵματα ἕστο); and he stood above Achilles.[68]

The description of the dream figure of Patroclus in the *Iliad* is borrowed for the description of the dream figure Chaereas in Chariton.

Homeric echoes are also found in a couple of dream reports in other Greek novels. Longus' *Daphnis and Chloe* 3.28.1 contains a Homeric echo from the *Odyssey* in describing the dreamer's response/reaction.[69] After the dream figure(s) departs, 'Daphnis jumped up cheerfully and, *with a lot*

---

65   Plato, *Cri.* 44a-44b (trans. mine; text LCL).
66   Homer, *Il.* 9.363.
67   Chariton, *Chaer.* 2.9.6 (modified trans. of Reardon; text Blake).
68   Homer, *Il.* 23.66-67 (modified trans. of Murray, LCL).
69   This Homeric echo is identified by Christopher Gill in his translation of Longus' *Daphnis and Chloe* in *Collected Ancient Greek Novels* (ed. B. P. Reardon; Berkeley: University of California Press, 1989), 315 n. 57.

of whistling, drove the goats to the pasture (ῥοίζῳ πολλῷ ἥλαυνε τὰς αἶγας εἰς τὴν νομήν).'[70] This echoes the *Odyssey* where the Cyclops, 'with much whistling directed the fat goats to a mountain (πολλῇ δὲ ῥοίζῳ προ 'ς ὄρος τρέπε πίονα μῆλα).'[71] The description of the dream figure in the *Aethiopica* 5.22.1-2 is virtually a string of Homeric allusions and echoes that are various descriptions of Odysseus:[72]

> But as I slept, a vision of an old man appeared to me. Age had withered him (*Od.* 13.397ff) almost to a skeleton, except that his cloak was hitched up to reveal a thigh that retained some vestige of strength of his youth (*Od.* 18.67-68). He wore a leather helmet on his head (*Il.* 10.261), and his expression was one of cunning (*Od.* 13.332) and many wiles (*Od.* 1.1); he was lame in one leg, as if from a wound of some kind (*Od.* 19.392ff).

The fashioning of dream narratives with quotations and echoes of Homer further demonstrates the literary character of dreams. It also provides another case in point of how the dream narrative invites a degree of literary creativity.

The Double-Dream Report

The inventiveness of dreams can also be shown by the literary elaboration of the dream report known as the double-dream report.[73] The double-dream narrative involves two characters who each have a dream. The two dreams can be identical, similar or entirely different, but they are connected in some way to 'produce what may be called a "circumstance of mutuality" between the two dreamers.'[74] Thus, the double-dream narrative provides a more sophisticated and engaging literary device for plot development.

The first example of a double-dream narrative comes from Josephus' *Jewish Antiquities* 11.326-335. The high priest Jaddus has received news that Alexander the Great is approaching Jerusalem with his army. Jaddus had previously defied Alexander and so was in fear of the impending encounter. Having called upon the people to pray, Jaddus also prayed and offered sacrifices requesting God's help. While in the temple, he falls asleep and receives the following dream:

---

70   Longus, *Daphn.* 3.28.1 (Gill; text Edmond, LCL).

71   Homer *Od.* 9.315 (modified trans. of Murray, LCL).

72   See J. R. Morgan's note to his translation of Heliodorus in *Collected Ancient Greek Novels* (ed. B. P. Reardon; Berkeley: University of California Press, 1989), 462 n. 144.

73   Alfred Wikenhauser, 'Doppelträume,' *Bib* 29 (1948): 100–111; and Hanson, 'Dreams and Visions,' 1414–1419.

74   Hanson, 'Dreams and Visions,' 1414–1419.

God commanded him during sleep to take courage and adorn the city with wreaths and to open the gates and go out to meet them, and that the people should be in white garments and he himself with priests should be in the robes prescribed by the laws, and that they should not look to suffer any harm, for God was watching over them.[75]

Jaddus obeys the dream command and goes out with the people to meet Alexander and his army. The tension of the scene is heightened by Josephus' portrayal of the army, who 'thought to themselves that the king in his anger would naturally permit them to plunder the city and put the high priest to a shameful death.'[76] But when Alexander sees the people in their white clothing and Jaddus in his priestly garb, especially the priestly headdress with the name of God inscribed upon it, he prostrated before the divine name and greeted Jaddus. This highly unusual and unexpected act is explained by Alexander:

> It was not before him that I prostrated myself but the God of whom he has the honor to be high priest, for it was he whom I saw in my sleep as he is now, when I was at Dium in Macedonia, and, as I was considering with myself how I might become the master of Asia, he urged me not to hesitate but to cross over confidently, for he himself would lead my army and give over to me the empire of the Persians. Since, therefore, I have beheld no one else in such robes, and on seeing him now I am reminded of the vision during my sleep and the exhortation, I believe that I have made this expedition under divine guidance and that I shall defeat Darius and destroy the power of the Persians and succeed in carrying out all the things which I have in mind.[77]

Thus, the dream of Jaddus inspires actions that cause Alexander to recall his own dream, which moves Alexander to spare Jaddus and the Jewish people. The 'circumstance of mutuality' exists in the people's salvation and in Alexander's opportunity to worship the God that exhorted him to begin his military conquest. Moreover, the double-dream narrative is the literary device by which Josephus writes the Jewish people and their God into the world history of Alexander and the Greeks.[78] Apart from the historical questions that are raised by this account,[79] the double-dream narrative itself betrays literary creativity.

The second illustration of the double-dream report is found in the *Roman Antiquities* of Dionysius of Halicarnassus. In Book 1.57, the

75 Josephus, *A.J.* 11.327 (Marcus, LCL).

76 Josephus, *A.J.* 11.330 (Marcus, LCL).

77 Josephus, *A.J.* 11.333-335 (modified trans. of Marcus, LCL).

78 Erich S. Gruen, *Heritage and Hellenism: The Reinvention of Jewish Tradition* (Berkeley: University of California Press, 1998), 193–199.

79 Erich S. Gruen, *Heritage and Hellenism*, 195, is quite forward in his evaluation of Josephus' account: 'It is outright fabrication .... The tale is a fiction.'

legendary Aeneas has moved his troops into the territory ruled by Latinus and he is taking materials from the land to establish a town. When Latinus hears of this, he leads his army near to where Aeneas is settling. As Latinus is encamped for the night and planning to attack Aeneas the following morning, both he and Aeneas have dreams that will prove beneficial:

> Now when he had determined these things, a certain divinity (δαίμων) of that region appeared to him in his sleep and said to him the Greeks should be received into his land to dwell with his own subjects, adding that their coming was a great advantage to him and a benefit to all the Aborigines alike. And the same night Aeneas's household gods appeared to him and admonished him to persuade Latinus to grant them of his own accord a settlement in the part of the country they desired and to treat the Greek forces rather as allies than as enemies. Thus the dream (τὸ ὄναρ) hindered both of them from beginning an engagement. And as soon as it was day and the armies were drawn up in order of battle, heralds came to each of the commanders from the other with the same request, that they should meet for a conference; and so it came to pass.[80]

The narrator explains the mutual benefit of the two dreams: a battle is averted and a peace accord is established. For the larger plot, however, the two dreams effect a relationship between Greeks and Latins and initiate the ultimate founding of the city of Rome. The literary device of the double-dream narrative functions well for enacting such momentous events.

Finally, the Acts of the Apostles provides two examples of a double dream-vision report. The accounts are not dreams, however, but visions. I include them here because Acts is a Christian text and it serves as a reminder – and preliminary perspective for the appendix – that dreams and visions represent the same phenomenon that occurs while one is either asleep (dream) or awake (vision).[81]

The first double dream-vision in Acts involves Ananias and Saul (Paul). The dream-vision report directly follows the account of Paul's encounter with Christ as he was traveling to Damascus and his subsequent blindness (9.1-9). The vision is narrated as follows:

> Now there was a certain disciple in Damascus named Ananias, and the Lord said to him in a vision (ἐν ὁράματι), 'Ananias.' And he said, 'I am here, Lord.' And the Lord said to him, 'Ananias, Get up and go to the gate that is called Straight and seek in the house of Judas one named Saul of Tarsus. For behold, he is praying and he sees a man in a vision

---

80 Dionysius of Halicarnassus, *Ant. rom.* 1.57.3-4 (modified trans. of Cary, LCL).

81 This position is conveyed in the terminology of Hanson: dream-vision report and double dream-vision report.

named Ananias coming and laying his hands upon him so that he might see again.' And Ananias responded, 'Lord, I have heard from many about this man, how much evil he has done to your saints in Jerusalem; and here he has authority from the chief priests to bind all the ones who call upon your name.' And the Lord said to him, 'Go, for this one is a chosen vessel for me to bring my name before Gentiles and kings and the children of Israel. For I will show him what is how much he must suffer for my name.' And Ananias departed and entered the house and put his hands upon him and said, 'Brother Saul, the Lord has sent me, Jesus who you saw on the road while coming here, so that you may see again and be filled with the Holy Spirit.' And immediately something fell from his eyes like scales, and he could see again, and he got up and was baptized and receiving food he regained his strength.[82]

This double dream-vision is notable for the way in which one vision is narrated within another dream-vision report; the report of Saul's vision is embedded in the vision message given to Ananias. The two visions work together so that the infamous persecutor of the church, Saul, is now received and served by a would-be victim with healing, baptism and nurture. Ananias also benefits with the revelation that Saul is no longer a threat. But Luke also artistically utilizes the double dream-vision to include God in this 'circumstance of mutuality' and those who will now hear the name of Jesus because of Paul's mission.

In Acts 10, Luke provides another double dream-vision that involves a Gentile 'God-fearer' named Cornelius and the apostle Peter. The first vision narrated is the one granted to Cornelius:

> At about the ninth hour of the day he saw clearly in a vision (ἐν ὀράματι φανερῶς) an angel of God coming to him and saying to him, 'Cornelius.' And he stared at him and being afraid he said, 'What is it, Lord?' And he said to him, 'Your prayers and almsgivings have gone up as a memorial before God. And send now men to Joppa and summon a certain Simon who is called Peter. This one is being entertained by a certain Simon, a tanner, whose house is by the sea.' And when the angel who spoke to him departed, he called two of his servants and a devout soldier of those who was a close companion to him, and having described everything to them he sent them to Joppa.[83]

The scene then shifts to Joppa, where Peter is praying on a rooftop. As he is praying, he falls into a trance and has the following vision:

> He saw the heavens open and some object descending like a large piece of cloth being let down upon the earth by the four corners. And on it there were all kinds of animals and reptiles of the earth and birds of the sky. And there came a voice to him, 'Get up, Peter, kill and eat.' But

82   Acts 9.10-19.
83   Acts 10.3-8.

> Peter said, 'By no means. Lord, for I have never eaten anything defiled
> and unclean. And the voice again a second time came to him, 'What
> God has cleansed, you do not consider defiled.' And this happened three
> times, and immediately the object was taken up to heaven.[84]

As Peter is pondering the meaning of the vision, Cornelius' messengers
arrive at Simon's house and relate the request to return with them to
Cornelius. Peter accepts the invitation, and the Gentile Cornelius
describes his vision to him. Peter learns his own lesson, announcing
that, 'God has shown me that I should not call anyone defiled or
unclean.'[85] Peter then preaches the gospel, after which the Holy Spirit
comes upon all who heard Peter's preaching and are baptized.

The 'circumstance of mutuality' effected by these visions is Cornelius'
hearing of the gospel, experiencing the gift of the Holy Spirit, and
receiving baptism; and Peter is prepared for his encounter with the Gentile
Cornelius, gaining a new understanding about the character of God and
the implications of the gospel. Like the double dream-vision in Acts 9, this
'circumstance of mutuality' is more inclusive than simply Cornelius and
Peter. The Cornelius event becomes the critical impetus for the church
recognizing the place of the Gentiles among God's people.[86] In fact, the
double dream-visions of Acts 9 and 10 themselves function in tandem to
motivate the events that will ultimately determine the decision of Gentile
inclusion in Acts 15. The literary artistry of Luke is on full display in his
utilization of the double dream-visions in Acts 9 and 10.

The double-dream narrative proves particularly helpful in illustrating
the inventiveness of dreams. As a sophisticated literary device that
facilitates plot development at critical points, the double-dream report
attracts embellishment and invention.[87]

Dreams and 'Rewritten Bible'

The inventiveness of dreams can also be demonstrated by noting their
presence in the Jewish literary tradition referred to as 'Rewritten Bible.'
'Rewritten Bible' refers to a literary development in Middle Judaism that
reworks and retells biblical stories through a diverse combination of

---

84   Acts 10.11-16.
85   Acts 10.28.
86   Acts 15.1-28, esp. 7–11 and 13–18.
87   For other texts that contain double dream-vision reports, see Livy, *Hist. Rome* 8.6.9-
11; Tacitus, *Hist.* 4.43-84; Athenaeus, *Deipn.* 13.575; Achilles Tatius, *Leuc. Clit.* 4.1.4-8.
Longus, *Daphn.* 1.7.1-3; Heliodorus, *Aeth.* 8.11.1-9; Petronius, *Sat.* 104; Apuleius, *Metam.*
11.6; *Acts Thom.* 29–34; *Acts John* 18–19. References given by Hanson, 'Dreams and
Visions.' 1415 n. 82; I have added the Achilles Tatius and Heliodorus references.

verbatim reproduction, paraphrase, expansion, addition and omission.[88] Though adapted to a variety of genres and motivated by a diversity of social and intellectual concerns,[89] a primary characteristic of 'Rewritten Bible' is literary creativity.[90] Dreams constitute one way in which this embellishment and refashioning of the Jewish scriptures is achieved. The three 'Rewritten Bible' texts that are treated here are the *Genesis Apocryphon* (1QapGen), Pseudo-Philo's *Biblical Antiquities*, and Ezekiel the Tragedian's *Exagoge*.

The *Genesis Apocryphon* (1QapGen) was among those first manuscripts discovered in Cave 1 of Qumran, and already in 1966 was the subject of a full length commentary by Joseph Fitzmyer, which was revised in 1971. The text is written in Aramaic and was composed sometime during the first century B.C.E. and first century C.E.[91] Fitzmyer's description of the *Genesis Apocryphon* is worth repeating, for it reinforces the notion that a fundamental characteristic of these kinds of texts (i.e., 'Rewritten Bible') is literary creativity:

> We stress then the independent character of this composition. Though it depends on the biblical text of Genesis and displays at times traits of targumic and midrashic composition, it is in reality a free reworking of the Genesis stories, a re-telling of the tales of the patriarchs.... . The Genesis Apocryphon represents then an example of late Jewish narrative writing, strongly inspired by the canonical stories of the patriarchs, but abundantly enhanced with imaginative details.[92]

These imaginative details include three dreams that have been added to embellish the biblical text.

The first dream in the *Genesis Apocryphon*[93] comes as an embellishment to the narrative of Genesis 12.10–13.1, which tells the story of Abraham and Sarah's sojourn into Egypt because of a famine. In the biblical story,

---

88   Brant Pitre, 'Rewritten Bible,' in *The Westminster Dictionary of New Testament and Early Christian Literature and Rhetoric*, by David E. Aune (Louisville, Ky.: Westminster John Knox, 2003), 410–414 (esp. 412).

89   George W. E. Nickelsburg, 'The Bible Rewritten and Expanded,' in *Jewish Writings of the Second Temple Period: Apocrypha, Pseudepigrapha, Qumran Sectarian Writings, Philo, Josephus* (ed. M. E. Stone; vol. 2 of *The Literature of the Jewish People in the Period of the Second Temple and the Talmud*; CRINT Section Two; The Netherlands: Van Gorcum, Assen, 1984), 89–90; Gruen, *Heritage and Hellenism*, chs. 4–5; and Craig A. Evans, 'The Genesis Apocryphon and the Rewritten Bible,' *RevQ* 13 (1988): 154–162.

90   See Gruen, *Heritage and Hellenism*, ch. 4.

91   For introductory matters, see Joseph A. Fitzmyer, *The Genesis Apocryphon of Qumran Cave I: A Commentary* (2d rev. ed.; BibOr 18a; Rome: Biblical Institute Press, 1971), 1–41; and Bruce N. Fisk, 'Genesis Apocryphon (1QapGen),' *DNTB* 398–401.

92   Fitzmyer, *The Genesis Apocryphon*, 10–11.

93   Since the manuscript is significantly corrupt at places, especially at the beginning, it would perhaps be more precise to say the first dream in the *extant Genesis Apocryphon*.

it is before they enter Egypt that Abraham recognizes Sarah's beauty as a
potential threat to his life and so instructs her to say that she is his sister;
otherwise the Egyptians will kill him if they know that she is his wife. In
the *Genesis Apocryphon*, a dream narrative has been added to the
beginning of the narrative unit. After Abraham enters Egypt, he has a
dream, which is narrated by Abraham as follows:

> I, Abram, had a dream, on the night of my entering into the land of
> Egypt and I saw in my dream [that there wa]s a cedar, and date-palm
> (which was) [very beautif]ul; and some men came intending to cut down
> and uproot the cedar, but leave the date-palm by itself. Now the date-
> palm remonstrated and said, 'Do not cut down the cedar, for we are
> both from the family.' So the cedar was spared with the help of the date-
> palm, and [it was] not [cut down].[94]

When Abraham awakes from the dream, he not only tells the dream to
Sarah, but he also interprets the dream. Abraham explains that men will
seek to kill him but spare Sarah. Presumably based on the intervention of
the date-palm in the dream, Abraham asks Sarah to say that Abraham is
her brother.

The function of this dream narrative is interesting in a couple of ways.
First, by its placement at the beginning of the narrative unit, the dream
foreshadows the plot and sets in motion the action of the plot. According
to the interpretation given by Abraham, the dream portends the threat to
Abraham and the saving intervention of Sarah. Moreover, the dream and
its interpretation provides the impetus for Sarah's less than truthful
statement that Abraham is her brother, a statement that actually leads to
a further development of the plot: Pharaoh's taking of Sarah. Though this
part of the plot is not signified by the dream, perhaps it increases the
interest and anticipation of the reader as the reader continues in hope of
its resolution.

Second, the dream and its interpretation elicit an emotional response
from Abraham and Sarah that introduces an element of inevitability into
the narrative. The text reads that Abraham was 'frightened by this dream'
and that 'Sarai wept at my words that night.'[95] The dream portends that
Abraham will be saved by the intervention of Sarah; and so the dream
could be understood as God's instruction or guidance to save Abraham, a
reading that seems evident in Abraham's interpretation of the dream and
the consequent plan based on the dream. This sense of guidance and
divine intervention via a dream is the norm in Jewish literature. But
Abraham and Sarah's emotional response suggests that their attention is

---

94 1QapGen XIX, 14–17 (Fitzmyer).
95 1QapGen XIX, 18 and 21 (Fitzmyer); see also XX, 10–11 and 16 for other atypical
emotional responses of Abraham.

not on the deliverance but on the inevitable threat and peril that lies ahead of them. This anticipation and concern for the unavoidable circumstances is characteristic of dreams in the Greek novels, and represents one of several novelistic features introduced into the scriptural story.[96]

The second dream in the *Genesis Apocryphon* is also found in this narrative unit, though it is not narrated. In response to Abraham's prayer that Sarah be protected, God sends unspecified ailments upon Pharaoh and his household. Pharaoh's representative Hirqanos finds Abraham and begs his service in healing Pharaoh, 'for [he had seen me] in a dream.'[97] The dream should be understood as another intervention by God that ironically puts Pharaoh, who has unknowingly wronged Abraham by taking his wife, in position of seeking Abraham's favor. Abraham will not only have Sarah returned to him, but Pharaoh will reward him with gifts (XXI, 31).

The third dream comes as an addition to the retelling of Genesis 13.14-18, in which God tells Abraham to survey the promised land and restates the promise of progeny. In the *Genesis Apocryphon*, God's communication to Abraham takes place in a dream: 'God appeared to me in a vision of the night and said to me ... .'[98] The dream message only includes the command to survey the promised land, which Abraham promptly does the next day. After Abraham's survey of the land, God then reaffirms to him the promise of numerous descendants. In light of the biblical story, the dream report not only clarifies the means by which God speaks to Abraham, but it also emphasizes Abraham's faithful response to the divine instruction, which is lacking in the Genesis text. Thus the dream narrative, with its formal feature of a response, provides a literary device that facilitates Abraham's response to God's command and so enhances the biblical story.

Another example of 'Bible Rewritten' is Pseudo-Philo's *Liber antiquitatum biblicarum* (*Biblical Antiquities*), which retells the biblical story from Adam to the death of Saul.[99] This retelling, interestingly, both abridges and expands the scriptures, omitting large sections of the original

---

96   Other novelistic features introduced to the biblical story of Abraham and Sarah in the *Genesis Apocryphon* include an *ekphrasis* of Sarah, the emphasis on the threat to Sarah's chastity, and the accentuation of divine intervention. I analyzed these novelistic features in a paper, 'The Romance of Abraham and Sarah: Novelistic Features in the *Apocryphon of Genesis*' (paper presented at the annual meeting of the Society of Biblical Literature, San Antonio, Tex., November, 2004).

97   1QapGen XX, 22 (Fitzmyer). It is unclear in the text whether the dream was Pharaoh's or Hirqanos'.

98   1QapGen XXI, 8 (Fitzmyer).

99   Though originally written in Hebrew in the first or second century C.E., the text was translated into Greek and then into Latin; it survives only in Latin manuscripts. For introductory issues, see D. J. Harrington, 'Pseudo-Philo,' in *Old Testament Pseudepigrapha*

narrative while at the same time adding material. Dreams are affected by both of these literary techniques. For example, in retelling the Joseph saga, Pseudo-Philo includes the statement that Pharaoh had a dream (8.10), but unlike the biblical narrative the dream is not narrated nor is Joseph's detailed interpretation given. The dream narrative is simply reduced to a reference. Our concerns, however, are the five dreams that have been added to the original scriptural narrative.

The first additional dream is found in the story of Moses' birth. The scripture story is embellished by reporting a dream of Moses' sister Miriam. The dream is narrated as a report by Miriam to her parents:

> I have seen this night, and behold a man in a linen garment stood and said to me, 'Go and say to your parents, "Behold, he who will be born from you will be cast forth into the water; likewise through him the water will be dried up. And I will work signs through him and save my people, and he will exercise leadership always."' And when Miriam told of her dream, her parents did not believe her.[100]

As the above discussion on dreams and encomium indicates, dreams are a common motif of birth narratives in Greco-Roman literature revealing the future destiny of a notable person. The birth story of Moses invites this kind of literary-rhetorical embellishment, and Miriam's dream fulfils this convention. Miriam's dream proleptically represents Moses' divine mission and leadership as well as alluding to two critical events in his life, his being placed in an ark in the Nile and the parting of the Red Sea. The dream also provides the context for expressing two major themes of *Biblical Antiquities*: God's 'saving' activity and the issue of leadership.[101]

Pseudo-Philo also mentions certain dreams experienced by Pharaoh's daughter (9.15), though they are not narrated. In the biblical story, Pharaoh's daughter comes to the Nile to bathe and by happenstance finds baby Moses in the ark (Exod 2.5). In *Biblical Antiquities* her decision to come to the Nile to bathe is motivated by the dreams that she has seen; her presence at the Nile is in response to the divinatory function of dreams. Thus, this literary addition highlights the providential aspect of Moses' preservation.

Although it is not an extra-scriptural dream, the dream of Balaam in Numbers 22 is significantly expanded in *Biblical Antiquities*. The biblical narrative relates how God spoke to Balaam commanding him not 'to curse the people, for they are blessed' (22.12; NRSV). This communica-

---

(ed. J. H. Charlesworth; 2 vols.; Garden City, N.Y.: Doubleday, 1985), 2.297-303; Howard Jacobson, *A Commentary on Pseudo-Philo's Liber antiquitatum biblicarum* (2 vols.; AGJU 31; Leiden: E. J. Brill, 1996), 1.195-280.

100   *L.A.B.* 9.10 (Harrington, *OTP*).

101   Frederick J. Murphy, *Pseudo-Philo: Rewriting the Bible* (New York: Oxford University Press, 1993), 59.

tion is implicitly related as a dream, for the encounter is introduced with Balaam's direction to Balak's messengers, 'stay here tonight' (22.8; NRSV), and concludes with the comment, 'so Balaam rose in the morning' (22.13; NRSV). In *Biblical Antiquities*, the dream phenomenon is made more explicit by introducing Balaam as an interpreter of dreams (18.2) and stating that God spoke to Balaam at night (18.4). More significant is Pseudo-Philo's expansion of the dream message (18.5-6). The dream not only warns Balaam not to curse Israel, but it also provides an opportunity to rehearse the blessing and covenant relationship between God and Israel. In the dream God recalls the promise of progeny for Abraham, the gracious response to Abraham's willingness to sacrifice Isaac, the special counsel to Abraham regarding the wickedness of Sodom and Gomorrah, and the blessing conferred to Jacob while wrestling with the angel. This expansion illustrates how God has blessed and chosen Israel, but these memorable episodes from the biblical story have not been narrated in *Biblical Antiquities*. Pseudo-Philo presents a highly condensed version of the ancestral narratives in chapter 8, but none of these specific instances of divine blessing are related or mentioned. Thus, the dream becomes a literary device by which gaps in the previous narrative are filled as well as a warrant for the command. As a command-warning dream, the dream of Balaam corresponds to dreams in Greco-Roman literature; but the emphasis on and review of past events is an unusual development of the dream report.

This kind of development is also seen in Pseudo-Philo's representation of Joshua's covenant renewal speech. The biblical text introduces Joshua's speech with reference to the gathering of all the tribes of Israel (24.1) and to Joshua's speaking to them, 'Thus says the LORD' (24.2; NRSV). Pseudo-Philo, however, presents Joshua's speech as inspired and revealed in a dream:

> And on the sixteenth day of the third month all the people along with women and children gathered together before the Lord in Shiloh, and Joshua said to them, 'Hear, O Israel. Behold I am establishing with you a covenant of this Law that the LORD established for your fathers on Horeb. And so wait here this night and see what God will say to me on your behalf.' And while the people were waiting that night, the LORD appeared to Joshua in a dream vision and said to him, 'According to these words I will speak to this people.' And Joshua rose up in the morning and gathered all the people and said to them, 'The LORD says this: ...'[102]

The speech that Joshua then gives is the message that God revealed to Joshua in the dream as indicated in the conclusion, 'these are the words

---

102 *L.A.B.* 23.2-4a (Harrington, *OTP*).

that the Lord spoke to me this night.'[103] Like the dream of Balaam, the
message of Joshua's dream greatly elaborates the original, biblical speech
with a rehearsal of God's past dealings with Israel (23.4-11), but it also
announces God's continued, future faithfulness if Israel keeps the divine
covenant (23.12-13). There is very little of the biblical speech present in
Pseudo-Philo's recasting of it,[104] thus providing Pseudo-Philo a context
for expressing his particular theological interests.[105] By depicting the
origin of the speech in a dream, the speech – and so Pseudo-Philo's ideas –
achieves a greater authority and explains the means by which God
communicated to Joshua.

The inventiveness of dreams is also evident in the way Pseudo-Philo
describes the final testament of the priest Eleazar as being first received in
a dream.[106] This testamentary dream is part of the larger Kenaz narrative
(25–28), which is an embellishment of the biblical text that only mentions
Kenaz in Judges 3.9, 11 as the father of Othniel. The setting is the last
days of Kenaz before his death and the assembly of the people, including
Phinehas, the son of the priest Eleazar (28.1). Phinehas asks permission to
relate, 'the word that I heard from my father when he was dying ... while
his soul was being taken away.'[107] After Kenaz agrees to hear first from
Phinehas, Phinehas recounts Eleazar's message:

> While my father was dying, he commanded me, saying, 'These words
> you will say to the sons of Israel, "When you gathered together in the
> assembly, the LORD appeared to me three days ago in a dream by night
> and said to me, ..." '[108]

The dream message, as God's word, then foretells the corruption and
unfaithfulness of Israel and the subsequent anger and sorrow of God. The
response of Kenaz and the people is one of lamentation, and sometime
later in the evening Kenaz enters a trance and begins to prophesy. Just as
Eleazar's final testament is inspired in a dream-vision, the final testament
of Kenaz is inspired through a prophetic trance. The divinatory nature of
dreams and prophecies contribute to the authority of these final
testaments.

---

103   *L.A.B.* 23.13c (Harrington, *OTP*).

104   *L.A.B.* 23.4b, 5b, 8a, 9, 11, 14a (Harrington, *OTP*).

105   For a discussion of how the speech reflects the concerns of Pseudo-Philo, see
Murphy, *Pseudo-Philo*, 108–113.

106   Flannery-Dailey has shown how the 'testamentary dream' is a uniquely Jewish
development of the dream report (Frances Lynn Flannery-Dailey, 'Standing at the Heads of
Dreamers: A Study of Dreams in Antiquity' [Ph.D. diss., The University of Iowa, 2000], ch.
5). Cf. *T. Levi* 2.5–5.7; 8.1-18; *T. Naph.* 5.1–6.10 (cp. 7.1); *T. Jos.* 19.1-11; *4 Ezra* 11.1–12.51;
13.1–14.26; *2 Bar.* 36.1–43.2; *2 En.* 1.3-10; 70.3-13; and *4QVisions of Amram*[a-f] (4Q543–548).

107   *L.A.B.* 28.3a (Harrington, *OTP*).

108   *L.A.B.* 28.4a (Harrington, *OTP*).

The final illustration of dreams in 'Rewritten Bible' comes from the *Exagoge* by Ezekiel the Tragedian. The *Exagoge* is a departure from our consideration of prose narratives, but its inclusion here is intended to demonstrate the diverse forms for which the literary activity of 'Rewritten Bible' could be adopted; it also provides an opportunity to exhibit a memorable invented dream. This dramatic tragedy, written in Greek, survives only in quotations from Eusebius, Clement of Alexandria and Pseudo-Eustathius. The provenance and date of the work are difficult to settle, though Alexandria in the second century B.C.E. is often suggested.[109]

The *Exagoge* retells the story of Moses in dramatic form. One of the more interesting embellishments of the biblical story is the dream of Moses and its interpretation by Moses' father-in-law. In terms of the plot, the dream report takes place just prior to Moses' encounter with God in the burning bush. Moses relates the dream to his father-in-law as follows:

> On Sinai's peak I saw what seemed to be a throne
> so great in size it touched the clouds of heaven.
> Upon it sat a man of noble mien,
> Becrowned, and with a scepter in one hand
> while with the other he did beckon me.
> I made approach and stood before the throne.
> He handed o'er the scepter and he bade
> me mount the throne, and gave to me the crown;
> then he himself withdrew from off the throne.
> I gazed upon the whole earth round about;
> things under it, and high above the skies.
> Then at my feet a multitude of stars
> fell down, and I their number reckoned up.
> They passed by me like armed ranks of men.
> Then I in terror wakened from the dream.[110]

It has been argued that Moses' dream portends his future deification, since the dream describes Moses ascending a throne that God has occupied.[111] But the interpretation set forth by Moses' father-in-law states that the dream signifies Moses' future leadership and authority and that he will be

---

109 For introductory issues, see R. G. Robertson, 'Ezekiel the Tragedian,' in *Old Testament Pseudepigrapha* (ed. J. H. Charlesworth; 2 vols.; Garden City, N.Y.: Doubleday, 1985), 2.803-807; Gruen, *Heritage and Hellenism*, 128 n. 68.

110 Ezek. Trag. 68–82 (Robertson, *OTP*). Robertson's translation is an attempt to render the text in iambic pentameter. I have not modified it for this reason, but it should be noted that the dream is introduced with the conventional δοκέω: ἔ < δο > ξ' ὄρους κατ' ἄκρα Σιν < αί > ου θρόνον μέγαν τιν' εἶναι ('It seemed on the peak of Mt. Sinai that there a great throne'). Also, the last line (89) reads 'from sleep' (ἐξ ὕπνου) not 'from the dream.'

111 P. W. van der Horst, 'Moses' Throne Vision in Ezekiel the Dramatist,' *JJS* 34 (1983): 24–27. Most interpreters believe the 'man of noble mien' of Moses' dream signifies God; see Gruen, *Heritage and Hellenism*, 123.

responsible for a future dynasty, though not of his own.[112] Dreams that prefigure an individual's future glory and reign are common in Greco-Roman literature. Ezekiel the Tragedian participates in this literary tradition by supplementing the biblical story with a dream narrative.

Summary

Several ancient sources refer to inventing dreams. This section has attempted to identify this practice in specific instances of Greco-Roman literature. By looking at literary imitation of dreams, Homeric quotations and allusions in dreams, the double-dream report and dreams in 'Rewritten Bible', it seems that dreams are a literary *locus* for creativity, embellishment and literary license. As stated above, the inventive character of dreams does not negate the reporting of actual dreams or traditions about dreams. It does, however, highlight that in the narration of dreams ancient authors shaped, fashioned and utilized dreams according to their own literary concerns.

Conclusion

This chapter represents the first part of an analysis of the literary character of dreams in Greco-Roman literature, particularly prose narratives. In this chapter, this literary facet of dreams was described and demonstrated in three ways. First, dreams in Greco-Roman literature are narrated or reported according to a compositional pattern. The dream narrative is an identifiable literary type with repetitive formal features. This formal pattern contributes to the character of dreams as a literary convention in ancient literature. Second, dreams are occasionally discussed in the Greco-Roman rhetorical tradition in connection with encomium and style. The very context of literary-rhetorical considerations betrays that dreams are being approached and understood in literary-rhetorical terms. And finally, the references to the invention of dreams by ancient rhetoricians suggest that there is an artistic, creative quality to dream narratives. Dreams attract a variety of inventive adaptations, depending on the author's literary purposes and interests. Thus, a proper understanding of dreams in the ancient Mediterranean world must take into account and fully appreciate their literary character and dimensions.

112   Ezek. Trag. 85–86.

Chapter Four

THE ANCIENT, LITERARY CONTEXT OF DREAMS, PART II: THE LITERARY FUNCTIONS OF DREAMS

The present chapter continues the literary analysis of dreams in Greco-Roman literature by analyzing the function of specific dream narratives. The dream narratives will come from a sampling of Greco-Roman histories, biographies and fiction. It should be carefully noted that the presence or function of dreams is *not* an indicator of genre. It is perhaps no exaggeration to suggest that dreams are found in every form of Greco-Roman literature: epics, dramas, histories, biographies, philosophical treatises, medical treatises, novels, letters, dialogues, allegories, inscriptions, etc. The focus here, however, is on prose narratives, and these three genres are the most apt representatives of prose narrative in Greco-Roman literature. Thus, genre is an organizational device for this chapter, not an argument for the function of dreams.

As this analysis of dream narratives will be facilitated by attending to the form of dreams, it is helpful to review the literary form of the dream narrative.[1] The four formal features of the dream narrative are (1) *scene-setting*, (2) *dream terminology*, (3) *dream proper* and (4) *reaction* and/or *response*. The *scene-setting* can include: (a) the identification of the dreamer, along with a sketch of his or her character; (b) the place where the dream occurs; (c) the time in which the dream occurs; (d) the mental state of the dreamer; and (e) the activity of sleeping. The *dream terminology* usually comes after the *scene-setting*, but its placement can vary. The *dream proper* includes three types: (a) visitant dream, (b) auditory dream, and (c) symbolic dream. The *dream proper* is often introduced by δοκέω. The dream narrative concludes with the dreamer's *reaction* (waking, amazement, perplexity, fear, interpretation, etc.) and/or *response*, taking some course of action based on the *dream proper*. The following outline is given again as a reference guide to the form of the dream report:

1   John S. Hanson, 'Dreams and Visions in the Graeco-Roman World and Early Christianity,' *ANRW* 23.2: 1395–1427.

1   *Scene-setting*
    a. identification of dreamer, along with a sketch of his or her character
    b. place
    c. time
    d. mental state of dreamer
    e. sleep
2.   *Dream terminology*
3.   *Dream proper* (three types) – often introduced by δοκέω
    a. Visitant dream – dream figure visits to deliver message
        i.   identification of dream figure
        ii. description of dream figure
        iii. position of dream figure
        iv. message
        v. departure of dream figure
    b. Auditory dream – dream message only heard
    c. Symbolic dream – scene or event described; interpretation required
4.   *Reaction* and/or *response* of dreamer

With this compositional pattern of dreams in mind, we now turn to analyzing dream reports in selected Greco-Roman texts.

Dreams in Greco-Roman Histories

This section will analyze dreams in two texts that are representative of Greco-Roman histories: Herodotus' *Histories* and Josephus' *Jewish War*. Dreams in some other histories are as follows: Appian (*Bell. civ.* 1.11.97; 1.12.105; 2.16.115; 4.14.110; *Hist. Rom.* 8.1.1; 8.20.136; 11.9.56; 12.2.9; 12.4.27); Diodorus Siculus (*Bib. hist.* 13.97.6; 16.33.1; 17.103.7); Tacitus (*Ann.* 1.65; 2.14; 11.4; 12.13; *Hist.* 4.83); Dionysius of Halicarnassus (*Ant. rom.* 1.56.5; 1.57.4 [2 ×]; 3.67.3; 5.54.2; 7.68.3-5 [3 ×]; 20.12.1-2); Livy 8.5; and 2 Maccabees 15.11-17.[2]

---

2   It is interesting to note that Thucydides has no dream narratives. Polybius mentions three dreams (5.108; 10.4-5; 10.11), but he is suspicious of dreams (12.24) and these dreams are not typical literary dreams. The dream in 5.108 is simply a reference to a dream and is highly 'psychological'; the dream in 10.4-5 is actually a contrived dream (cf. Suetonius, *Claud.* 37.1-2 and Philo, *Mos.* 1.268 for other contrived dreams); and the dream in 10.11 is embedded in a speech and may also be understood as a contrived dream by Polybius.

Herodotus' Histories[3]

Dating from the fifth century B.C.E., Herodotus' *Histories* represents the Greek classical period and so is outside the time frame for this survey of dreams in Hellenistic literature. The influence of this text on the literary activity of the Hellenistic period, however, makes its inclusion justified.[4] In addition, the dreams in Herodotus offer a helpful variety of the literary functions of dreams. The *Histories* provides an account of the 'barbarian' aggressions against the Greeks and so is structured around the sequence of these barbarian kings, beginning with Croesus and ending with Xerxes. This simple description of the *Histories*, however, obscures its encyclopedic-like treatment of various subjects, such as geography and local histories and customs, and its attempt to describe and understand a variety of human, cultural experiences.

It is often pointed out that all the dreams in Herodotus are experienced by eastern rulers,[5] though this tendency has not been satisfactorily explained.[6] There are seventeen dream narratives or references to dreams in Herodotus and each one will be analyzed in the following survey.

The dream of Croesus (*Hist.* 1.34). The dream of the Lydian king Croesus comes after an extended narrative concerning the wise Athenian Solon, who is the guest of Croesus (1.30-33). Croesus shows Solon his vast treasures with the certainty that Solon would declare him the most blessed man in the world; but the wise Solon measures blessedness by how one ends his life, not one's present fortune. Croesus dismisses Solon, regarding him as quite foolish. At this point, the dream report is given:

> But after Solon's departure, the anger of God (ἐκ θεοῦ νέμεσις) fell heavily on Croesus, as I guess, because he supposed himself to be blest beyond all other men. At once, as he slept, a dream stood by [him] (εὕδοντι ἐπέστη ὄνειρος), which revealed (ἔφαινε) the truth of the evil that was about to happen to his son. Croesus had two sons, one of whom was wholly undone, for he was deaf and dumb, but the other,

---

3 Translations of Herodotus are mine or modified translations of Godley, LCL. For introductory issues, see *Brill's Companion to Herodotus* (ed. E. J. Bakker, I. J. F. de Jong, and H. van Wees (Leiden: Brill, 2002); John P. A. Gould, 'Herodotus,' *OCD* 696–698; Klaus Meister, 'Herodotos,' *DNP* 5.470-475.

4 Meister, 'Herodotos,' 5.474.

5 For example, see Peter Frisch, *Die Träume bei Herodot* (Beiträge zur klassischen Philologie 27; Meisenheim am Glan: Verlag Anton Hain, 1968), 52.

6 For example, Keely Kristen Lake, 'Vergil's Dreams and Their Literary Predecessors' (Ph.D. diss., University of Iowa, 2001), 101, states that 'the eastern rulers are transgressors and their dreams are part of the divine warning system against attacking the Greeks.' This statement, however, does not account for all the dreams in Herodotus. Moreover, it is a deceptive dream that actually prompts Xerxes to commence his military campaign against the Greeks (7.12-14, 17-18, 19).

whose name was Atys, was in every way far pre-eminent over all of his years. Now it was this Atys that the dream signified (σημαίνει . . . ὁ ὄνειρος) to Croesus that he would be struck and killed by a spear of iron. So, Croesus awoke, thought to himself about the message, and greatly dreaded the dream (καταρρωδήσας τὸν ὄνειρον).

The *scene-setting* establishes the time of the dream (after Solon's departure) and the identity of the dreamer (Croesus), and it mentions the activity of sleep. The character of Croesus is also important in setting the scene for this dream. Croesus (falsely) thinks that he is the most blessed, which demonstrates his foolishness and arrogance. Most dream narratives, when they describe the character of the dreamer, mention the dreamer's virtue, but Croesus' dream functions within the larger plot of divine retribution. The type of dream (*dream proper*) is somewhat ambiguous. The language of 'standing by' (ἐφίστημι) suggests that it is a visitant dream, but the term φαίνω has a more visual connotation, perhaps indicating a symbolic dream. If it is a symbolic dream, its interpretative nature is secondary, for Herodotus as narrator explicitly states what the dream signifies: the death of Croesus' son Atys by an iron spear. It is interesting to note that the *dream proper* is interrupted by a narrative aside that informs the reader about Croesus' two sons. The *reaction* to the dream is described in terms of waking from the dream, considering the dream and fearing the dream. Croesus' *response* to the dream receives the most attention. Herodotus tells how Croesus takes one precaution after another to prevent the fate of Atys that was portended by the dream (1.34-42). And yet, it is one of these preventive actions that actually leads to the death of Atys by an iron spear (1.45). The irony of this set of circumstances is not lost on the reader, who, given the predictive quality of dreams, anticipates its fulfillment despite Croesus' attempts to prevent it; the dream is determinative. The dream functions in two ways: first, the dream predicts death, which is a common motif associated with dreams; and second, it contributes to the plot development of the divine punishment of the ill-character Croesus.[7]

The dreams of Astyages (Hist. 1.107-108). In the account of the Persian king Cyrus, Herodotus reports two dreams concerning the birth of Cyrus that portend his future sovereignty and distinction. Both dreams are symbolic and experienced by Cyrus' grandfather Astyages before Cyrus' birth. The first dream report begins with the simple clause, 'Astyages thought in [his] sleep . . .' (ἐδόκεε Ἀστυάγης ἐν τῷ ὕπνῳ), thus identifying the dreamer (Astyages), indicating the activity of sleep and introducing

---

7   Frisch, *Die Träme bei Herodot*, 21–22, argues that the dream is not about Croesus' arrogance but the inescapability of fate. This interpretation, however, sets up an unnecessary dichotomy between character and fate.

the *dream proper* with the customary δοκέω. The *dream proper* is a symbolic dream of Astyages' daughter Mandane, 'urinating so much that it filled his own city and overflowed all of Asia.' The *reaction* of Astyages is twofold. First, he submits the dream to the magi for interpretation. Herodotus does not relate to his readers the interpretation provided by the magi, but he does describe Astyages' second reaction: 'he was afraid' (ἐφοβήθη) and, 'he feared the vision' (διδοικὼς τὴν ὄψιν). His *response*, then, is to marry his daughter to a Persian named Cambyses, because Astyages, the Median king, perceives the Persian Cambyses to be of a lesser distinction and, therefore, a lesser threat. The reader is left to infer the meaning of the dream.

The second dream is reported immediately after the first one. The *scene-setting* and *dream terminology* are given in one sentence: 'in the first year [of Mandane's marriage] Astyages saw another vision' (ὃ Ἀστυάγης τῷ πρώτῳ ἔτει εἶδε ἄλλην ὄψιν). Like the first dream of Astyages, the *dream proper* is a symbolic dream and is introduced by δοκέω: 'It seemed that from the pudendum of his daughter came forth a vine, and the vine covered all of Asia.' Once again, Astyages *reacts* by consulting the dream interpreters. As with the previous dream report, Herodotus does not give the interpretation but narrates the *response* of Astyages: he brings Mandane, who is now pregnant, back from Persia and keeps her under guard, because he 'wants to destroy the child that comes from her.' At this point, Herodotus finally reveals the meaning of the dream given by the dream interpreters: 'the offspring of his daughter would rule instead of [Astyages].' This delay in giving the meaning of the symbolic dreams has the rhetorical effect of confirming or correcting the meaning tentatively determined by the reader.

Astyages' plot to have the baby killed is foiled by a series of events, and eventually Cyrus does establish an empire over that of Astyages. The portents of the dreams prove to be determinative and are fulfilled.

The dream of Cyrus (*Hist.* 1.209). Herodotus' story of Cyrus ends with an account of Cyrus' death, which is predicted in a dream but misinterpreted by Cyrus. The *scene-setting* mentions both the place (beyond the Araxes River in the country of the Massagetae) and the time (night). The *dream terminology* is 'he saw the following vision' (εἶδε ὄψιν ... τοιήνδε). The *dream proper* is a symbolic dream with the conventional δοκέω: 'Cyrus in his sleep seemed to see the eldest of Hystaspes' sons having wings upon his shoulders, and one of these wings was overshadowing Asia and the other one Europe.' It should be noted that the *dream proper* includes a narrative aside that informs the reader about Hystaspes' eldest son, Darius, and his circumstances at the time of the dream. The *reaction* of Cyrus is described as 'awaking' and 'thinking to himself about the vision.' His interpretation of the dream is that Hystaspes' son Darius is planning a coup against his

reign. Herodotus rhetorically emphasizes Cyrus' certainty of the interpretation by having Cyrus recount verbatim the dream to Hystaspes and
stating, 'The gods are concerned about me, even showing me beforehand
everything that is coming.' Cyrus' certainty, however, is undermined when
Herodotus relates to the reader the real meaning of the dream: 'But the
daimon (ὁ δαίμων) predicted for him that he himself was about to die in
this place and that his kingdom would be transferred to Darius' (1.210).
Herodotus then relates how Cyrus was killed in a battle with the
Massagetae (1.211-214). In Greco-Roman literature, dreams often predict
or are associated with the death of an individual.

The dream of Sabacos (*Hist.* 2.139). Sabacos was an Ethiopian king who
invaded Egypt and ruled there for fifty years. Herodotus relates how the
end of his reign was prompted by a dream.

> The final departure of the Ethiopian, they say, happened in this way.
> Having seen the following vision in [his] sleep he departed and fled (ὄψιν
> ἐν τῷ ὕπνῳ τοιήνδε ἰδόντα αὐτὸν οἴχεσθαι φεύγοντα). It seemed
> (ἐδόκεε) that a man who stood over him counseled him to bring together
> all the priests in Egypt and to sever them in two. Having seen this vision,
> he said that he supposed it to be a manifestation sent to him by the
> gods, that he might commit sacrilege and so be punished by gods or
> men. He would not act so, he said, but otherwise, for the time foretold
> for his rule over Egypt, after which he was to depart, was not fulfilled:
> for when he was still in Ethiopia the oracles (τὰ μαντήια) which are
> inquired of by the people of that country declared to him that he was
> fated to reign fifty years over Egypt. Seeing that this time was now
> completed and that the vision of the dream troubled him (αὐτὸν ἡ ὄψις
> τοῦ ἐνυπνίου ἐπετάρασσε), Sabacos departed Egypt of his own accord.

Herodotus' presentation of this dream has several interesting qualities.
First, Sabacos' *response* and the consequence of the dream (departing
Egypt and ending his reign) are mentioned at the beginning of the dream
report. This alteration has the effect of 're-locating' the reader's
anticipation of the narrative. Usually the reader's anticipation is
connected with how the dreamer's response or the subsequent events of
the plot will fulfill the dream. In this case, however, the outcome is known
beforehand, and so the anticipation is the dream itself: what kind of
dream would prompt Sabacos to end his reign of Egypt? This dream is
also interesting because of the seeming incongruence between the *dream
proper* and Sabacos' response. The *dream proper* is a visitant dream that
advises Sabacos to execute all the Egyptian priests. In a conventional
dream report, the message of the dream is heeded by the dreamer; if it is
not obeyed, negative consequences usually follow. Sabacos, though, does
not act in accordance to the message but decides to leave Egypt rather

than commit sacrilege and face the subsequent, inevitable punishment. The incongruence, however, is resolved when Herodotus notes in the end that before Sabacos came to Egypt prophetic oracles had revealed that his reign would be fifty years. Thus, the dream is really about prompting the action that fulfills the oracles. The connection between prophecy and dreams is not uncommon in Greco-Roman literature and will be important in the study of dreams in the Gospel of Matthew.

The dream of Sethos (*Hist.* 2.141). The dream of the Egyptian king, Sethos, functions to provide assurance of victory in battle. The *scene-setting* is elaborated by explaining the predicament. The Egyptian soldiers desert Sethos because he has confiscated their land. When the Assyrian general Sanacharib threatens Egypt, Sethos enters the temple and prays to the god. The *scene-setting* describes the mental state of the dreamer Sethos and refers to sleep: 'as he was lamenting sleep fell upon [him] (ὀλοφυρόμενον δ᾽ ἄρα μιν ἐπελθεῖν ὕπνον).' The *dream proper* is a visitant dream that is introduced by δοκέω: 'and it seemed in a vision that the god stood over [him] and assured him (καί οἱ δόξαι ἐν τῇ ὄψι ἐπιστάντα τὸν θεὸν θαρσύνειν) that he would suffer no disgrace by encountering the army of Arabia, for the [god] himself will send avengers.' The *reaction/response* of Sethos is described as 'trusting in this dream' (πίσυνον τοῖσι ἐνυπνίοισι) and encamping near the Assyrian army with those few Egyptians who would follow him. Herodotus then describes how in one night a horde of mice damaged the weapons of the Assyrian army, making an Egyptian victory certain. The association of dreams and battles is common in Greco-Roman literature.

The dream of Cambyses (*Hist.* 3.30). Herodotus narrates a series of acts that illustrate the impiety and madness of the Perisan king Cambyses. Cambyses' 'first evil act' is prompted by a dream. The *scene-setting* is important because it describes the character of the dreamer Cambyses as mad (μαίνομαι), and this madness finds expression in jealousy (φθόνος) of his brother Smerdis, whom Cambyses had sent to Persia from Egypt. The *dream proper* (ὄψιν ... ἐν τῷ ὕπνῳ) is a visitant dream introduced by δοκέω: 'It seemed (ἔδοξέ) that a messenger came from Persia and reported that Smerdis was placed on the royal throne with his head reaching to heaven.' Cambyses' *reaction* is twofold and interrelated: he (1) 'fears for himself' (δείσας περὶ ἑωυτοῦ), because he (2) interprets the dream to mean that Smerdis will assassinate him and become king. Cambyses *responds* by having Smerdis killed.

The dream of Cambyses is unusual in that Smerdis does not become king as the dream seems to indicate. The reader expects that the dream is determinative and will be fulfilled. This anomaly, however, may be explained by recognizing that the dream is part of the larger context of revealing the negative character of Cambyses. Thus, though the motif of the dream is a king's rule, the narrative function of the dream is related to revealing the negative character of Cambyses.

The dream of Polycrates's daughter (Hist. 3.124). As a kind of digression from the story of Cambyses, Herodotus narrates the murder of Polycrates, the esteemed tyrant of Samos, at the hands of Oroetes (3.120-126). This 'unholy act' (3.120) is presaged by a dream. The *scene-setting* has Polycrates preparing to visit Oroetes despite the warnings of diviners and friends. The unstated prophecies of the diviners are coupled with the dream of Polycrates' daughter, 'who saw the following dream vision (ἰδούσης τῆς θυγατρὸς ὄψιν ἐνυπνίου τοιήνδε): it seemed (ἐδόκεε) that [her] father, being in mid-air, was washed by Zeus and anointed by the sun.' The *dream proper* is a symbolic dream introduced by δοκέω. The daughter *responds* by trying to persuade her father not to visit Oroetes, but he does not listen to her counsel. Polycrates indeed meets his death, being murdered by Oroetes, though Herodotus does not narrate the manner of Polycrates' death. Oroetes has the body of Polycrates crucified, which according to Herodotus fulfills the dream: 'now with Polycrates hanging there, the daughter's entire vision was accomplished; for he was washed by Zeus when it would rain, and he was anointed by the sun when it brought out the moisture from his body' (3.125).

This dream report is interesting in several respects. First, the manner in which Herodotus narrates the story of Polycrates creates both certainty and anticipation. From the very beginning, the reader knows that Oroetes will murder Polycrates (3.120). Given this knowledge, the reader anticipates the death of Polycrates and reads the dream as an assured affirmation of this event. But the reporting of a symbolic dream without an immediate interpretation leaves the reader anticipating how the death of Polycrates will correspond to the dream vision. The reader is certain of Polycrates' death but uncertain as to the manner of his death as predicted by the dream. Herodotus makes sure this uncertainty is answered by explicitly stating how the dream forecasted Polycrates' demise. The dream is also noteworthy for its connection with prophetic oracles. Though less creative and explicit in its presentation, this dream report does link dreams and prophecies, which is not uncommon in Greco-Roman literature.

The dream of Otanes (Hist. 3.149). The dream of the Persian general Otanes is not narrated but simply mentioned. As part of his military campaign, Otanes had deported the entire population of the island of Samos. But because of a dream vision (ὄψιος ὀνείρου), along with a disease of the genitals, Otanes is moved to help re-colonize the island. The implication is that the dream and the disease convince Otanes that the gods are not pleased that the island was uninhabited. The dream functions as a medium of a divine command.

The dream of Hipparchus (5.56). As part of a long digression on the history of Athens (5.55-96), Herodotus recounts the death of Hipparchus, the tyrant of Athens, which is predicted in a dream. The dream report is actually retrospective in that Herodotus already states that Hipparchus was murdered, 'having seen a dream vision (ὄψιν ἐνυπνίου) which most clearly related (ἐναργεστάτην) that which befell him' (5.55). It is after this statement that Herodotus narrates the dream:

> Now the vision of Hipparchus's dream was this (ἡ μεν νυν ὄψις τοῦἹππάρχου ἐνυπνίου ἦν ἥδε): in the night before the Panathenaea Hipparchus thought (ἐδόκεε) that a tall and handsome man stood over [him] and spoke these riddling words:
>> Endure, Lion, the unendurable, suffering with an enduring heart;
>> No man who acts unjustly shall avoid vengeance.
>
> As soon as it was day, he imparted this vision to the dream interpreters; but after dismissing the dream he led the ceremonial procession in which he was killed.

The dream of Hipparchus is conventional in that it portends his death, but the way in which Herodotus reports this dream is interesting for its rhetorical effect. As stated, the fulfillment and meaning of the dream is reported before its narration, and Herodotus as narrator judges the dream to be the clearest indication (ἐναργής) of Hipparchus' fate. And yet, Hipparchus still requires the help of interpreters to ascertain the meaning of the visitant's enigmatic message. Without Herodotus' retrospective telling of the dream and authorial comment, the reader may well have shared in Hipparchus' confusion, especially given that the message was a riddle. Herodotus' literary strategy, however, provides the reader with a privileged position, so that Herodotus and the reader stand over against the imprudent Hipparchus, an evaluation underscored by the *response* of Hipparchus to ignore the message at his own peril. Though more sophisticated in its reporting, the dream functions as a prediction of Hipparchus' death.

The dream of Hippias (*Hist.* 6.107). Hippias was the exiled Athenian tyrant, who served as a guide for the Persian attack on Greece. While in service to the Persians, Herodotus reports that Hippias had a dream:

> In the previous night [Hippias] saw the following vision (ὄψιν ἰδὼν τοιήνδε): Hippias seemed (ἐδόκεε) to be lying with his own mother. He thus concluded from the dream (ἐκ τοῦ ὀνείρου) that he should return to Athens and recover his rule and so die an old man in his own mother-country.

The *scene-setting* assumes much of the context, mentioning only the time
(previous night) and introducing the dream terminology (ὄψις). The
dream proper is a symbolic dream introduced by δοκέω. The *reaction* of
Hippias is simply his interpretation that the dream signifies his eventual
return to power in Athens. Hippias' inference about the dream, however,
changes when he sneezes and looses a tooth in the sands of Marathon.
This omen causes Hippias to lament, 'this land is not ours, nor will we be
able to subdue it; my tooth has all the share of it that was for me.'
Hippias, then, changes his understanding of the dream: the dream and the
lost tooth signify defeat (6.108), which is subsequently narrated (6.111-
113).

The dream of Datis (*Hist.* 6.118). During his campaign, the Persian general
Datis, 'saw a vision in [his] sleep' (εἶδε ὄψιν ἐν τῷ ὕπνῳ). Herodotus says
that the exact nature of the vision was not known, but Datis' *response* to it
is underscored. Datis searches his ships and finds a cultic image of Apollo,
which had been taken as a spoil of war. Datis personally sails the statue
back to its proper place in the temple at Delos. The assumption is that the
dream revealed to Datis the sacrilege and commanded its return.

The *dream of Agariste* (*Hist.* 6.131). In a transitioning section, Herodotus
briefly mentions the symbolic dream of Agariste concerning her unborn
child: 'and being pregnant, she saw a vision in [her] sleep (καὶ ἔγκους
ἐοῦσα εἶδε ὄψιν ἐν τῷ ὕπνῳ). It seemed (ἐδόκεε) that she bore a lion, and
after a few days she bore Pericles to [her husband] Xanthippus.' The
report is truncated, lacking the *scene-setting* and *reaction/response*
features. The *dream proper* is symbolic, but an interpretation is lacking.
The birth of Pericles is not pertinent to Herodotus' narrative; he seems to
assume that readers know about the dream and how Pericles' future
corresponds to the dream. Lions are often the symbol of royalty and
conquerors.[8] It is a birth dream signifying the future rule of Pericles, and
as was noted in the previous chapter, this dream concerning Pericles was
an example in the *progymnasmata* of demonstrating the birth *topos* of an
encomium.

The dreams of Xerxes and Artabanus (*Hist.* 7.12-14, 17-18, 19). The
dreams of Xerxes and Artabanus stand at the critical juncture of
Herodotus' *Histories*,[9] even initiating the action that is central to

---

8   Cf. Plutarch, *Alex.* 2.3, and the comments by J. R. Hamilton, *Plutarch: Alexander* (2d
ed.; London: Bristol Classical Press, 1999), 3–4.
9   See Nick Fisher, 'Popular Morality in Herodotus,' in *Brill's Companion to Herodotus*
(ed. E. J. Bakker, I. J. F. de Jong, and H. van Wees; Leiden: Brill, 2002), 220, who states that
'Xerxes' decision to invade mainland Greece is the most elaborately deployed, important,

Herodotus' narrative. The Persian king, Xerxes, was intent on leading a military campaign against the Greeks until his uncle Artabanus in a long speech makes a case against such an expedition (7.10). The *scene-setting* of the dream report stresses the mental state of Xerxes and refers to the activity of sleeping: 'after evening it happened that Artabanus' opinion provoked Xerxes; and giving serious counsel [to this] during the night he concluded that no army would march against Greece. And having resolved these things anew he fell asleep.' Herodotus then introduces the dream with language and a comment that seems to deflect any thought that his presentation is biased: 'and then, supposedly, in the night he saw the following vision, (as it is said by the Persians) (καὶ δή κου ἐν τῇ νυκτὶ εἶδε ὄψιν τοιήνδε, ὡς λέγεται ὑπὸ Περσέων).' The *dream proper* is a visitant dream, whose message is given in direct discourse:

> It seemed (ἐδόκεε) to Xerxes that a tall and handsome man stood over [him] and said, 'Have you now decided, O Persian, not to lead an army against Greece, though you have already declared to assemble the Persian army? You do not do well by changing your decision, nor will the one [you see before you] pardon you for it. But do what you decided yesterday, and let that be your course.'

The *dream proper* concludes with the vision 'seeming to fly away' (ἐδόκεε ... ἀποπτάσθαι). Xerxes does not follow the counsel of the dream, however, and informs his army on the following day that they will not march against Greece (7.13). This non-response to the dream occasions another nocturnal visit.

> And when night came the same dream (τὠυτὸ ὄνειρον) again stood over Xerxes while he was sleeping and said, 'O son of Darius, have you so openly denounced the military campaign among the Persians and made no consideration of my words as though you heard no one beside [you]. Now do this right. If you do not march the army at once, this will be your outcome: just as you became great and mighty in a short time, you will be brought back low just as quickly.'

Xerxes' *reaction/response* to the dream is described as being greatly afraid (περιδεής), leaping out of bed, and sending for Artabanus.

Xerxes comes up with a plan to have Artabanus wear the royal attire, sit on the throne, and sleep in Xerxes' bed in order to deceive the dream in thinking that Artabanus is Xerxes. In doing this, Xerxes hopes to confirm the truthfulness of the dream (7.15). After much protest, Artabanus agrees and follows through with Xerxes' proposal, 'hoping to prove wrong what Xerxes said' (7.17). Herodotus narrates:

---

and over-determined decision in the *Histories*.' See also, Thomas Harrison, *Divinity and History: The Religion of Herodotus* (Oxford Classical Monograph; New York: Clarendon Press, 2000), 132.

> The same dream (τὠυτὸ ὄνειρον) that visited Xerxes came to
> Artabanus while he was sleeping and stood over him and said, 'Are
> you that person who is dissuading Xerxes to march the army against
> Greece, as though you are concerned for him? But neither hereafter nor
> in the present will you escape punishment for trying to change what
> must take place. It has been made known to Xerxes himself what he
> must suffer if he disobeys.' After these things, it seemed to Artabanus
> that the dream threatened [him] by attempting to burn his eyes with hot
> irons.

Artabanus *reacts* with a loud cry and jumping up out of bed and *responds*
by recounting the dream to Xerxes and urging him to lead the army
against the Greeks.

The fourth and final dream of this series comes to Xerxes after he has
begun to make preparations for the military campaign. Herodotus'
narration of this dream is unusual in that he states the interpretation of
the dream as part of the *scene-setting*: '[A] third vision happened in [his]
sleep (τρίτη ὄψις ἐν τῷ ὕπνῳ ἐγένετο), which the magi when hearing it
interpreted to refer to the whole earth and to enslaving all people.' The
dream proper is a symbolic dream and is introduced with *dream
terminology* and the conventional δοκέω:

> Now the vision was this (ἡ δὲ ὄψις ἦν ἥδε): It seemed (ἐδόκεε) to Xerxes
> that he was crowned with an olive bough, and from the olive bough
> branches spread upon the whole earth, but then the crown that was
> placed upon his head disappeared.

The dream report is also unusual in that the *response* is not by the dreamer
Xerxes but the army who hears the magi's interpretation and is enthused
by its prospect.

The function of this series of dreams has been discussed in the previous
chapter. Herodotus seems to have modeled his dreams after the deceiving
dream of Agamemnon in Homer's *Iliad*. In obedience to the command of
the dream figure, Xerxes decides to invade Greece, an action that will
eventually end in failure. Dreams related to battles and wars are common
in Greco-Roman literature, but the functions are usually to encourage the
dreamer and to predict accurately victory or defeat. The dreams of Xerxes
and Artabanus, however, deceivingly prompt actions that will bring
disaster.

Summary. Herodotus narrates eight symbolic dreams (1.31; 1.107-108
[2×]; 1.209; 3.124; 6.107; 6.131; 7.19) and six visitant dreams (2.139;
2.141; 3.30; 5.56; 7.12-14, 17); two dreams are not narrated (3.149; 6.118).
In reporting these dreams, Herodotus is highly consistent in using the
term ὄψις; the two exceptions being ὄνειρος in 1.34 and 7.17. Also,
Herodotus always introduces the *dream proper* with δοκέω. The dreams in

Herodotus have a range of functions. Dreams portend the future greatness of an individual at his birth (1.107-108; 6.131), indicate one's future reign or loss of rule (2.139; 3.30), provide divine command-warnings (3.149; 6.118), predict victory or defeat in battle (2.141; 7.12-14, 17, 19 [deceptive]) and presage death (1.34; 1.209; 3.124; 6.107). Moreover, the dreams contribute to the characterization of individuals as well as prompt the narrative's plot movement. Herodotus also provides some examples of dream reports with narrative asides (1.34; 1.209) and of dreams linked with prophetic oracles (3.124; 2.139).

Josephus' Jewish War[10]

Josephus wrote his *Jewish War* at the end of Vespasian's reign (ca. 79 CE), though book 7 was written near the end of the first century. On the surface, *Jewish War* is an account of the Jewish rebellion against Rome, which ended in the destruction of the Jerusalem temple. But as characteristic of ancient historical monographs, it is a multifaceted, literary work that attempts to provide lessons about political, social, cultural and theological issues. Steven Mason identifies four principal themes operating in *Jewish Wars*: (1) the noble service of the Judean ruling class; (2) the insidious problem of civil/political strife (*stasis*); (3) the Romans as the agent of the Jewish God to punish the Judeans; and (4) Jews as an honorable people with an honorable history.[11]

The reports of dreams in *Jewish Wars* are most likely drawn from the sources used by Josephus, except, of course, for those dreams that he alleges he experienced himself. The use of sources, however, does not preclude Josephus' shaping or altering these dream reports for his own purposes. As much of the material in *Jewish War* is also found in his later *Antiquities*, it is interesting to compare the dreams in *Jewish War* with their reporting in *Antiquities*.

The *dreams of Herod the Great* (*J.W.* 1.328 [= *A.J.* 14.451]). In recounting the military exploits of Herod the Great, Josephus refers to certain 'dreams' that Herod experiences concerning the death of his brother Joseph. The dreams themselves are not narrated, but in *Jewish War* the reporting of them contains some formal features of the dream-vision narrative. The *scene-setting* feature identifies Herod as the dreamer and specifies 'Daphne, near Antioch' as the place where the dreams occur. The *dream terminology* is the plural ὄνειροι, which precludes Josephus from providing the narration of multiple *dreams proper*. Instead of the dream

---

10 Translations of Josephus are mine or modified translation of Thackeray, LCL. For introductory issues, see Steve Mason, *Josephus and the New Testament* (2d ed.; Peabody, Mass.: Hendrickson Publishers, 2003); and Louis H. Feldman, 'Josephus,' *ABD* 3.981-998.

11 Mason, *Josephus and the New Testament*, 68–99.

proper, Josephus simply states that the dreams, 'clearly presaged (σαφεῖς
... προσημαίνουσιν) the death of his brother.' The dreamer's *reaction/
response* is described as Herod 'leaping out of bed disturbed' at the exact
moment when the messengers enter with the news of his brother's death.

The motif of the dreams is common, portending the death of someone.
The reporting of the dreams, however, is unusual in that Josephus
narrates the death of Joseph (1.323-327) before mentioning Herod's
dreams. The customary pattern is to report a predictive dream and then
narrate its fulfillment. The effect is one of anticipation and suspense as the
reader continues with the narrative, curious as to how exactly the
prediction will come to pass. This literary effect is foiled by Josephus'
narrative arrangement of describing Joseph's death before the predictive
dreams. And yet, this arrangement allows for the narrative nicety of
Herod awaking from one of these disturbing dreams just as the
messengers of the misfortune arrive. Thus, the emphasis shifts from the
event of Joseph's death to the character of Herod, who quickly sets out to
avenge his brother's death.[12]

Josephus repeats this reference to Herod's dreams in *Jewish Antiquities*
14.451. Although the basic account is the same, there are some differences
in the reporting of the dreams, which consequently alters the narrative
effect. First, the paragraph begins with those who report the news of
Joseph's death; their arrival does not coincide with Herod's reaction to
one of the dreams as in *Jewish War*. As a matter of fact, the formal feature
of Herod's reaction to the dreams in *Jewish War* is missing in the
Antiquities account. Also, there is no *scene-setting* in the *Antiquities*
account. The reference to 'Daphne of Antioch' is connected to where the
messengers inform Herod of his brother's death; it is not related to the
reference to Herod's dreams. Thus, the formal features of the dream
report present in the *Jewish War* account are omitted in *Antiquities*. In
Antiquities, it simply states that Herod expected such news 'because of
certain visions of dreams that distinctly indicated (διά τινας ὀνείρων
ὄψεις τρανῶς προφαινούσας) the death of his brother.' In *Antiquities*,
the reference to Herod's dreams seems incidental to the narrative.

The dream of Archelaus (J.W. 2.112-113 [*= A.J.* 17.345-348]). Josephus
ends the Archelaus material in *Jewish War* (2.1-116), and in *Antiquities*
(17.200-355), by reporting a dream of Archelaus. Josephus first relates the
circumstances under which Augustus revoked Archelaus' rule and exiled
him to Gaul (2.111), specifically noting that this banishment happened in
the ninth year of his reign. He then narrates the dream, but only
offhandedly linking it to the narrative by the simple expression φασίν ('it

---

12   See *J.W.* 1.336-339, 342, which explicitly links his victory in battle with the motive of
avenging his brother's death.

is said'). The *scene-setting* assumes much of the narrative but does indicate the general time at which the dream occurs: 'before [Archelaus] was summoned by Caesar.' The *dream terminology* is ὄναρ with the frequently used δοκέω introducing the *dream proper*: 'it seemed (ἔδοξεν) that he saw nine full, large ears of corn being devoured by oxen.' Archelaus' *response* to the dream is to seek help in interpreting the symbolic dream: 'he sent for diviners (μάντεις) and certain ones of the Chaldeans and inquired what they thought it signified.' These professionals differ in their interpretations, which Josephus does not describe, but Josephus does recount the interpretation of a certain Essene named Simon:

> A certain Simon, of the sect of the Essenes, said that in his view the ears of corn denoted a period of time and the oxen a change of circumstances because the plowing [by the oxen] changes the field; he would therefore rule for as many years as there were ears of corn and would die after various changes of circumstances.

Josephus ends the section by noting that Archelaus was summoned to Rome for his trial just five days after hearing Simon's interpretation.

The dream is a symbolic, predictive dream that signifies the fate of Archelaus' rule, which is a common motif of dreams. Once again, Josephus deviates from the conventional pattern of first narrating the dream and then describing the manner in which it is fulfilled. In terms of narrative discourse, the dream report does not foreshadow an event; it is a flashback that fills out the narrative in a retrospective fashion.

It is interesting to note that in *Antiquities* (17.345-348) the dream of Archelaus is more integrated into the narrative than in *Jewish War*. The dream is still reported after the fact, and is mostly identical in terms of content, but its relation to the context is more explicit. Josephus describes the messenger of Augustus, who summons Archelaus to Rome to give an account of his brutal reign, as relating the news while Archelaus is feasting with his friends (17.344). Josephus then states that 'before being summoned to come up to Rome, Archelaus described to his friends the following dream (ὄναρ τοιόνδε) that he saw.' The implication is that Archelaus recounts the dream to his friends at the banquet just prior to the arrival of the messenger. Whereas in *Jewish War* the dream is introduced with the minimal φασίν ('it is said'), in *Antiquities* the feast is the context of both the reporting of the dream and the fulfillment of the dream.

The dream of Glaphyra (*J.W.* 2.114-116 [= *A.J.* 17.349-353]. Immediately after narrating the dream of Archelaus, Josephus 'believes it is fitting to mention the dream (τό ὄναρ) of his wife Glaphyra.' In addition to indicating the place and time of the dream (not long after her arrival in Judea; 2.116), the *scene-setting* includes a review of Glaphyra's marriage history (2.114-115) so that the content of the dream will make sense. Glaphyra was first married to Archelaus' brother Alexander, who eventually was killed by his father Herod the Great. She then marries the Lybian king Juba. After Juba's death, Archelaus divorces his wife Mariamne in order to marry the now widowed Glaphyra. With the *dream terminology* (τό ὄναρ) given at the beginning of this section (2.114), the *dream proper* simply begins with δοκέω:

> It seemed (ἔδοξεν) that Alexander stood beside (ἐπιστάντα) her and said, 'The Libyan marriage was sufficient for you, but not content with that you returned to my house to take a third husband, and O audacious woman, this one my brother. However, I will not overlook this outrage (τὴν ὕβριν), but I will reclaim you though you may not wish it.' After describing the dream, she lived barely two days.

Though in a vague manner, this visitant dream announces to Glaphyra the consequence of her transgression: death. The dream report is somewhat abridged in that it lacks any description of the dreamer's *reaction/response*. Instead, the fulfillment of the dream is promptly and modestly stated, making explicit the meaning of the ambiguous dream message.

The dream of Glaphyra in *Antiquities* is similar in terms of the larger context and setting, but the *dream proper* has been expanded, creating a more dramatic representation and a fuller understanding of why Josephus relates the dream:

> And being married to Archelaus she saw the following dream (τοιόνδε ὄναρ): It seemed (ἐδόκει) that Alexander was standing by her, and when she saw him she rejoiced and enthusiastically embraced him. But he considered her at fault and said, 'Glaphyra, you prove the saying that declares, 'A women is not to be trusted.' For though you were betrothed and married to me as a virgin and we had children, you forgot [these things] and betrayed my love by desiring a second marriage. Nor was this the extent of your outrage (ὕβρεως), but you had the audacity to have a third bridegroom lie down with you; and you came into my house indecently and imprudently by agreeing to marry Archelaus, your own brother-in-law and my brother. However, I myself will not forget your [first] goodwill, and I will remove every reproach by making you as my own, as you were [before].' She described these things to her female friends, and after a few days her life came to an end.

In this version of Glaphyra's dream, the emotions and intensity of the transgression are much more pronounced. The appearance of Alexander brings joy to Glaphyra and arouses her to embrace him, but Alexander suppresses her *reaction* by reproaching her and offering a highly descriptive account of her treachery. This description leaves the reader with a greater impression of her offense.

Moreover, in *Antiquities* Josephus provides a rationale for including the dreams of Archelaus and Glaphyra (17.354): they concern royal persons, and they provide examples of the immortality of the soul and God's providence in human affairs. Then, as if anticipating an objection, he states, 'Such things can be disbelieved by anyone, but while having his own opinion he should not hinder the one who adds them for the purpose of virtue (ἐπ' ἀρετὴν).' This explanation may provide a clue to explaining the differences between the dreams in *Jewish War* and *Antiquities*. In *Jewish War*, the dreams of Archelaus and Glaphyra seem incidental to the narrative; but in *Antiquities* both dreams are more integrated into the narrative, and Glaphyra's dream is elaborated.

The research of Steve Mason is most helpful here: according to Mason, *Jewish War* is less concerned with the reigns of Herod's sons, 'focusing rather on the turbulence that arose in Judea' which led to the war with Rome.[13] Thus, the postscript-like reports of the dreams of Archelaus and Glaphyra in *Jewish War* reflect the perspective of that work. *Antiquities*, on the other hand, has a different purpose than *Jewish War*: to illustrate 'that, according to the ancient and noble constitution of the Jews, those who stray from the law come to a disastrous end.'[14] For Josephus, Herod's family provides ample illustrations of this thesis, and the dreams of Archelaus and Glaphyra in *Antiquities* contribute to the dramatic demonstration of that argument.

The dreams of Josephus (J.W 3.351-354). Josephus himself was involved in the first Jewish war against Rome as a military leader in Galilee. Hunted and besieged by the Romans, Josephus surrendered to Nicanor, the representative of the Roman general Vespasian. In his *Jewish War*, Josephus describes, in the third person, how he came to the decision to surrender.

> But as Nicanor was persistently urging his proposals and Josephus became aware of the threats of the hostile crowd, he remembered [his] dreams during the night (τῶν διὰ νυκτὸς ὀνείρων), in which God prefigured (προεσήμανεν) to him the misfortunes (τάς συμφοράς) that were about to come upon the Jews and the future of the Roman rulers. Now concerning the interpretation of dreams (περὶ κρίσεις ὀνείρων) he was skilled in discerning the ambiguous statements of the Deity (τὰ ἀμφιβόλως ὑπὸ τοῦ θείου λεγόμενα); and he was certainly not ignorant of the prophecies of the sacred books as he himself was a priest and a descendant of priests. And then at that hour, becoming inspired (ἔνθους γενόμενος) and comprehending the dreadful images (τὰ φρικώδη ... φαντάσματα) of [his] recent dreams, he offered this silent prayer to

13 Mason, *Josephus and the New Testament*, 154.
14 Mason, *Josephus and the New Testament*, 155.

> God, 'Because it seems good to you, the Creator, that the Jewish people
> fade away, and all fortune pass to the Romans, and you have chosen my
> soul to speak about the things that are about to take place, I willing give
> myself to the Romans and stay alive, and I am giving witness not as a
> traitor but I am your servant.'

Josephus does not narrate the dreams, but the references to interpretation
and dream images (φάντασμα) suggest symbolic dreams. The immediate
response of Josephus is to surrender to the Romans, but the function of
the dreams is more significant than simply to direct Josephus to surrender.
In linking these dreams and their interpretation with inspiration and the
prophecies of Scripture, Josephus seems to infer that the dreams signify
the fulfillment of the biblical prophecies. This inference is supported by
the common convention in Greco-Roman literature in which dreams and
oracles contribute to the fulfillment of one or the other.Thus, the dreams
and their relation to prophecies contribute to a major theme of the *Jewish
War*: like ancient Assyria and Babylon, the Romans are instruments of
God's judgment upon the Jewish people.[15]

Steve Mason also observes that the dreams of Josephus occur at the
midpoint of *Jewish Wars*, a pattern that seems to be present in Josephus's
other works.[16] As such, the dreams occur at a critical moment of the
narrative and Josephus' life, revealing the Roman victory as God's will
and prompting Josephus to surrender.

Summary. There are four reports of dreams in Josephus' *Jewish War*, two
non-narrated (1.328; 3.351-354) and two narrated (2.112-113; 2.114-116).
The two non-narrated dream references use the plural term ὄνειροι to
indicate the dream phenomenon, while the two narrated dream reports
use the term ὄναρ with δοκέω introducing the *dream proper*. Two dreams
signify the impending death of someone (1.328; 2.114-116), and one dream
portends the loss of one's rule (2.112-113); and yet, each of these three
dreams also functions to demonstrate the character of the dreamer.
Though the fourth dream (2.351-354) has a familiar function in
connection with a battle or war, its more central function is its
contribution to a critical narrative moment. This dream also is associated
with the fulfillment of prophecies.

---

15 Mason, *Josephus and the New Testament*, 81–88.

16 Steve Mason, *Life of Josephus: Translation and Commentary*, vol. 9 of *Flavius
Josephus: Translation and Commentary* (ed. S. Mason; Leiden: Brill, 2001), 104 n. 927. The
prophetic dreams of Daniel (Book 10) stand at the center of his twenty volume *Antiquities*; a
decisive dream is narrated about midpoint in Josephus's *Life* (208–209).

Dreams in Greco-Roman Biographies

The following survey of dreams in Greco-Roman biographies will consider the Acts of the Apostles,[17] Plutarch's *Parallel Lives*, and Suetonius' *Lives of the Caesars*. Other ancient biographies that contain dream reports or references to dreams are Diogenes Laertius (*Vit. phil.* 1.117; 2.35; 3.2; 3.5),[18] Philostratus (*Vit. Apoll.* 1.5; 1.9; 1.10; 1.23; 1.29; 4.11; 4.34; 8.7.v; 8.12),[19] Lucian (*Peregr.* 26.2), Soranus (*Vit. Hipp.* 4.7), and *Life of Aesop* (6–9; 29 [cf. 30; 33]).[20]

Acts of the Apostles[21]

Written sometime between the end of the first century C.E. and the first half of the second century C.E., the Acts of the Apostles is included in the New Testament canon and is the second volume of the Third Gospel, the Gospel of Luke. It narrates the ministry and life of the early church – with emphasis on the apostles Peter and Paul – as it fulfills the command of Jesus to preach the gospel to the whole world (1.8). This narrative contains four dream reports.

Before examining the dreams individually, it should be noted that the dreams, along with visions, collectively have a function within the narrative of Acts. In Acts 2, the speech of Peter interprets the Pentecost event, in which the Holy Spirit came upon the early believers, as the fulfillment of the prophecy of Joel. The prophecy is quoted and partially reads, '... and your young men will see visions (ὁράσεις ὄψονται) and your old men will dream dreams' (ἐνυπνίοις ἐνυπνιασθήσονται; 2.17). The subsequent narrative includes both visions (9.3-9 [cf. 22.6-11; 26.12-18]; 9.10-17; 10.3-8 [cp. 10.30-33]; 10.9-16 [cf. 11.4-11]; 22.17-23) and dreams (16.6-10; 18.9-11; 23.11; 27.23-26). The Joel prophecy not only interprets retrospectively the Pentecost event, but it also interprets

---

17   The genre of Acts is greatly debated and still lacks a scholarly consensus. It is interesting that a case has been made for each of the genres considered in this chapter: history (Gregory E. Sterling, *Historiography and Self-definition: Josephos, Luke-Acts, and Apologetic historiography* [NovTSup 64; Leiden: Brill, 1992]); biography (Charles H. Talbert, *Literary Patterns, Theological Themes, and the Genre of Luke-Acts* [Missoula, Mont.: Scholars Press, 1974], and Richard A. Burridge, *What Are the Gospels? A Comparision with Graeco-Roman Biography* [2d ed.; Grand Rapids, Mich.: Eerdmans, 2004], 237–39, 275–279), and novel (Richard I. Pervo, *Profit with Delight: The Literary Genre of Acts of the Apostles* [Philadelphia: Fortress Press, 1987]).

18   In addition to dream reports, Diogenes Laertius also includes certain philosophers' teachings about dreams: *Vit. phil.* 6.43; 8.32; 10.32; 10.135.

19   In addition to these dream reports or references, see 2.37 for teaching regarding dreams.

20   There are no dream narratives in Tacitus, *Life of Agricola*; Philo, *Life of Moses* (1.268 and 1.289 are contrived dreams); Porphory's *Life of Plotinus*; or Satyrus, *Life of Euripides*.

21   Translations of Acts are mine.

proleptically the ensuing ministry of the early church. Thus, visions and dreams have a programmatic function in Acts: they are signs of the continued, spirit-empowered apostolic ministry that was initiated at Pentecost. Also, this association of dreams and prophecy would be familiar to an ancient audience.

The dream of Paul (16.6-10). This dream comes about as Paul and his companions, Silas and Timothy, are seeking to proclaim the gospel on the so-called 'second missionary' journey. Their efforts, however, are hindered by the Holy Spirit; they were prevented (κωλύω) to preach in Asia (v. 6) and were not permitted (ἐάω) to go into Bithynia (v. 7). So, they enter the city of Troas, where Paul has the following dream:

> And during the night a vision appeared to Paul (καὶ ὅραμα διὰ τῆς νυκτὸς τῷ Παύλῳ ὤφθη). There stood a certain man of Macedonia begging him and saying, 'Cross over to Macedonia and help us.' And when he had seen the vision, we immediately attempted to go over to Macedonia concluding (συμβιβάζοντες) that God had called us to preach the gospel to them.

The *scene-setting* includes the circumstances of being divinely hindered in their missionary journey, and it identifies the place (Troas) and time (night) of the dream and the dreamer (Paul). The *dream terminology* is ὅραμα. The *dream proper* is a visitant dream of a certain Macedonian man who requests Paul's help. The *response* is an immediate attempt to comply with the dream message.[22] This response, however, does not come without some discernment of what the vision intends. The missionaries infer (συμβιβάζω) that the night vision means God is calling them to evangelize Macedonia. Thus, the message of the dream is not straightforward and is most likely understood in connection with their experience of divine hindrance in Asia and Bithynia. The function of the dream is a divine directive that advances the gospel across the Aegean Sea and thus contributes to the fulfillment of Jesus' command at the beginning of Acts: 'you will be my witnesses in Jerusalem and in all Judea and Samaria and to the end of the earth' (1.8).

The dream of Paul (18.9-11). Acts 18.1-17 describes Paul's ministry in Corinth, where his experience with the Jews has been both positive and negative. On the one hand, Paul has experienced opposition and insult from the synagogue (vv. 4–6). But on the other hand, he has been united

---

22   The 'Western' text of Acts, as witnessed in Codex Bezae, provides a reading that fills out the response element by specifically noting that Paul told his companions about the dream: 'thus, when he had gotten up [Paul] related (διηγήσατο) to us the vision, and we perceived (ἐνοήσαμεν) that the Lord had called us to preach the gospel to the ones in Macedonia.'

with the Jewish-Christian couple Aquila and Priscilla (vv. 2–3) and has converted the official of the synagogue, Crispus (v. 8). Moreover, Paul has established a house-church right beside the synagogue (v. 7), which no doubt intensified the conflict between Paul's ministry and the ministry of the synagogue. It is in this context that Paul receives a dream:

> In the night through a vision the Lord said to Paul (εἶπεν δὲ ὁ κύριος ἐν νυκτὶ δι᾽ ὁράματος τῷ Παύλῳ), 'Do not fear, but speak and do not be silent; because I am with you and no one will put [a hand] on you to harm you, [and] because there are many of my people in this city.' And he resided there a year and six months teaching among them the word of God.

This dream narrative is introduced with one clause that identifies the time of the dream (night), the *dream terminology* (ὅραμα), and the dreamer (Paul). The dream functions to encourage Paul in continuing his ministry in Corinth. Paul *responds* by staying in Corinth a year and a half instructing the believers. Thus, the dream is a command-encouragement dream that prompts Paul's lengthy ministry in Corinth.

The dream of Paul (23.11). Paul has been at the center of several disturbances in Jerusalem (21.7ff; 22.22ff; 23.6ff) and is in Roman custody for his own safety. As he is in Roman custody, Paul experiences a dream:

> Now on the following night the Lord stood by him and said (τῇ δὲ ἐπιούσῃ νυκτὶ ἐπιστὰς αὐτῷ ὁ κύριος εἶπεν), 'Take courage! For just as you testified about me in Jerusalem, in the same way it is also necessary that you testify in Rome.'

The *scene-setting* assumes much of the context and is minimal: 'on the following night.' There is no *dream terminology* but the position of the dream figure is noted ('standing by him'), which is a feature common in visitant dream reports. The function of the dream is two-fold: (1) to encourage Paul in his present circumstance, and (2) to foretell Paul's eventual arrival and testimony in Rome. Rhetorically, the prediction of Paul testifying in Rome provides the reader with an anticipation of its fulfillment, an anticipation that will be intensified as the plot continues with several circumstances that threaten Paul's Roman destination.[23]

The dream of Paul (27.23-26). This dream is actually reported in a speech by Paul. Paul is aboard a ship being taken as a prisoner to Rome. The sea voyage has proved to be quite difficult with raging storms causing the crew to throw provisions overboard. Paul addresses those on board in order to encourage them:

---

23 For example, the conspiracy to kill Paul (23.12-31), Paul's lengthy imprisonment in Caesarea (24.22-27), and Paul's difficult sailing and shipwreck (27.1–28.10).

I urge you now to take courage, for there will not be one loss of life
from among you but [only] the ship. For in this night (ταύτη τῇ νυκτὶ)
an angel of the God to whom I belong and whom I worship stood by me
(παρέστη ... μοι) and said, 'Do not fear, Paul, it is necessary that you
stand before Caesar. And behold, God has graciously given you all
those who are sailing with you.' Therefore, take courage, men! For have
faith in God that it will be in the same way as it was spoken to me.

Once again, there is no *dream terminology*, but the time (night) and
reference to the position of the dream figure ('standing by me') are
common features of a dream narrative. The *dream proper* is a visitant
dream by an angel of God, and Paul's *response* is one of trust in the dream
message. Like the previous dream narrative, this dream functions to give
encouragement to Paul and the other travelers and to predict his
testimony before the emperor in Rome.

Summary. The four dream reports in the Acts of the Apostles are all
visitant dreams experienced by Paul; two visitations from 'the Lord' (18.9-
11; 23.11), one from an 'angel of God' (27.23-26), and one from a 'man of
Macedonia' (16.6-10). One dream is a command-directive dream that
gives guidance for further evangelization (16.6-10). Three of the dreams
function to provide encouragement to Paul and/or others (18.9-11; 23.11;
27.23-26). Two of these same dreams also predict Paul's witness in Rome
(23.11; 27.23-26).

The dream of 27.23-26 raises questions, however, since its fulfillment –
testifying before Caesar – is not narrated. The book of Acts ends with
Paul under house arrest, 'preaching the kingdom of God and teaching the
things about the Lord Jesus Christ [to those who visited him] with all
boldness and without hindrance'; there is no appearance before Caesar.
An ancient audience, though, would expect the fulfillment of the dream
prediction. And yet, it is exactly that anticipation which dreams provoke
in readers that allows Luke to end Acts in such an open-ended manner.
Charles Talbert nicely describes the rhetorical nature of this open-
endedness:

> Narrative suspension is a literary device whereby the author, by failing
> to bring certain narrative data to their resolution, hinders the closure of
> the narrative world for the reader. The closure must be achieved by the
> reader, who does so by finishing the story in consonance with its plot.[24]

---

24   Charles H. Talbert, *Reading Acts: A Literary and Theological Commentary on The
Acts of the Apostles* (New York: Crossroad, 1997), 235. Cf. also Robert C. Tannehill, *The
Narrative Unity of Luke-Acts: A Literary Interpretation* (2 vols.; Minneapolis: Fortress Press,
1990), 2.353-357.

In regard to appearing before Caesar, the literary device of the dream narrative (prediction) functions in tandem with the literary device of narrative suspension (imagined fulfillment).

Plutarch's Parallel Lives[25]

Generally dated during the reign of the Roman emperor Trajan (98–117 C.E.), Plutarch's *Parallel Lives* (παράλληλοι βίοι)[26] is a series of comparative biographies of celebrated Greeks and Romans. His purpose in writing *Parallel Lives* is to display the virtue – and sometimes vice – of these great figures so as to reveal their character (*Alex.* 1.2-3). Such demonstrations of virtue are in turn to be admired and emulated (*Tim.* praef.; *Per.* 1.1–2.4). Plutarch follows a general pattern in narrating his *Lives*: family and birth; education and entrance into public life; greatest moments; changes in fortune; and latter years and death.[27] Where it fits his purposes, Plutarch includes dream narratives; and as Frederick Brenk observes, Plutarch often manipulates the dream reports of his sources for biographical purposes, emphasizing the psychological state and decision-making process of the dreamer.[28]

This survey of dreams in Plutarch only looks at the biographies of Themistocles, Alexander, and Caesar, though the summary will cross-reference other dreams in Plutarch's *Lives*.

The dream of Themistocles (*Them.* 26.2-4). This dream comes at a time when Themistocles is a fugitive, having been accused of treason by the Athenians. At the time of the dream, however, he is receiving hospitality from a certain Nicogenes. The dream report is preceded by a meal scene, in which a servant becomes inspired and prophesies, 'night shall speak; night shall counsel; night shall give victory.' The dream report immediately follows:

> And after these things Themistocles went to bed and saw a dream (ὄναρ). It seemed (ἔδοξεν) that a serpent wound itself along over his body and crept up to his neck. Then as soon as it touched his face it

25 Translations of Plutarch are mine or modified translation of Perrin, LCL. The following works are helpful introductions to Plutarch's *Parallel Lives*: Barbara Scardigli, ed., *Essays on Plutarch's Lives* (Oxford: Clarendon Press, 1995); Timothy E. Duff, *Plutarch's Lives: Exploring Virtue and Vice* (Oxford: Oxford University Press, 1999); R. H. Barrow, *Plutarch and His Times* (Bloomington, Ind.: Indiana University Press, 1967), 51–65; and Donald Andrew Frank Moore Russell, 'Plutarch,' *OCD* 1200–1201.

26 The designation 'Parallel Lives' comes from Plutarch himself; see *Thes.* 1.1 and *Pel.* 2.4.

27 Russell, 'Plutarch,' 1201.

28 Frederick E. Brenk, 'The Dreams of Plutarch's Lives,' *Latomus* 34 (1975): 336–349, esp. 338, 343–347.

became an eagle and enveloped him with its wings and lifted him on
high and bore him a long distance, when there appeared as it were a
golden herald's wand, on which it set him securely down, freed from
helpless terror and distress.

There is no interpretation offered for this symbolic dream, but its meaning
is unfolded in the subsequent narrative. In order to get Themistocles out
of the country safely, the host Nicogenes has Themistocles placed in a
mobile tent that was routinely used to transport women so that they
would not be seen. Plutarch explains that this custom came about because
the Persians 'are savage and harsh in their jealous watchfulness over their
women.' So, at every instance when the traveling party was stopped and
questioned, Themistocles' servants simply replied that they were carrying
one of the king's prized Hellenic women; and Themistocles was securely
led out of Greece. The dream portends Themistocles' deliverance from his
present, threatening circumstance. Also, as in other Greco-Roman
literature, the dream is associated with prophecy.

The dream of Themistocles (*Them.* 30.1-3). The context for this dream
report is a plot against Themistocles' life. Plutarch relates how Pisidian
mercenaries were waiting in a village called the Lion's Head
(Λεοντοκέφαλος) to assassinate Themistocles. The dream report is then
given:

> It is said that while he was lying down at midday the mother of the gods
> appeared in a dream and said (τὴν μητέρα τῶν θεῶν ὄναρ φανεῖσαν
> εἰπεῖν), 'O Themistocles, avoid a head of lions (κεφαλῆς λεόντων), so
> that you may not come upon a lion. And in return for this I demand of
> you [your daughter] Mnesiptolema to be my handmaiden.'

The *reaction* of Themistocles is characterized as 'being greatly confused'
(διαταράσσω), but nonetheless he *responds* by supplicating to the goddess
and taking another route to bypass the Lion's Head. The assassins adjust
their plans, but through a series of events occasioned by his detour, their
plot is foiled and Themistocles is saved.

The *dream proper* is a visitant dream by the 'mother of the gods,' who is
known by several names such as Rhea, Cybele, or Dindymené.[29] The
message, given in direct discourse, is both a warning and command. The
warning comes as a riddle and wordplay on the village's name Lion's
Head (Λεοντοκέφαλος), the name of which the reader has already been
introduced. Themistocles is to avoid κεφαλὴ λεόντων so as not to
encounter a λέων. Though initially confused by the riddle, Themistocles
presumably discerns its meaning and heeds its warning. The command is
that Themistocles gives his daughter to the ministry of the goddess in

---

29 See note by Perrin, LCL.

return for the divine protection. Themistocles not only complies with this command, but he also builds a temple in honor of the goddess. Like the dream in 26.2-3, this dream also functions to deliver and protect Themistocles.

Dreams of Olympias and Philip (Alex. 2.2-3.). Following the conventions of encomiastic rhetoric, Plutarch begins his *bios* of Alexander the Great by relating his ancestry (2.1) and the circumstances of his birth (2.1–3.5), which includes two dreams by his father and mother. Having stated that Philip and Olympias, Alexander's parents, were betrothed (ἁρμόζω), the *scene-setting* and the *dream proper* are recounted:

> On the night before they were to come together in the bride-chamber, the bride thought (ἔδοξε) that a peal of thunder and a lightning bolt fell upon her womb, and from the lightning strike a great fire was kindled, and then after having burst into flames everywhere it was extinguished.

The second dream follows directly upon the report of the first one:

> At a later time after the marriage, Philip saw a dream (εἶδεν ὄναρ): he was putting a seal on [his] wife's womb; and the emblem of the seal, as he thought, had the image of a lion.

Olympias' dream is not given an interpretation, but the dream can be interpreted in light of Alexander's life: he conquers the world in a short time but dies at a young age. Also, the lightning may suggest a birth of divine origin. This possibility is more evocative when Plutarch shortly recounts how Philip often saw a snake sleeping near Olympias, thinking that she might be 'the partner to a superior being' (κρείττονι συνούσης; 2.4). Philip's dream, on the other hand, is submitted to the diviners (μάντεις) for interpretation. They conclude that the dream indicates a need for Philip to be guarded of his marriage, but the famed diviner, Aristander of Telmessus, rightly interprets the dream to signify the pregnancy of Olympias, 'since no seal is put upon what is empty and the child conceived would have a bold and lion-like nature.' Both dreams are a motif common to birth stories, which function to portend the future greatness and distinction of the unborn child.

The dream of Dareius (Alex. 18.4). In recounting the military campaigns of Alexander, Plutarch describes a dream that comes to the Persian king Dareius. The *scene-setting* includes the mental state of the dreamer: Dareius was quite optimistic about his military engagement against Alexander, for 'a certain dream (τινος ὀνείρου θαρρύνοντος αὐτον) had encouraged him.' Before narrating the *dream proper*, however, Plutarch discloses that Dareius' encouragement is misplaced, because the magi have interpreted the dream, 'for favor rather than according to the truth' (πρὸς χάριν ... μᾶλλον ἢ κατὰ τὸ εἰκός). Thus, the fulfillment and meaning of the dream are insinuated before its reporting. The *dream proper* is introduced by the customary δοκέω:

It seemed (ἔδοξε) that the Macedonian battle lines were engulfed with a fire, and that Alexander, wearing a robe that he himself [i.e., Dareius] used to wear when he was a royal courier, was serving him; and [then] Alexander went into the temple of Belus and disappeared.

In contrast to the magi's favorable interpretation, the dream actually signifies Alexander's conquering army, rule of Asia and sudden, but glorious, end. For the reader of Plutarch's *Alexander*, the proper interpretation of Dareius' dream has already been provided in light of the dream of Olympias (2.2). The fire of the Macedonian battle lines is a manifestation of the all-encompassing fire initiated by the lightning bolt in Olympias' dream. Also, both the dreams of Olympias and Dareius signify a swift end to Alexander's life. Thus, in addition to the dream being a common motif of battles and future reign, the dream of Dareius also functions within the narrative as a confirmation and partial fulfillment of Olympias' dream.

The dreams of Alexander and the Tyrians (*Alex.* 24.3-5). In recounting Alexander's siege of the city of Tyre, Plutarch reports two dreams of Alexander and a dream of 'many Tyrians'; all the dreams signify Alexander's inevitable capture of Tyre. The first dream of Alexander is initially reported with the *scene-setting* indicating the time of the dream: during the besieging of Tyre. Although the figure of Heracles is present, the *dream proper* should be considered a symbolic dream: '[Alexander] saw a dream (εἶδεν ὄναρ): Heracles was stretching out his hand to him from the wall and calling him.' The dream report lacks a *reaction/response* of the dreamer or an interpretation; the narrative simply continues by reporting immediately the dream of the Tyrians:

And it seemed (ἔδοξεν) to many of the Tyrians during [their] sleep that Apollo said that he was going away to Alexander because the events in the city were not pleasing to him.

This dream report does include a *response*: the Tyrians fastened the statue of Apollo to its pedestal, considering the god a deserter (αὐτομολουντων) and an Alexandrite (Ἀλεξανδριστῆς). Both these dreams contribute to the understanding that Alexander's military endeavor is sanctioned and assured by the divine.

The second dream of Alexander is another symbolic dream, and its reporting is given directly after the response of the Tyrians:

And Alexander saw another vision during [his] sleep (ἑτέραν δὲ ὄψιν Ἀλέξανδρος εἶδε κατὰ τοὺς ὕπνους): it seemed (ἐδόκει) to him that a satyr (σάτυρος) appeared and mocked him at a distance. [Alexander] attempted to take him but he escaped; but finally, after much coaxing and chasing, [the satyr] surrendered.

The dream is then interpreted by the diviners, who base their interpretation on the word satyr (σάτυρος); the diviners say, 'Tyre will be yours' (Σὴ γενήσεται Τύρος). Thus, all three dreams portend Alexander's victory and conquest of the city of Tyre, which is subsequently narrated (25.1-2).

The dream of Alexander (Alex. 26.3). This dream of Alexander provides inspiration and instruction about where to establish a new city in Egypt that would come to be known as Alexandria. The context for the dream is two-fold. First, as part of the spoils of defeating the Persian king Dareius, Alexander receives a small, valuable coffer in which he places his copy of Homer's *Iliad* (26.1). Second, Plutarch notes that after his conquest of Egypt, Alexander intends to begin construction of the new city on a location advised by his architects. Plutarch then reports the dream as follows:

> Then, in the night as he was sleeping, he saw a marvelous vision (ὄψιν εἶδε θαυμαστήν): A man with very grey hair and an honorable appearance seemed (ἔδοξεν) to be standing by him and speaking these words:
>   'Now, there is an island in much-dashing sea,
>   in front of Egypt; And they call it Pharos.'
> Thus, he immediately rose up and went to Pharos (which then was still an island, a little above the Canobic mouth of the Nile, but now it has been joined to the mainland by a causeway).

The *scene-setting* of this visitant dream assumes much of the context and simply states the time of the dream (night) and the activity of sleep. The *dream terminology* is notable for its further description with an adjective, ὄψις θαυμαστή. The *dream proper* includes the conventional δοκέω, but it does not introduce the dream as expected. Instead, it is positioned after the description of the dream figure, which has the effect of emphasizing the visitant, who is none other than Homer.[30] Not only does the description bring to mind Homer, but the reader also recognizes the identity as Homer with the mention of Homer's *Iliad* in the previous paragraph (26.1), and the dream message itself, which is a quotation from the *Odyssey* (4.354). Alexander's *reaction* is described in terms of 'rising up [out of bed]' (ἐξανίστημι), and after a narrative aside, Plutarch relates Alexander's *response* of having the city established at Pharos in

---

30   J. R. Hamilton, *Plutarch: Alexander* (2d ed.; London: Bristol Classical Press, 1999), 67.

accordance with the dream (24.4). On the one hand, the dream functions in the narrative as instruction on the best location of Alexander's city; but on the other hand, the dream contributes to the glory and legend of the great city of Alexandria.

The dream of Caesar (*Caes.* 32.6). This dream is reported in relation to Caesar's decisive crossing of the Rubicon River, which initiated a civil war that would ultimately leave him the sole ruler of the Roman world. Plutarch goes to great lengths to portray Caesar's inner struggle to take that 'fearful step' (ἡ δεινός; 32.4). Caesar eventually makes the decision to cross into Italy with resolve and abandonment with the infamous words, 'let the die be cast' (32.6). It is after Plutarch's narration of the crossing that he relates the following:

> Now it is said that on the night before the crossing he saw an unlawful dream (ὄναρ ἰδεῖν ἔκθεσμον), for he seemed (ἐδόκει) to be having incestuous intercourse with his own mother.

Other writers report that this dream took place earlier in Caesar's life, while he was a quaestor serving in Spain.[31] Moreover, they offer a favorable interpretation of the dream: to rule over one's country or empire. Plutarch, however, has relocated the dream to the Rubicon crossing and has not offered an interpretation. Not only does the dream contribute to Plutarch's depiction of Caesar's anxiety and uncertainty about the crossing, it also draws the reader into this psychological apprehension. By ending this critical juncture in the story of Caesar with this dream, Plutarch makes the prudence of Caesar's decision to march into Italy much more ambiguous, especially with his characterization of the dream as 'unlawful' (ἔκθεσμος) and his not offering an interpretation. As Frederick Brenk states, 'The immediate tone is one of anxiety, lawlessness, and ruthlessness.'[32] Perhaps the ambiguity of the dream's meaning reflects the imprecision of judging Caesar's achievement: Caesar was triumphant in the civil war but was assassinated before he could experience the benefits of his rule.[33]

The dream of Calpurnia (*Caes.* 63.5-7). Plutarch reports the dream of Caesar's wife, Calpurnia, as a part of his larger recounting of the

---

31 Suetonius, *Jul.* 32.9 and Cassius Dio, *Hist. Rom.* 41.24.

32 Brenk, 'The Dreams of Plutarch's Lives,' 346.

33 Cf. Plutarch, *Caes.* 69.1: 'At the time of his death Caesar was fully fifty-six years old, but he had survived Pompey not much more than four years, while of the power and dominion which he had sought all his life at so great risks, and barely achieved at last, of this he had reaped no fruit but the name of it only, and a glory which had awakened envy on the part of his fellow citizens' (Perrin, LCL). Noted in Brenk, 'The Dreams of Plutarch's Lives,' 346.

'wondrous signs and apparitions' (σημεῖα θαυμαστὰ καὶ φάσματα; 63.1) that foreshadowed Caesar's death. Plutarch recounts how on the night before his death, Caesar noticed his wife 'uttering indistinct words and inarticulate groans in her sleep; for it seemed (ἐδόκει) that she was holding her murdered husband in her arms and wailing for him.' The lack of a full dream report may be due to Plutarch's narrating the events according to Caesar's perspective. There are several portentous circumstances that Caesar fails to heed or consider, but Calpurnia's dream gives him pause. At her request, he consults the diviners (οἱ μάντεις) who confirm through sacrifices the unfavorable omen. Caesar then decides to stay at home and send Anthony to the senate. But the dream proves fateful, and through a set of circumstances Caesar goes to the senate where he is assassinated. As is common in Greco-Roman literature, the death of an individual is portended by a dream.

The dream of Cinna (*Caes.* 68.2-3). After the death of Caesar and the reading of his will, which benefited every Roman citizen, a riot broke out against the conspirators, fueled by gratitude for Caesar's generous benefaction. Plutarch recounts how a friend of Caesar's, a certain Cinna, became a victim of the unrest. This fate was portended in a dream. The *scene-setting* identifies the dreamer (Cinna), the time of the dream ('the previous night'), and the dream terminology ('a strange vision'; ὄψιν ... ἄτοπον). The *dream proper* is a symbolic dream introduced by δοκέω:

> For it seemed (ἐδόκει) that he was invited to a dinner by Caesar and that when he excused himself Caesar led him by the hand, though Cinna was not wanting to go and resisted.

The reporting of the *reaction* to the dream is delayed until it is noted that Cinna decided to go to hear the reading of Caesar's will in spite of his 'misgivings (ὑφορώμενός) arising from his vision.' An interpretation of the dream is not offered, but the event of Cinna being mistaken for one of Caesar's assassins and thereby being killed by the mob explains the dream: Cinna follows Caesar in death. Thus, by presaging the death of Cinna the dream functions similarly to other dreams in ancient literature.

Summary. Of the dreams surveyed here in Plutarch's *Lives*, eight are symbolic dreams (*Them.* 26.2-4; *Alex.* 2.2-3 [2 ×]; 18.4; 24.3-5 [2 ×]; *Caes.* 32.6; 68.2-3; cf. *Cim.* 18.2-4; *Per.* 3.2; *Alc.* 39.1-2; *Ant.* 16.3; *Eum.* 6.4-7), two are visitant dreams (*Them.* 30.1-3; *Alex.* 26.3; cf. *Arist.* 11.5; 19.2; *Per.* 13.8; *Rom.* 2.4), and one is not narrated (*Caes.* 63.5-7; cf. *Ant.* 22.2). The dream terminology for these dream reports includes ὄναρ (*Them.* 26.2-4; 30.1-3; *Alex.* 2.3; 24.3; *Caes.* 32.6; cf. *Cim.* 18.2-4; *Per.* 13.8), ὄψις (*Alex.* 24.4-5; 26.3; *Caes.* 68.2-3; cf. *Alc.* 39.1-2; *Eum.* 6.4-7), and ὀνείρος (*Alex.* 18.4); and seven dream propers are introduced by δοκέω (*Them.* 26.2-4;

Alex. 2.2; 18.4; 26.3; *Caes.* 32.6; 63.5-7; 68.2-3; cf. *Arist.* 11.5; 19.2; *Cim.* 18.2-4; *Per.* 3.2; *Alc.* 39.1-2; *Eum.* 6.4-7). The functions of these dreams vary. The two dreams in *Themistocles* function to protect the dreamer (26.2-4; 30.1-3; cf. *Ant.* 22.2; *Rom.* 2.4). The dreams in *Alexander* all relate to his future reign or greatness (2.2-3 [2 ×]) or victory in battle (18.4; 24.3-5 [2 ×]; cf. *Arist.* 11.5; *Eum.* 6.4-7), with the exception of one dream that is a command-directive dream as to the where to establish the city of Alexandria (26.3). Two dreams in *Caesar* portend death (63.5-6; 68.2-3; cf. *Arist.* 19.2; *Cim.* 18.2-4; *Alc.* 39.1-2; *Ant.* 16.3), while one dream is uncharacteristically ambiguous (32.6) – though the dream prompts action at a critical juncture in the narrative of *Caesar*.

Suetonius' Lives of the Caesars[34]

Suetonius' *De vita Caesarum* (or *Caesares*) was published around 120 C.E. and offers an evaluation of twelve Roman emperors in light of social and philosophical expectations of imperial conduct. Though varied in how each life is treated, the *Caesares* generally follows a three part pattern: (1) an account of family, birth, childhood, education, early career and ascension to power; (2) an analysis of the performance as emperor by non-chronological, thematic essays; and (3) an account of removal from power and death with an epilogue of honors or other random appendices.[35] In general, dreams are reported by Suetonius in relation to the first part, which usually portends an emperor's good fortune and future reign, and the third part, which usually portends the end of an emperor's reign or his death. This review of dreams in Suetonius is facilitated by considering dreams in *Divus Julius* and *Divus Augustus*; other dreams in the *Caesares* will be noted in the summary.

The dream of Julius Caesar (Jul. 7.2). While serving as a quaestor in Spain, Julius Caesar sees a statue of Alexander and bemoans that he has done nothing noteworthy at the same age when Alexander had conquered the world. So, he requests a discharge in order to pursue more ambitious endeavors back in Rome. Suetonius then relates that Julius had a dream.

> When he was dismayed by a dream (*somnio*) the following night – for he thought that he had offered violence to his mother – the diviners

---

34 Translations of Suetonius are from Rolfe, LCL; a few of these translations have been slightly modified. For introductory matters of Suetonius' *Lives of the Caesars*, see Andrew Wallace-Hadrill, *Suetonius* (2d ed.; London: Bristol Classical Press, 1995); R. G. Lewis, 'Suetonius' "Caesares" and Their Literary Antecedents,' *ANRW* 33.5.3623-3674; and Keith R. Bradley, 'Suetonius (Gaius Suetonius Tranquillus),' *OCD* 1451–1452.

35 Lewis, 'Suetonius' "Caesares",' *ANRW* 33.5.3641; see also Bradley, 'Suetonius,' 1452. It should be noted that even in the beginning and ending accounts of some *vitae*, chronology is disrupted in favor of topical discussions.

(*coniectores*) inspired him with high hopes by their interpretation, which was: that he was destined to rule the world, since the mother whom he had seen in his power was none other than the earth, which is regarded as the common parent of all mankind.[36]

By placing the *dream proper* as a parenthetical statement between the introductory genitive absolute clause and the main clause, Suetonius downplays the *dream proper* and emphasizes the interpretation. The form of the dream report is distorted because of this narrative arrangement. The *reaction* is actually mentioned first ('dismayed') along with a reference to the time of the dream ('following night') in the genitive absolute clause. The *dream proper* is a symbolic dream that portends, according to the professional interpreters, the future reign of Julius.

The dreams of Julius and Calpurnia (*Jul.* 81.3). In this chapter, Suetonius reports a number of 'unmistakable signs' (*evidentibus prodigiis*; 81.1) that indicated the murder of Julius. Among these omens, Suetonius reports the dreams of Julius and his wife, Calpurnia:

> In fact the very night before his murder he saw (*visus est*) now that he was flying above the clouds, and now that he was clasping the hand of Jupiter; and his wife Calpurnia thought (*imaginata*) that the pediment of their house fell, and that her stabbed husband was in her arms.

Suetonius relates these dreams simply as part of the popular traditions surrounding the death of Julius Caesar, and he assumes his readers are familiar with them.

The dreams of Augustus (*Aug.* 91). As a part of a larger section in which Suetonius illustrates Augustus' positive attitude toward religious matters (90–96), chapter 91 touches upon Augustus' respect for dreams by providing some examples of significant dreams. The first example is a reference to a dream by a friend of Augustus (91.1).

> At the battle of Philippi, though he had made up his mind not to leave his tent because of illness, he did so after all when warned by a friend's dream (*amici somnio monitus*); fortunately, as it turned out, for his camp was taken and when the enemy rushed in, his litter was stabbed through and through and torn to pieces, in the belief that he was still lying there ill.

The *dream proper* is not narrated, but it in some way communicates a warning that Augustus' life is in danger. The emphasis is on Augustus'

---

36 Cf. Artemidorus, *Onir.* 1.78, who provides a similar interpretation of a dream in which one has intercourse with his mother: 'it is also fortunate for every demagogue and public figure, for a mother signifies one's native country.'

response to the dream, which results in being delivered from the threat. The dream functions to protect Augustus.

The other dream that Suetonius uses to demonstrate Augustus' respect for dreams is a cultic dream (91.2). Once again, a narration of the *dream proper* is lacking, though one may infer that it is a visitant dream.

> Being in the habit of making constant visits to the temple of Jupiter the Thunderer, which he had founded on the Capitol, he dreamed (*somniavit*) that Jupiter Capitolinus complained that his worshippers were being taken from him, and that [Augustus] replied that he had only given him the Thunderer for his porter; and accordingly he presently fastened bells to the gable of the temple, because these commonly hung at gates of great houses.

It is uncertain whether the dream appears to Augustus during one of his visits to the temple, but – as shown in Chapter Two – such an experience was quite common in the Greco-Roman world. The *dream proper* is a visitant dream and includes a reply by Augustus, but the form of indirect discourse lessens the dramatic portrayal of the dream proper. Once again, the emphasis is on Augustus' *response* of attaching bells to the temple in order to attract more worshippers.

Dreams concerning Augustus' future greatness (*Aug.* 94). In this chapter, which is still in the context of Augustus' positive attitude toward religion, Suetonius recounts the various portents that signified Augustus' 'future greatness and uninterrupted good fortune' (*futura magnitudo et perpetua felicitas*; 94.1). Among these portents are several dreams.

The first two dreams described by Suetonius are the dreams of Augustus' mother and father, Atia and Octavius (94.4). The dreams are symbolic dreams and occur while Atia is pregnant with Augustus.

> Atia, before she gave him birth, dreamed (*somniavit*) that her vitals stretched to the stars and spread over the whole extent of land and sea. And his father Octavius dreamed that the sun rose from Atia's womb.

These dreams are further examples of the birth *topos* developed by dream reports.

Octavius experiences another dream after Augustus was born (94.5). While leading an army through Thrace, Octavius consults diviners about his new born son. The diviners offer libation at an altar that results in an omen that had never before occurred except for Alexander the Great. Octavius then experiences a symbolic dream.

> The very next night he saw a vision (*videre visus*) that his son appeared to him in a guise more majestic than that of mortal man, with the thunderbolt, sceptre, and insignia of Jupiter Optimus Maximus, wearing

a radiant crown and mounted upon a laurel-wreathed chariot drawn by twelve horses of surpassing whiteness.

This dream functions in association with the libation omen to signify Augustus' future reign; an association of dreams and other divinatory practices, particularly oracles, is common in Greco-Roman literature.

Suetonius also recounts three dreams by prominent Romans when Augustus was a youth. Two dreams are experienced by the Roman consul, Quintus Catulus, and are reported together (94.8):

> After Quintus Catulus had dedicated the Capitol, he had dreams (*somniavit*) on two nights in succession: first, that Jupiter Optimus Maximus called aside one of a number of boys of good family, who were playing around his altar, and put in the fold of his toga an image of Roma, which he was carrying in his hand; the next night he saw the same body in the lap of Jupiter of the Capitol, and that when he had ordered that he be removed, the god warned him to desist, declaring that the boy was being reared to be the guardian (*tutorem*) of his country.

Suetonius then relates that on the next day Catulus meets Augustus for the first time and is amazed at the striking resemblance between Augustus and the boy in the dream.

The final dream of these portents is the dream experienced by the famed orator Cicero (94.9). While accompanying Gaius Caesar to the Capitol, Cicero describes a dream that he had the previous night: 'a boy of noble countenance was let down from heaven on a golden chain and, standing at the door of the temple, was given a whip by Jupiter.' Just as Cicero finishes recounting the dream and enters the Capitol, he sees for the first time Augustus, who was with Julius Caesar, and recognizes him as the boy in the dream.

Summary. In Suetonius' *Caesares*, there are both symbolic (*Jul.* 7.2; 81.3 [2 ×]; *Aug.* 94.4 [2 ×]; 94.5; 94.8; 94.9; cf. *Cal.* 57.3; *Nero* 46.1; *Vesp.* 5.5; 25; *Dom.* 15.3; 23.2) and visitant (*Aug.* 91.2; cf. *Tib.* 74; *Galb.* 4.3; 18.2; *Vesp.* 7.2) dreams; some dreams are not narrated (*Aug.* 91.1; cf. *Nero* 7.1; *Galb.* 9.2; *Otho* 7.2). As stated in the introduction to Suetonius, most dream reports in the *Caesares* either portend an emperor's future good fortune and reign (*Jul.* 7.2; *Aug.* 91.1; 94.4 [2 ×]; 94.5; 94.8; 94.9; cf. *Galb.* 4.3; 9.2; *Vesp.* 5.5; 7.2; 25) or signify the end of his reign and/or his death (*Jul.* 81.3 [2 ×]; cf. *Tib.* 74; *Cal.* 57.3; *Nero* 46.1; *Galb.* 18.2; *Otho* 7.2; *Dom.* 15.3; 23.2). The dreams (91.1; 91.2) that illustrate Augustus' respect for religion are exceptions to this pattern.

Dreams in Greco-Roman Fiction

The following analysis of dreams in Greco-Roman fiction will be based on two Greek novels and two Christian apocryphal Acts. Unlike the previous summaries, which followed each text, this section will have only two summaries, one summarizing the Greek novels and the other summarizing the apocryphal Acts.

Chariton's Chaereas and Callirhoe[37]
Chariton's romance novel was written in the first or second century C.E. As characteristic of other romance novels, Chariton tells the fictional love story of his protagonists Chaereas and Callirhoe in terms of their beauty and falling in love, their marriage, their separation and subsequent adventures that present various threats to their lives and marriage, and their eventual reunion. Dream narratives are one of the literary devices employed by Chariton to develop this plot.

The dreams of Theron and Leonas (1.12.5, 10). Theron is a bandit who raids a tomb to acquire its valuables. In addition to the treasure, he finds alive the protagonist Callirhoe, who had been placed there after it was assumed that she was dead. Theron resolves to return to his ship the following day and throw Callirhoe into the sea. That night, however, he has a dream: 'when he fell asleep he saw a dream (κοιμηθεὶς δὲ ἐνύπνιον εἶδε), a closed door; so he decided to wait for that day.' As a consequence, Theron delays the drowning of Callirhoe one day, and during that day he becomes acquainted with a certain Leonas, the administrator (διοικητής) of the widower Dionysius' household. Sensing an opportunity, Theron proposes the sale of Callirhoe to Leonas for Dionysius' services. Leonas responds, 'some god has delivered you to me to be my benefactor. Why, you are setting out before me in reality what I dreamed about (ὠνειροπόλουν)!'

This episode is an example of a double-dream report; two people have separate dreams which prompt a circumstance that is mutually beneficial.[38] Theron's symbolic dream is minimally narrated. The *scene-setting* simply states the activity of sleeping; the *dream terminology* is ἐνύπνιον; and the *dream proper* (closed door) is merely an appositional phrase to ἐνύπνιον. The emphasis is on Theron's *response*, his decision to postpone his killing of Callirhoe. Leonas' dream is not narrated but only referenced

---

37 Translations of Chariton are modifications of the translation by B. P. Reardon in *Collected Ancient Greek Novels* (ed. B. P. Reardon; Berkeley: University of California Press, 1989), 21–124. Also, see his introduction to Chariton for introductory issues and bibliography (17–21).

38 For a discussion of the double-dream report, see above pp. 70–74.

(ὀνειροπολέω). Though both Theron and Leonas benefit from their respective dreams, the real function of the dreams is to benefit Callirhoe: she will not be thrown into the sea. On the other hand, this change in circumstances also advances the plot to a greater threat to Chaereas and Callirhoe's love: Callirhoe's eventual marriage to Dionysius.

The dream of Dionysius (2.1.2). In some respects, the dream of Dionysius is also connected with the two previous dreams. After having purchased Callirhoe from the bandit Theron, Leonas comes to his master Dionysius to give him the good news about the newly obtained servant. Before Leonas can tell him, however, Dionysius describes to Leonas a dream that he has experienced.

> 'This is the first good night's sleep I have had since my poor wife died. For I indeed clearly saw her (εἶδον αὐτὴν ἐναργῶς) as if I were awake, though she was taller and more beautiful. I thought (ἔδοξα) that it was the first day of our married life; I was bringing her home after our wedding, from my estate by the sea, and you were singing the wedding song.' Leonas cried out before his master had even finished: 'You're a lucky man, sir, asleep and awake! You're just going to hear the very thing you've dreamed about.'

The *dream proper* is a symbolic dream in which a scene is being acted out. As interpreted by the character Leonas, the dream portends Dionysius' future love and relationship with Callirhoe. Just as Leonas sings the wedding song in the dream, he now announces the good news of acquiring the beautiful Callirhoe.

The dream of Callirhoe (2.3.5). Callirhoe has been taken to the country estate of Dionysius, but Dionysius has not yet met her. As Dionysius is traveling to the estate, 'during that night Callirhoe beheld Aphrodite (ἡ Καλλιρόη τῆς νυκτὸς ἐκείνης θεασαμένη τὴν Ἀφροδίτην), and decided to pay homage to her again.' Callirhoe then goes to the local temple of Aphrodite where Dionysius has also decided to visit. Thus, this first, chance meeting between Dionysius and Callirhoe is occasioned by a night vision of Aphrodite. It is uncertain whether this vision is while Callirhoe is asleep or awake, but the night setting suggests a dream.[39] The dream is a literary device that motivates character action that in turn develops the plot. Moreover, the cultic setting of the dream would be familiar for a Greco-Roman audience.

---

39 Reardon actually translates θεασαμένη τὴν Ἀφροδίτην as 'had a dream about Aphrodite.'

The dream of Callirhoe (2.9.1-6). Callirhoe discovers she is pregnant with Chaereas' child. She is separated from Chaereas and is the newly purchased slave of Dionysius. She anguishes over the decision to either kill the unborn child or allow it to live. At this point in the narrative, a dream report is given.

> All night long [Callirhoe] considered these things (ταῦτα λογιζομένη δι᾽ ὅλης νυκτὸς), and as she did so, sleep stole over her momentarily, and a vision of Chaereas (εἰκὼν Χαιρέου) stood over her, like him in every way, like him in stature and fair looks and voice, and wearing just such clothes. As he stood there, he said, 'I entrust our son to you, my wife.' He wanted to say more, but Callirhoe jumped up and tried to embrace him. So on her husband's advice, as she thought, she decided to rear her child.

The *scene-setting* of this dream narrative notes the time in which the dream occurs (night), the mental state of the dreamer Callirhoe (considering these things), and the activity of sleep. 'These things' refer to the immediate context in which Callirhoe is contemplating whether or not to kill her unborn child. The *dream proper* is a visitant dream that identifies the dream figure (Chaereas) and describes his appearance and position. The dream message is given in direct discourse. Callirhoe's *reaction* is her impulse to embrace the image of Chaereas, which results in the message being interrupted. She *responds* to the dream by deciding to keep her unborn child. On the one hand, the dream functions to protect the child of Callirhoe and Chaereas, but the dream also contributes to plot development. The decision to keep the child leads Callirhoe to marry Dionysius, who is led to believe the child is his. This situation creates a new development in the novel's plot that will need to be resolved.

The dreams of Callirhoe (3.7.4; 4.1.1-3). These two dreams are treated together because they contribute to the same development in the plot. The first dream report comes right after the narration of Chaereas being placed in chains after his ship is attacked 'in the middle of the night, set on fire, and destroyed' (3.7.3). The dream is reported as follows:

> Chaereas stood over Callirhoe in a dream (Καλλιρόη δὲ ὄναρ ἐπέστη Χαιρέας), chained and trying to approach her but unable to do so. She uttered in her sleep a loud, piercing cry of distress, 'Come to me, Chaereas!'

Hearing of Chaereas for the first time, Dionysius, Callirhoe's recently wedded husband, asks who she is calling for. Callirhoe explains that Chaereas is her first husband and that the chains in her dream signify that he is dead. She grieves deeply for Chaereas and in turn Dionysius becomes jealous. The reader, of course, knows that Callirhoe has misinterpreted the dream. Her dream came at the same time Chaereas was captured and so reveals his actual circumstances.

The second dream report comes after Callirhoe has been falsely told that Chaereas died in the ship attack:

> So Callirhoe spent that night weeping and wailing, mourning for Chaereas – though he was still alive. But for a short time she slept, and she saw a dream (μικρὸν δὲ καταδραθεῖσα ὄναρ ἑώρα): [she saw] a band of barbarian robbers bringing torches, and the ship ablaze, and herself rescuing Chaereas.

Because of Callirhoe's continued dreaming of Chaereas, Dionysius, as an act of self-service, suggests that Callirhoe erect a tomb for Chaereas. Callirhoe is persuaded and invites the whole town to observe a mock funeral for Chaereas. In attendance is Mithridates, who later becomes the ally of Chaereas and the adversary of Dionysius and schemes to reunite Chaereas and Callirhoe (see 4.2-7). Thus, the two dreams, along with Callirhoe's continuous grieving, initiate actions that eventually will result in the reuniting of Chaereas and Callirhoe.

The dream of Callirhoe (5.5.5-7). Dionysius has accused Mithridates, the Persian governor of Caria, of a conspiracy to seduce Callirhoe, which is not true but misconstrued as Mithridates was acting on Chaereas' behalf. The accusation has found a hearing before the Babylonian king. On the night before the trial, Callirhoe experiences a dream:

> She spent the whole day lamenting despondently to herself like this. When it came night she saw a dream (νυκτὸς δὲ ἐπελθούσης ὄναρ ἔβλεπεν): [she saw] herself in Syracuse entering Aphrodite's shrine, still a maiden; then returning from there and seeing Chaereas and her wedding day. She saw Syracuse all decked out with garlands and herself being escorted by her father and mother to the bridegroom's house. She was on the point of embracing Chaereas when she suddenly started up from her sleep. She called Plangon ... and told her about the dream (τὸ ὄναρ). Plangon replied, 'Take courage, madam; you should be glad! You have seen a good dream (καλὸν ἐνύπνιον); you will be freed from all your worries; for just as it seemed to you in the dream, in the same way it will happen while you're awake ...'.

The *scene-setting* describes her mental state (lamenting), the time of the dream (night), and the *dream terminology* (ὄναρ). The *dream proper* is a symbolic dream that re-enacts a past event: the wedding day of Chaereas and Callirhoe. Callirhoe's *reaction* is twofold: (1) she attempts to embrace Chaereas; and (2) she recounts the dream to her maidservant, Plangon. Plangon provides a general, but positive, interpretation. Though the dream rehearses a past event, the meaning of the dream is prospective,

foreshadowing the reunion of Callirhoe and Chaereas and their eventual
return to their homeland.[40]

The dream of the Babylonian king (6.2.2). The court scene has now shifted
from a case between Mithridates and Dionysius to a case between
Dionysius and Chaereas: who is Callirhoe's rightful husband? Before the
trial begins, the Babylonian king orders sacrifices because 'a dream set
over me and the royal gods are demanding sacrifice' (ὄναρ μοι ... ἐπιστὰν
βασίλειοι θεοὶ θυσίας ἀπαιτοῦσι). The emphasis is on the king's *response*,
which is an elaborate religious ceremony even sacrificing for the first time
to the god Eros. Such cultic command-dreams are common in the Greco-
Roman world,[41] but the sacrifice to Eros has a particular implication for
the plot: the will of Eros will be fulfilled to the benefit of Chaereas and
Callirhoe.

Longus' Daphnis and Chloe[42]

Written in the second century C.E., Longus' romance is a pastoral novel
that depicts the love story of the couple Daphnis and Chloe. Like the
dream narratives in Chariton, the dreams in Longus prompt actions and
circumstances that advance the plot.

The dream of Dryas and Lamon (1.7.1–8.2). When Daphnis is fifteen and
Chloe is thirteen, both their fathers, Lamon and Dryas, experience an
identical dream. Though the fathers have the dream separately, the dream
is reported only once.

> Dryas and Lamon in a single night saw the following dream (ὁ Δρύας
> καὶ ὁ Λάμων ἐπὶ μιᾶς νυκτὸς ὁρῶσιν ὄναρ τοιόνδε τι): they thought
> (ἐδόκουν) that the Nymphs – the ones in the cave where the spring was,
> where Dryas found his child – were handing Daphnis and Chloe over to
> a very pretty boy, with a very arrogant manner, who had wings growing
> from his shoulders and carried little arrows and a miniature bow. The
> boy touched both of them with a single arrow, and for the future he
> commanded that Daphnis look after the herd of goats, and Chloe to
> look after the flock of sheep. Having seen this dream (τοῦτο τὸ ὄναρ
> ἰδόντες), they were upset at the thought that the children were to
> become shepherds and goatherds, although their tokens had promised

---

40 Suzanne MacAlister, *Dreams and Suicides: The Greek Novel from Antiquity to the
Byzantine Empire* (London: Routledge, 1996), 35.
41 See above, pp. 29–32.
42 Translations of Longus are modifications of the translation by Christopher Gill in
Collected Ancient Greek Novels (ed. B. P. Reardon; Berkeley: University of California Press,
1989), 288–348. Also, see his introduction to Longus for introductory issues and
bibliography (285–288).

greater things. . . . After sharing with one another the dream and making
a sacrifice in the Nymph's shrine to 'the winged boy' (they did not know
his name), they sent the children out as shepherds with the flocks.

The *scene-setting* of this dream report identifies the dreamers (Dryas and
Lamon), the time of the dream (night), and the *dream terminology* (ὄναρ).
The *dream proper* is a symbolic dream that is introduced by the
conventional δοκέω. Although it is a symbolic dream, it includes a
command, which is more characteristic of a visitant or auditory dream.
The dream indicates that Daphnis and Chloe will be the 'victims' of Eros
and experience the 'sickness' of love. The dream also becomes the medium
by which Eros commands that the children become shepherds. The initial
reaction of Dryas and Lamon is one of detesting (ἔχθω), for they were
hoping for more from their discovered children than a pastoral life. They
respond, however, with sacrifice and obedience. Thus, the dream functions
to foreshadow the subsequent love between Daphnis and Chloe; it also
reveals the source of that love, Eros. This love is initiated when they
discover one another tending to their respective herds, an occasion
brought about by the command in the dream.

The dreams of Daphnis and Chloe (2.10.1). Daphnis and Chloe are
experiencing the 'pain' (ἀλγέω; 2.8.3) of love – not eating nor sleeping,
and having a 'fire' within them. An older acquaintance, Philetas, reveals to
them the remedies (φάρμακα; 2.8.5) for love: kisses, embraces and
intercourse. The reference to dreams is then made in this context: 'While
thinking about these things – as you might expect – they also saw erotic
dreams (καὶ ὀνείρατα ἑώρων ἐρωτικά) about kisses and embraces; and
what they hadn't done in the day, they did in their dreams (ὄναρ): they lay
naked with one another.'

An ancient audience would recognize these dreams as sexual dreams
that derive from dreamers' passions and therefore are not divinatory or
significant. The professional dream interpreter Artemidorus states it this
way:

> To have sexual intercourse with a woman with whom one is familiar
> and on intimate terms, if the dreamer is sexually attracted to and
> desirous of the woman, predicts (προαγορεύει) nothing at all because
> his desire for her has been aroused (οὐδὲν προαγορεύει διὰ τὴν
> ἐπιτεταμένην ἐπιθυμίαν).[43]

In the context of the narrative, however, these dreams could function as
'healing' dreams, for they provide the antidote for the illness of love:

---

43 Artemidorus, *Onir.* 1.78 (White). Interestingly, this is the exception to the rule. This
statement comes in the context of explaining how sexual dreams are indeed significant (i.e.,
predict the future), see 1.78-80; 4.4; 4.20; 4.65.

kisses, embraces and intercourse. As shown in Chapter Two, healing dreams were common in the Greco-Roman world.

The dream of Daphnis (2.23.1–24.1). Chloe has been kidnapped by a group of Methymnean soldiers, and Daphnis blames the Nymphs (2.22.1-4). At this point, Daphnis falls asleep and has a dream:

> While he was talking in this way out of his tears and pain, a deep sleep overtook him. And three Nymphs stood by (ἐφίστανται) him; they were tall, beautiful women, half-naked and barefooted, their hair flowing free – just like their images. At first, they seemed to be feeling sorry for Daphnis. Then the eldest spoke encouraging (ἐπιρρωννύουσα) him. 'Don't blame us, Daphnis. We care about Chloe even more than you do. We were the ones who took pity on her when she was a child, and when she was lying in this cave, we saw to it that she was nursed. Even now we have paid attention to her situation and made sure she won't be carried off to Methymna to become a slave and won't become part of the spoils of war. You see Pan over there, his image set up under the pine, who's never received from you even the honor of some flowers – well, we've asked him to be Chloe's protector. He's more used to army camps than we are, and he's already left the country and fought a number of wars. And when he attacks the Methymneans, they won't find him a good enemy to have. Don't make yourself anxious. Get up and show yourself to Lamon and Myrtale. Like you, they're lying on the ground, thinking that you are part of the plunder too. Chloe will come to you tomorrow, with the goats and with the sheep, and you will graze together and play the pipes together. All your other affairs will be taken care of by Eros.' Seeing and hearing such things, Daphnis jumped up out of his sleep; weeping with pleasure and pain, he kneeled down before the images of the Nymphs and promised that if Chloe were rescued, he would sacrifice the best of the she-goats.

The *scene-setting* indicates Daphnis' mental state (talking out of his tears and pain) and notes that he has fallen asleep. The *dream proper* is a visitant dream, with the dream figures being described. The message of the dream is given in direct discourse and encourages Daphnis by assuring him that Pan will protect Chloe and that Chloe will be with him the following day. Daphnis *reacts* by jumping up (ἀναπηδάω) from his sleep and *responds* by sacrificing to both the Nymphs and Pan (2.24.2). Thus, the dream functions to encourage Daphnis by revealing the character and will of the divine to save Chloe.

The dream of the Methymnean general, Bryaxis (2.26.5–28.1). With Chloe being held captive by the Methymneans, Pan begins to disturb the soldier-bandits by many 'apparitions and noises' (φανατάσματα καὶ ἀκούσματα; 2.26.5). The Methymneans know that Pan is the cause of the various commotions, but they do not know the reason. The Methymnean general, Bryaxis, then has a dream.

> Around midday, the general – not without divine aid (οὐκ ἀθεεὶ) – fell asleep, and Pan himself appeared (ὤφθη) and spoke in the following way: 'Most unholy and impious of men, what madness has driven you to act so recklessly? You've filled the countryside I love with war; you've driven off herds of cows, goats, and sheep that are under my care; you've dragged from the altars a girl whom Eros wants to make the subject of a story; and you showed no shame before the Nymphs when they watched what you did, or before me – Pan. If you sail on with these spoils, you'll never see Methymna, nor will you escape this piping that has made you so panic-stricken. Instead I shall sink your ship and make you food for the fish unless, immediately, you hand back Chloe to the Nymphs and the flocks to Chloe, both the goats and the sheep. So get up and put the girl ashore, together with the animals I spoke of. I myself will be your guide on sea, and hers on land.' Bryaxis (that was the general's name) was very disturbed (τεθορυβημένος); he jumped up (ἀναπηδᾷ), summoned the ships' captains, and ordered them to look for Chloe among the captives as soon as possible.

The *scene-setting* indicates the time of the dream (midday), the identity of the dreamer (the general), and the activity of sleep. A specific *dream term* is absent, but the verb ὤφθη denotes a visionary experience. The *dream proper* is a visitant dream of the god Pan, whose message is given in direct discourse. Pan commands that Chloe and her flock be set free and warns of the consequences if his will is not heeded. After describing the general's *reaction* (disturbed), the dream report concludes by noting the general's obedient *response* to the dream, finding and releasing Chloe. Thus, this command-warning dream functions to protect and rescue Chloe and to continue the love 'story' of Daphnis and Chloe.

The dream of Daphnis (3.27.1–28.1). Daphnis is dejected because he can not financially compete with Chloe's rich suitors. This problem is resolved when Daphnis 'again calls the Nymphs for help' and has a dream.

> While sleeping in the night (καθεύδοντι νύκτωρ), they stood (αἱ ἐφίστανται) by him in the same form as before, and again it was the eldest who spoke. 'Another god is taking care of Chloe's marriage. But we shall give you a present that will bring Dryas round. The boat that belonged to the young Methymneans – the one whose willow shoot your goats once ate – was blown far out to sea on that memorable day. But in the night a wind from the sea made the water rough, and the boat was cast ashore on the rocks of the headland. The boat itself and the bulk of the cargo were destroyed. But a purse, with three thousand drachmas in it, was thrown out by the waves and is lying, covered with seaweed, near a dead dolphin; that's why none of the passersby even goes near it,

because they're keeping away from the stench of the decay. But you go up to it, and once you're there, pick it up, and once you've picked it up, use it as a present. For the time being, it is enough for you not to seem poor; later on, you will actually be rich.' Saying this, they departed (συναπῆλθον) with the night. Now that it was day, Daphnis jumped up cheerfully (περιχαρής) and, with a lot of whistling, drove his goats to pasture.

The *scene-setting* is minimal (sleeping at night) but assumes Daphnis' plea to the Nymphs for help. Like the dream of 2.23.1–24.1, the *dream proper* is a visitant dream by the Nymphs with the eldest Nymph delivering the message. The message instructs Daphnis as to the location of a large sum of money. This money will allow Daphnis to compete with the other suitors. The *dream proper* ends with a description of the Nymphs 'departing' (συναπέρχομαι). Daphnis *reacts* with a joyful (περιχαρής) disposition and *responds* by searching and finding the money as instructed by the Nymphs (2.24.2-3). The dream, thus, functions as a command-directive revealing the location of money. As such, this dream also contributes to the plot's resolution and development; it provides a solution to Daphnis' predicament and results in Daphnis presenting the money to Dryas (Chloe's father) and so acquiring the promise of Chloe (3.29-30).

The dream of Dionysophanes (4.34.1-3). The noble Dionysophanes has recently discovered that he is the real father of Daphnis. In order to provide an honorable wedding for the couple, it is necessary also to find Chloe's real parents. With this problem at hand, Dionysophanes has a dream:

> Dionysophanes, after much thought (μετὰ φροντίδα πολλὴν), fell into a deep sleep and had the following dream (ὄναρ ... τοιόνδε γίνεται): It seemed (ἐδόκει) that the Nymphs were begging Eros to give his consent at last to their marriage and that Eros unstrung his little bow and took off his quiver. Eros then told Dionysophanes to ask all the best of the Mytileneans to come to a feast, and when he had filled the last mixing bowl, to show each person the tokens of Chloe's identity – and then sing the wedding song. After seeing and hearing these things, Dionysophanes got up at daybreak and gave orders for the preparation of a glittering feast – drawing on the resources of the land and the sea, the marshes and the rivers – and invited as his guests all the best of the Mytileneans. When it was already night and the mixing bowl had been filled to make the libation to Hermes, a servant brought in the tokens on a silver tray and carried them round from left to right, showing them to everyone.

The *scene-setting* notes the identity of the dreamer (Dionysophanes), his mental state (much thought), and the activity of sleep. The dream terminology is ὄναρ, and the *dream proper* is introduced by δοκέω. The *dream proper* is a visitant dream, though the beginning of the dream is a bit peculiar in that Dionysophanes is simply an on-looker to a conversation between the Nymphs and Pan. Pan, however, then addresses Dionysophanes, commanding him to host a feast for the leading citizens and show them the tokens of Chloe. Dionysophanes *responds* by doing exactly what Pan commanded. This obedience results in Chloe's real parents being discovered (4.34.4) and the couple being married (4.38). This dream, therefore, is a command-dream functioning to bring about plot resolution.

Summary

This summary of the Greek novels will deviate from the manner of the other summaries in this chapter. This deviation is predicated upon the distinctive character of the Greek novels, which are defined by the form of their plot – a combination of love and adventure. This plot is succinctly described by Reardon:

> Hero and heroine are always young, wellborn, and handsome; their marriage is disrupted or temporarily prevented by separation, travel in distant parts, and a series of misfortunes, usually spectacular. Virginity or chastity, at least in the female, is of crucial importance, and fidelity to one's partner, together with trust in the gods, will ultimately guarantee a happy [reunion].[44]

It is in service of this formal plot that dreams function in the Greek novels; that is, dreams contribute to the development of the plot by creating circumstances that relate to (1) the initial love and/or marriage of the hero and heroine, (2) the separation or threat to the relationship, or (3) the happy reunion of the couple.[45]

In the case of Chariton's *Chaereas and Callirhoe*, there are no dreams connected to the circumstances of the couple's initial love or marriage. There are five dreams, however, that move the plot to separation or threat, which is epitomized by Callirhoe's marriage to Dionysius: the dreams of Theron and Leonas that bring about the sale of Callirhoe (1.12.5, 10);[46] the dream of Dionysius that foreshadows his marriage to

---

44   B. P. Reardon, 'Introduction' to *Collected Ancient Greek Novels* (ed. B. P. Reardon; Berkeley: University of California Press, 1989), 2.

45   This observation draws upon the work of Suzanne MacAlister, *Dreams and Suicides*, 19–52, who studies the dreams in the Greek novels according to Mikhail Bakhtin's analysis of the narrative framework of the Greek novels.

46   One the one hand, the dream of Theron actually protects Callirhoe from death, and so it could be seen as a more positive development in the plot. In the story world of the novels, however, death is a preferable option to separation from one's lover, a situation that now Callirhoe finds herself in by being sold to Leonas.

Callirhoe (2.1.2); Callirhoe's dream of Aphrodite, which prompts her chance meeting with Dionysius (2.3.5); and the dream of Callirhoe in relation to her unborn child, which brings about her marriage to Dionysius (2.9.6). Chariton contains four dreams that advance the plot or foreshadow the reunion of Chaereas and Callirhoe: Callirhoe's two dreams of Chaereas in chains and a victim of a pirate attack (3.7.4; 4.1.1-3);[47] the dream of Callirhoe that foreshadows her reunion with Chaereas (5.5.5-7); and the dream of the Babylonian king, which results in a sacrifice to Eros (6.2.2).

The dreams in Longus can also be read according to the novelistic plot structure.[48] The initial love and meeting of Daphnis and Chloe is foreshadowed and prompted by the dream of Dryas and Lamon (1.7.1-8.2). There are no dreams that prompt actions that lead to separation or threat, but four dreams do provide protection or aid in the face of various threats and thus keep the plot moving towards its intended resolution: the dream of Daphnis, which reveals Chloe's deliverance from the Methymneans (2.23.1–24.1); the dream of the Methymnean general that commands Chloe's release (2.26.5–28.1); the dream of Daphnis, which reveals the location of money and allows Daphnis to compete with other suitors (3.27.1–28.1); and the dream of Dionysophanes, which prompts the discovery of Chloe's real parents and so allows the couple to marry properly (4.34.1-3).

Thus, on the one hand, dreams in the Greek novels are formally and functionally comparable to dreams in other Greco-Roman prose literature; they are symbolic or visitant dreams that portend future events or command certain actions. But on the other hand, these dream narratives in the Greek novels are literary devices that function primarily in plot development, prompting circumstances that contribute to the formal plot structure of the romance novels.[49]

---

47   In one sense, these two dreams could be understood as relating to the separation/threat of Chaereas and Callirhoe, since they reveal the actual circumstances of Chaereas – Callirhoe even misinterprets the chains to mean Chaereas is dead. But as stated in the discussion of these two dreams, Dionysius' response to her dreaming actually initiates actions that will contribute to the eventual reunion of the couple.

48   Unlike the other novels, the couple's separation in Longus is not a physical separation but an intimate separation, which is not overcome until the couple is finally married. Thus, the novel does not work towards a happy reunion as much as an anticipated marriage union.

49   Dreams in other Greek romance novels include Xenophon of Ephesus, *Eph. Tale* 1.12.4; 2.8.2; 5.8.5-9; Achilles Tatius, *Leuc. Clit.* 1.3.3-5; 2.23.4-5; 4.1.5-8; 7.12.4; 7.14.2, 5–6; Heliodorus, *Aeth.* 1.18.2-5; 2.16.1-2; 3.11.4–12.1; 4.8.4; 4.16.7; 5.22.1-4; 9.25.1; 10.3.1-2.

Acts of Thomas[50]

The *Acts of Thomas* is a Christian, apocryphal tale of the apostolic ministry of Judas Thomas – the supposed twin brother of Jesus – in India. Written in the beginning of the third century, the *Acts of Thomas* is structured around thirteen 'acts' (i.e., miracles, conversion stories, wonder deeds, etc.) including the apostle's martyrdom, though the last six 'acts' take place in the court of an Indian king named Misdaeus. Within these thirteen acts, there are three dream narratives.

The dream of Thomas (Acts Thom. 29). This dream comes at the end of the second episode (17–29). The apostle Thomas is fasting because the following day is the Lord's day (ἡ κυριακή). The dream report is then given as follows:

> Now as night came and he was sleeping, the Lord came and stood at his head and said (τῆς δὲ νυκτὸς ἐπιούσης καὶ καθεύδοντος αὐτοῦ ἐλθὼν ὁ κύριος ἔστη πρὸς τῇ κεφαλῇ αὐτοῦ λέγων), 'Thomas, get up at dawn and bless all them; and after the prayer and service depart down the eastern road two miles, and there I will exhibit by you my glory. For because of your departing, many will take refuge in me, and you will put to shame the nature and power of the enemy.' And getting up from his sleep he spoke to the believers who were with him.

Though a *dream terminology* is lacking, the phenomenon is clearly a dream. The dream report begins (*scene-setting*) by noting the activity of sleep and ends (*reaction*) with the depiction of waking from sleep. Also, the *dream proper* has the description of the dream figure 'standing at his head,' which is a formal feature sometimes present in a visitant dream report. The dream figure is 'the Lord' (Christ) who commands Thomas to travel a specific route so that Christ's glory will be manifested. On the road, Thomas will discover a man killed by his son and raise him from the dead (30–38). Thus, on the one hand, the dream is a familiar command dream, giving a divine directive to the apostle; but on the other hand, the dream also moves the narrative plot, prompting action that leads to the next miraculous 'act' of the apostle (30–41) and demonstrations of the Lord's glory. Thus, based on the dream report the reader anticipates this next display of Christ's power.

---

50 Translations of *Acts of Thomas* are mine or modified translation of Drijvers, 'The Acts of Thomas', in *New Testament Apocrypha* (ed. W. Schneemelcher; trans. R. McL. Wilson; 2 vols.; rev. ed.; Louisville, Ky.: Westminster/John Knox Press, 1992), 2.322-411. For introductory matters, see Drijners, 'The Acts of Thomas,' 322–339; and A. F. J. Klijn, *The Acts of Thomas: Introduction, Text, and Commentary* (2d rev. ed.; NovTSup 108; Leiden: Brill, 2003), 1–15.

The dream of Charisius (*Acts Thom.* 91). This dream is part of the larger story that leads to Thomas' martyrdom. A noblewoman named Mygdonia, who is the wife of the king's brother, hears the gospel as proclaimed by Thomas (87–88). In response to it, she becomes a believer and commits to chastity. This commitment leads to a situation in which she will not eat nor sleep with her husband Charisius. As Charisius is sleeping in another bed, he has a dream:

> And when he arose from his sleep, he said, 'My lady Mygdonia, listen to the dream that appeared to me (τοῦ ὀνείρου τοῦ ὀφθέντος μοι). I saw myself reclining near king Misdaeus, and a full table was set before us. And I saw an eagle coming down from heaven and carry off from before me and the king two partridges, which it took away to its nest. And it again came to us and hovered over us. And the king commanded that a bow be brought to him. And the eagle again carried off from before us a pigeon and a dove. The king shot an arrow at it, and it passed through it from one side to the other. But the arrow did not harm it, and being uninjured it flew to its nest. And having awakened from sleep I am terrified and deeply troubled (καὶ διυπνισθεὶς ἐγὼ ἔμφοβός εἰμι καὶ περίλυπος), because I had tasted of the partridge but it did not allow me to put any more [of it] in my mouth.' And Mygdonia said to him, 'Your dream is good, for you eat partridges every day, but perhaps that eagle has not tasted a partridge until now.'

This symbolic dream is a creative allegory of the subsequent narrative. A. F. J. Klijn notes that the eagle is often identified with God or Christ.[51] Christ is the pierced, but not injured, eagle who takes for himself two partridges, a pigeon, and a dove. The partridge that Charisius tastes but does not consume is his wife Mygdonia, who has been converted. The other partridge is presumably the king's wife Tertia, who will also be converted (134–138). The pigeon and the dove are the king's son Vizan and his wife Mnesara respectively, who will also become believers (139–158). Thus, the dream foreshadows the plot development in which other royal persons will be converted.

The dream of Mnesara (*Acts Thom.* 154–155). Vazan, the king's son, has become a believer and is visiting the apostle Thomas in prison. He is requesting that the apostle come to his house and heal his wife Mnesara. Thomas agrees and tells Vazan to go ahead and prepare for his coming. When Vazan arrives at the house, he meets his wife Mnesara, who was about to go to the prison. Vazan asks how she was able to get out of bed, and she responds by mentioning a dream that she had:

---

51 Klijn, *The Acts of Thomas*, 170.

'This young man laid his hand upon me and raised me up, and I saw a dream (ὄναρ εἶδον) that I should go where the stranger is residing and I would be completely healthy.' Vazan said to her, 'What young man is with you?' And she said, 'Do you not see the one on my right hand leading me?'

At that moment Thomas and the other believers enter the house. When Mnesara sees the apostle, she says, 'Have you come, our savior from troublesome diseases? You are the one that I saw in the night handing me over to this young man to lead me to the prison.'

The dream is referenced in relation to a young man that only Mnesara can see. The young man has strengthened her enough to get out of bed, which allows her to obey the dream command to go where the stranger is. In dramatic fashion, the dream figure, who delivered Mnesara to the young man in the first place, is revealed to be none other than the apostle himself. The dream is a command dream that facilitates both physical and spiritual healing (156–158).

Acts of Andrew[52]

The *Acts of Andrew* is another Christian apocryphal Acts that narrates the miraculous ministry of the apostle Andrew. Written in the third century, the textual tradition of *Acts of Andrew* is incredibly complex. I have followed MacDonald's 'eclectic' text, which is based primarily on Gregory's Latin epitome (GE) but includes sections from some Greek witnesses. The *Acts of Andrew* contains five dream reports.

The dream of Adimantus (Acts Andr. [GE] 13). Adimantus is the sick son of a certain Carpianus, who hears one of Andrew's young disciples preaching in a theater. The crowd in the theater begins to plead for the healing of Adimantus. Andrew, who is present in the theater, tells the *crowd* to 'bring him before us, and the Lord Jesus Christ will heal him so that you may believe.' The father then goes to the house and tells Adimantus that he will be healed. Adimantus responds by saying, 'my dream (*somnium*) has indeed come true, for I saw in a vision this man restoring me to health.' The son, then, gets up from the bed and runs to the theater, which amazes the crowd because they have not seen him walk

---

52   Translations of *Acts of Andrew* are from Dennis R. MacDonald, *The Acts of Andrew and The Acts of Andrew and Matthias in the City of the Cannibals* (Text and Translations 33; Christian Apocrypha 1; Atlanta, Ga.; Scholars Press, 1990), or a modification of MacDonald's translation. Introductory issues are addressed in MacDonald, *The Acts of Andrew*, 1–59; and Jean-Mark Prieur, 'The Acts of Andrew,' in *New Testament Apocrypha* (ed. W. Schneemelcher; trans. R. McL. Wilson; 2 vols.; rev. ed.; Louisville, Ky.: Westminster/John Knox Press, 1992), 2.101-118.

in twenty-three years. Thus, the dream encounter itself has provided the healing.

The dream is not a full dream narrative but a reference to a dream and its content. The dream seems to be a visitant dream in which the dream figure heals Adimantus. The dream figure itself is simply referred to as 'this man' (*virum hunc*), but given Andrew's declaration that Christ would heal him the dream figure mostly likely refers to Christ. This dream is reminiscent of the healing dreams of the Asclepius cult.[53]

The dream of Andrew (*Acts Andr.* [GE] 20). This dream of Andrew introduces a new section in the narrative. The dream report is this:

> The following night the blessed apostle saw a vision (*visum*) that he narrated to the other believers: 'My good friends, listen to my dream (*somnium*). I saw a great mountain raised on high with nothing earthly on it, and it so radiated with light that it seemed to illumine the world. And there standing with me, my beloved brothers, were the apostles Peter and John. Extending his hand to the apostle Peter, John raised him to the mountain's summit, turned, and asked me to ascend after Peter saying, 'Andrew, you will drink Peter's cup.' With his hands out-stretched, he said, 'Come to me and stretch out your hands to join my hands, and let your head touch mine.' When I did so, I discovered myself to be shorter than John. 'Would you like to know,' he then asked, 'to what this image you see refers, or who it is who speaks with you?' 'I long to know these things,' I said. 'I am the word of the cross,' he said, 'on which you soon will hang for the name of the one you proclaim.' He also told me many other things about which I can say nothing now, but which will become apparent when I approach this sacrifice. For now, let all who have received the word of God come together, and let me commend them to the Lord Jesus Christ, so that he may keep them untarnished in his teaching. . . .' When the believers heard these things they wept effusively, slapped their faces, and groaned (*Haec audientes fratres, flebant valde et cedebant palmis facies suas cum gemitu magno*).

This symbolic dream portends the death of Andrew. The presence of Peter and John lend authority and honor to Andrew as well as indicate the kind of death that Andrew will experience. The dream also serves as a revelation of further teaching, though not all the teaching is made public.[54] The reporting of this symbolic dream is somewhat modified from the conventional dream report. The content of the dream is narrated by the dreamer after the fact. This arrangement allows the reader to learn of

---

53   For the Asclepius cult, see above, pp. 32–34.

54   At least is not made public immediately. MacDonald, *Acts of Andrew*, 269 n. 59, states that Andrew does eventually reveal this teaching in the subsequent narrative as he approaches the cross.

the contents at the same time as the narrative audience. Moreover, this modification of the dream report allows the *reaction* to issue from those who hear the narration of the dream instead of the dreamer as is customary.

The dream of Lesbius (*Acts Andr.* [M 3b-6; L 34] 22). When Andrew enters the Achaean city of Patras performing miracles, the proconsul Lesbius considers Andrew a magician and a charlatan and intends to have him arrested and killed. At this point, Lesbius experiences a vision.

> At night an angel of the Lord stood over (νυκτὸς δὲ ἐπιστὰς ἄγγελος κυρίου) the proconsul Lesbius with a great manifestation and foreboding threat and said, 'What have you suffered from this stranger Andrew such that you wickedly contrived to lay hands on him and defraud the God he preaches? And now, behold, the hand of his Lord is on you, and you will be stricken until you know the truth through him.' The angel vanished from him and he was struck dumb.

Lesbius then has Andrew brought to him and mournfully repents of his intentions. Andrew heals Lesbius of his punitive ailment and declares, 'since you have believed so greatly in the one who sent me, you will be abundantly filled with knowledge.'

The *scene-setting* places the vision at night, which is suggestive of a dream but not determinative. The description of the visitant figure as 'standing over' Lesbius is also indicative of a dream vision, as well as the depiction of the dream figure 'vanishing.' The function of the dream is twofold. First, the dream provides protection for Andrew by intervening and punishing the one who is responsible for his imminent threat. Second, the dream provides the means by which Lesbius repents and becomes a believer.

The dream of Sostratus (*Acts Andr.* [GE] 26). Sostratus is the father of a certain Philopater, whom Andrew has raised from the dead after a shipwreck. As Andrew and others, including Philopater, are walking along, Sostratus comes along and recognizes Andrew, 'for he looked just like he had in the dream (*somnium*).' Sostratus then follows the apostle and becomes a believer. The dream is not narrated, nor is it certain what the dream revealed. Sostratus identifies Andrew as the dream figure and consequently receives salvation.

The dream of Andrew (*Acts Andr.* [M] 29).[55] After healing a household that had been attacked by demons, Andrew has the following dream:

---

55 As stated by MacDonald, *Acts of Andrew*, 305 n. 88, this dream is not found in Gregory's Epitome but in an eighth century ms. Thus, 'one cannot be certain that this section actually appeared in the ancient *AA*.'

> The blessed Andrew then saw a vision (ὅραμα). It seemed (ἔδοξεν) that
> the savior Christ was standing before him and saying to him, 'Andrew,
> place the Spirit upon Lesbius and give him your grace. And take up
> your cross and follow me, for tomorrow I will cast you from the world.
> Hurry to Patras.' And after awaking from sleep (διυπνισθείς), the
> apostle disclosed to those with him the dream vision (τὴν ὄψιν τοῦ
> ὁράματος).

The *scene-setting* identifies the dreamer (Andrew) and contains the *dream
terminology* ὅραμα. The *dream proper* is a visitant dream introduced by
δοκέω. The dream figure is identified as 'savior Christ' and a description
of the dream figure's position is mentioned ('standing before him'). The
message of the dream is primarily a threefold command: (1) take up the
cross and follow; (2) sanctify Lesbius (succession?); and (3) go to Patras.
The function of the dream, of course, relates to Andrew's martyrdom;
thus the dream predicts his death. Andrew's *response* is surprisingly
incomplete. Andrew does immediately enter Patras (30) and experience
martyrdom, but there is no account of Andrew passing on his grace to
Lesbius. This is particularly odd because the *response* is an important
element in the dream narrative. If the dreamer is faithful to the dream
message, it reveals a positive aspect of the dreamer. But if the dreamer
disregards the dream message and does not act accordingly, the dreamer is
characterized as foolish and usually reaps negative consequences. In other
words, an ancient audience would expect a narration of Andrew placing
the Spirit upon Lesbius. This omission may be further evidence that this
dream scene was not part of the original *Acts of Andrew*.

Summary

Dreams in the Christian apocryphal *Acts* of apostles are formally
equivalent to dreams in Greco-Roman literature. Visitant dreams are
predominant (*Acts Thom.* 29; 154–155; *Acts Andr.* 13; 22; 26; 29; cf. *Acts
John* 19; 21; *Acts Pet.* 1; 5; 6; 30; 40), though symbolic dreams are not
absent (*Acts Thom.* 91; *Acts Andr.* 20). The dream figure of the visitant
dreams is usually Christ (*Acts Thom.* 29; *Acts Andr.* 13 [?]; 29; cf. also *Acts
Pet.* 1; 5; 30) or the apostles (*Acts Thom.* 154–155; *Acts Andr.* 26; cf. also
Acts John 19; 21; *Acts Pet.* 6; 40). The functions of the dreams in the *Acts*
of apostles are several and are particularly suited to the nature of this
Christian literature. There are command-directive dreams that instruct the
apostles to go to specified places so that the gospel can be preached or
demonstrated for others (*Acts Thom.* 29; cf. also *Acts John* 18; *Acts Pet.* 1;
5). There are healing dreams (*Acts Thom.* 154–155 [partial]; *Acts Andr.* 13)
or dreams that direct the dreamer to an apostle, which results in healing
and/or conversion (*Acts Thom.* 154–155; *Acts Andr.* 26; cf. also *Acts John*
19; 21). Dreams also portend an apostle's martyrdom (*Acts Andr.* 20; 29).

Conclusion

This chapter has surveyed dream narratives in sample texts of historical, biographical and fictional Greco-Roman texts; it has been guided by a consideration of the form and function of the dream report. It can be concluded that dreams in these texts function at two levels. First, dreams function within the narrative in two primary ways: to portend the future and/or to reveal a divine imperative. In portending the future, dreams are connected with several motifs: birth (future greatness), future reign (fortune or loss), battle (victory or defeat) and death. This portending function of dreams can also generate a sense of promise and encouragement. Divine imperative dreams also deal with or result in some recurring motifs: healing, protection, establishment of a city or colony or cultic act. Second, dreams function at a narratological level, contributing to characterization and prompting plot development, including of critical narrative moments. This analysis of the form and function of dreams in Greco-Roman literature provides a necessary perspective by which to interpret how an ancient audience would understand the dreams in the Gospel of Matthew.

Chapter Five

DREAMS IN THE GOSPEL OF MATTHEW

The previous chapters have described and analyzed the ancient social and literary contexts of dreams in order to construct the beliefs, values and expectations an ancient audience would bring to a text that narrated dreams. The present chapter intends to read the dreams of the Gospel of Matthew in light of this construct; that is, to understand or 'make sense' of the Matthean dreams as an ancient audience would. Matthew's Gospel contains six references to dreams: five in the infancy narrative (1.20; 2.12, 13, 19, 22) and one in the passion narrative (27.19). Of these six references, only three are presented in what may be considered a dream report: 1.18b-24, 2.13-15, and 2.19-21.

An ancient audience would first read these dreams as part of the larger literary work of Matthew's Gospel: a *bios* of Jesus.[1] Given the literary character of this work and its narrative form, the Matthean dreams will be read in view of the larger Greco-Roman literary context of dreams. This literary analysis will be facilitated by attending to the form and function of Matthew's dreams. Thus, the first major section of this chapter will describe the literary form of the Matthean dreams demonstrating that they correspond to the conventional form of dream reports found in other Greco-Roman literature. The second major section will interpret the functions of Matthew's dreams, drawing upon the way dreams function in other literature and explaining their specific contribution to Matthew's narrative of Jesus. The chapter will conclude with some perspectives on the significance of dreams for Matthew's overall portrait of Jesus.

The Form of the Matthean Dreams

As stated previously, only three of the six references to dreams in the Gospel of Matthew are dream reports. In analyzing the form of these dreams, interpreters have generally followed one of three approaches.

---

1 Richard A. Burridge, *What Are the Gospels? A Comparison with Graeco-Roman Biography* (2d ed.; Grand Rapids, Mich.: Eerdmans, 2004), 185–212; Graham Stanton, *A Gospel for a New People: Studies in Matthew* (Louisville: Westminster/John Knox Press, 1993), 59–71.

First, some scholars simply identify the particularly repetitive pattern of Matthew's dreams without any awareness of or comparison with the dream form in other literature. For example, Raymond Brown describes the structure of Matthew's dreams as follows: (1) a genitive absolute clause connecting the dream to the narrative context; (2) appearance of an angel of the Lord; (3) the command of the angel; (4) a reason for the command; and (5) Joseph's obedience to the command.[2] Brown's description of the structure of Matthew's dreams is not inaccurate, but by not comparing the Matthean dreams with dreams in other literature this approach is deficient in two ways. First, it neglects the subtleties of the compositional pattern that Matthew's dreams exhibit; a comparison with dreams in other literature would highlight this compositional pattern. Second, this approach fails to recognize that dreams are a literary convention in Greco-Roman literature, and that by employing this literary convention Matthew is participating in the literary tradition and practices of his day. Thus, this approach to the form of Matthew's dreams is too isolated from the larger literary context of dreams and so lacks a more comprehensive interpretive framework.

The second approach to the form of Matthew's dreams concludes that the Matthean dreams are modeled upon the dreams found in the Old Testament, particularly the book of Genesis. The most detailed study of this sort is Robert Gnuse's 1990 *Novum Testamentum* article.[3] Gnuse argues that the dreams in Matthew's infancy narrative share 'deep structural similarities'[4] with the Elohist dreams that are found in Genesis. In other words, Gnuse claims that the Matthean dreams are literary

---

2 Raymond E. Brown, *The Birth of the Messiah: A Commentary on the Infancy Narratives in the Gospels of Matthew and Luke* (new updated ed.; New York: Doubleday, 1993), 108. Cf. also Tarcisio Stramare, 'I sogni di S. Giuseppe,' *CaJos* 19 (1971): 104–22; and Donald A. Hagner, *Matthew 1–13* (WBC 33A; Dallas: Word, 1993), 15. See Robert Gnuse, 'Dream Genre in the Matthean Infancy Narratives,' *Novum Testamentum* 32 (1990): 104–105, for a review of earlier such studies.

3 Gnuse, 'Dream Genre in the Matthean Infancy Narratives,' 97–120. Cf. also Alfred Wikenhauser, 'Die Traumgesichte des Neuen Testaments in religionsgeschichtlicher Sicht,' in *Pisciculi: Studien zur Religion und Kultur des Altertums* (ed. F. J. Dölger; Antike und Christentum 1; Münster: Aschendorff, 1939), 321; and George M. Soares Prabhu, *The Formula Quotations in the Infancy Narrative of Matthew: An Enquiry into the Tradition History of Mt. 1–2* (AnBib 63; Rome: Biblical Institute Press, 1976), 185–7, 223–5. The influence of Gnuse's study can be seen in Raymond Brown's endorsement of his conclusions in the supplement material in the new updated version of his *The Birth of the Messiah*, 599. Cf. also, Marco Frenschkowski, 'Traum und Traumdeutung im Matthäusevangelium: Einige Beobachtungen,' *JAC* 41 (1998): 31, who accepts Gnuse's study – though it does not appear to bear upon his investigation; and John Nolland, *The Gospel of Matthew: A Commentary on the Greek Text* (NIGTC; Grand Rapids, Mich.: Eerdmans, 2005), 97 n. 50.

4 Gnuse, 'Dream Genre in the Matthean Infancy Narratives,' 107.

imitations of dreams in sections of Genesis that modern scholars have identified as 'Elohist.' As shown in Chapter Three, literary imitation of dreams in Greco-Roman literature existed; but given the formal, conventional pattern of dream reports, it is difficult to demonstrate a dream narrative as an imitation of another literary dream. The following is a response to Gnuse, showing that he does not convincingly demonstrate Matthew's dependence upon the Elohist dreams.

First, Gnuse's claim that Matthew's dreams share 'deep structural similarities' with the Elohist dreams is not sufficiently demonstrated. Gnuse supports this claim with five points. (1) He compares the introductory formal features of the Elohist dreams (Gen. 20.3-8 [Abimelech]; 28.12-16 [Jacob]; 31.10-13 [Jacob]; 31.24 [Laban]; and 46.2-4 [Jacob/Israel]) and the Matthean dream reports.[5] The Elohist features are theophany, recipient, dream reference and time; the Matthew features are theophany, dream reference, recipient and place. Gnuse notes the switching of recipient and dream reference and the replacement of time with place, but such differences do not lead him to question the 'deep similarities' between the two dream formats. Moreover, I would note that this is the common pattern of dream reports in Greco-Roman literature when an introductory δοκέω is not used. (2) Gnuse notes that 'Matthean dream reports begin with the particle, "behold," which is reminiscent of the introductory "behold" (hennēh) in the Genesis dreams that initiate the auditory message.'[6] Once again, Gnuse acknowledges the different function of 'behold' in the two dream formats – introducing the entire dream report in Matthew but only the dream message in Genesis – but this difference is simply seen as 'incidental.' It is important to note that only the dream of Gen. 20.3 has the term 'behold'; thus, the reference to 'Genesis dreams' in the above quotation is not completely accurate. (3) Gnuse argues that 'both the Genesis and the Matthean dreams introduce the divine message with vocabulary designed to emphasize the auditory nature of the dream theophany: hebrew *wayyō'mer* and greek λέγων.'[7] A

---

5   Gnuse, 'Dream Genre in the Matthean Infancy Narratives,' 112.

6   Gnuse, 'Dream Genre in the Matthean Infancy Narratives,' 112.

7   Gnuse, 'Dream Genre in the Matthean Infancy Narratives,' 112. This claim raises a secondary problem with Gnuse's study. He argues that Matthew modeled his dreams upon the *Hebrew* text of Genesis. Gnuse notes that the Septuagint does not have λέγων but εἶπεν (Gen. 20.3; 28.12; 31.11; 31.24) or εἰπών (Gen. 46.2). Moreover, the Septuagint does not have Matthew's dream terminology (ὄναρ). The textual form of Matthew's 'Bible', however, is quite complex; and though the issue is still a point of debate among scholars, most would accord a role to the Septuagint in Matthew's use of the Jewish Scriptures. Gnuse does not seem to be aware of this issue. For Matthew's use and form of the Old Testament, see Maarten J. J. Menken, *Matthew's Bible: The Old Testament Text of the Evangelist* (BETL 173; Leuven: Leuven University Press, 2004), 1–10; Graham N. Stanton, *A Gospel for a New People: Studies in Matthew* (Louisville, Ky.; Westminster/John Knox Press, 1992), 353–358;

review of the dream reports analyzed in Chapter Four will show that the message of visitant dreams is also introduced with verbs of 'saying'; the dreams of Genesis and Matthew are not providing more emphasis than other dreams in other literature. (4) Gnuse claims that the dream messages of Matthew, which are assurance and command, fall within the range of the Genesis dream messages, which are assurance, promise, warning, and command.[8] Once again, the dream reports surveyed in Chapter Four reveal that this 'range' of dream messages is not limited to dreams in Genesis and Matthew; these are common motifs in dream reports of Greco-Roman literature. (5) Gnuse notes that 'formal termination concludes both the Genesis and Matthean dream reports: in Genesis the dream recipient is said to have awakened, whereas in Matthew Joseph arose from sleep.'[9] The differences are noted by Gnuse, but these 'formal terminations' are common features found in Greco-Roman dream reports. Thus, Gnuse's contention that the Matthean dream reports share 'deep structural similarities' with the Genesis dreams is untenable. The acknowledged differences, along with the conventional pattern of dream reports in the larger Greco-Roman literary context, cumulatively undermine his argument that the Matthean dreams represent a literary mimesis of the Genesis dreams.

A second problem with Gnuse's argument is the diversity of the Genesis dream accounts. While the dream reports in Matthew are admittedly terse and repetitive, the Genesis dreams are fairly diverse and more elaborate. For instance, some dreams, like Matthew's, are visitant dreams that report a dream figure's message (Gen. 20.3-8; 31.24; 46.2-4), while other dreams combine a symbolic dream with a visitant or auditory dream (Gen. 28.12-16; 31.10-13). Also, several of the dreams in Genesis include a dialogue between the dream figure and the dreamer (20.3-8; 31.10-13; 46.2-6), unlike the monologue of the Matthean dreams. Should not the symbolic dreams in the Joseph narrative of Genesis be included in this analysis? If Matthew is imitating dreams in Genesis, can we expect him to select dreams along the lines of modern source-critical theories? In the end, the dream reports in Genesis, including the so-called Elohist tradition, are too diverse to claim that Matthew is imitating 'the dreams' in Genesis. An argument for literary mimesis would be more convincing if one could identify a single Genesis dream which Matthew imitated.[10]

---

and R. T. France, *Matthew: Evangelist & Teacher* (Downers Grove, Ill.; InterVarsity Press, 1989), 172–176; and Soares Prabhu, *The Formula Quotations in the Infancy Narrative of Matthew*, 19.

   8   Gnuse, 'Dream Genre in the Matthean Infancy Narratives,' 112.

   9   Gnuse, 'Dream Genre in the Matthean Infancy Narratives,' 113.

   10   Soares Prabhu, *The Formula Quotations in the Infancy Narrative of Matthew*, 223–224 and 294–297, actually sets forth such an argument. In his reconstruction of the sources of Mt. 1–2, Soares Prabhu argues that the dream of Mt. 2.13-15 is 'probably the earliest in origin'

Thirdly, Gnuse does introduce the possibility of Matthew being 'influenced' by Greco-Roman dream reports; he even provides John Hanson's form critical study.[11] He concludes, however, that 'Greek dreams are far more complex [than biblical dreams], especially in terms of portraying the mental processes and attitudes of the dreamer.'[12] Unfortunately, Gnuse does not offer any examples of these 'complex' dream reports, nor does he unpack his description of 'complex.' His conclusion is questionable on two grounds. First, the initial Matthean dream narrative (1.18-25) contains two features of the Greco-Roman dream report as described by Hanson:[13] (1) a character sketch of the dreamer (Joseph is described as 'righteous' [δίκαιος]); and (2) the mental state of the dreamer (Joseph was 'reflecting upon these things' [ταῦτα . . . ἐνθυμηθέντος]).[14] On the other hand, none of the Elohist dreams have these formal features. In this case, the Greco-Roman dream reports provide a closer formal parallel than the biblical material. Second, dreams in Greco-Roman epics and dramas do tend to be highly dramatic and sometimes include a psychological dimension, which may be what Gnuse intends by the word 'complex.' But a review of the dream reports in Chapter Four – drawn from historical, biographical and fictional texts – will illustrate a number of dream reports that rival the Matthean dreams in terseness and simplicity. Gnuse ultimately presents an unnecessary dichotomy and uninformed caricature of the differences between Greco-Roman and Ancient Near Eastern dream reports.[15]

Thus, whereas the first approach to the form of Matthew's dreams is too isolated from the larger literary context of dreams, the second approach is too narrow in its comparative material (i.e., Old

---

(295) and is modeled upon Gen. 46.2-4 (LXX). The dreams of Mt. 2.19-23 and 1.18-25 respectively were in turn modeled upon Mt. 2.13-15. In terms of Mt. 2.13-15 being an imitation of Gen. 46.2-4, the argument is open to the same weaknesses as those of Gnuse's arguments.

11   John S. Hanson, 'Dreams and Visions in the Graeco-Roman World and Early Christianity,' *ANRW* 23.2: 1395–1427.

12   Gnuse, 'Dream Genre in the Matthean Infancy Narratives,' 103.

13   Hanson, 'Dreams and Visions,' 1406–7.

14   The form of Matthew's dreams will be given fuller attention below.

15   As provided in Chapter Three, the observations of Frances Flannery-Dailey and John Hanson are worth repeating here. In her study of dreams in Ancient Near Eastern, Greek and Roman, and Hellenistic Jewish literature, Frances Flannery-Dailey discovers a 'surprisingly standardized [pattern] across many cultures for millennia' ('Standing at the Head of Dreamers: A Study of Dreams in Antiquity' [Ph.D. diss., The University of Iowa, 2000], 1, see chs. 1–2); and Hanson, 'Dreams and Visions,' 1396: 'Especially in formal, literary ways, the fundamental character of dream-vision reports does not significantly change from the Homeric poets to the end of late antiquity. Further, there are striking parallels between dream-vision materials of the Hellenistic and Roman periods and those of earlier cultures such as Assyria, Egypt, and Israel.'

Testament).[16] A third approach that takes into account Matthew's larger Greco-Roman literary context is necessary.

This third approach has been recognized by others but has not been fully employed. For example, Davies and Allison state the following in their commentary on Matthew:

> Dreams were also of great importance in the Graeco-Roman world, and Matthew's story of Joseph can be profitably compared with the typical dream patterns found in the literature that that world produced. This is particularly true because the standard OT pattern is to state 'X dreams a dream' and then to give the contents only after the event, after the dreamer awakes; while in the Graeco-Roman materials, on the other hand, the contents of a dream are usually given concurrently with the dreaming, that is, given as the dream takes place.[17]

Except for the detail of Joseph 'reflecting upon these things' in 1.20,[18] the exegesis of Davies and Allison is not informed by the comparison that they suggest. Another example of the third approach is John Hanson, whose form critical analysis is adopted by this present study. Hanson comments that Matthew's dreams 'conform completely to formal expectations' when compared with the formal pattern of dreams in Greco-Roman literature.[19] He, however, does not demonstrate nor analyze how the Matthean dreams indeed correspond to Greco-Roman dream narratives. The following seeks to fill this form critical gap in the study of Matthew's dreams, demonstrating that the form of the dream narrative in Matthew corresponds to the form of dream reports in Greco-Roman literature.

The Form of Matthew 1.18b-25

Though the Gospel of Matthew begins with a genealogy of Jesus, it could be said that the narrative proper opens with a dream report. This dream narrative is as follows:

16 The study of Matthew's dreams by Frances Flannery-Dailey, 'Standing at the Head of Dreamers: A Study of Dreams in Antiquity,' can also be placed in the second approach, for she limits her comparative material to Jewish texts of Second Temple Judaism. See Chapter One for a discussion of this work.

17 W. D. Davies and Dale C. Allison, *The Gospel According to Saint Matthew* (3 vols.; ICC; Edinburgh: T & T Clark, 1988), 1.207. Though the first part of this statement – comparing Matthew's dreams to those in the Greco-Roman world – is warranted, the second part of the quotation is mistaken. Only the dreams of Joseph and Daniel in the Old Testament follow the pattern described by Davies and Allison, but other Old Testament dreams follow the pattern set forth by Hanson (cf. Gen. 20.3-8; 28.10-21; 31.10-13; 31.24; 46.1-5; Num. 22.20-21; Judg. 7.13-14; 1 Kings 3.4-15). Davies and Allison show no awareness of Gnuse's study.

18 Davies and Allison, *The Gospel According to Saint Matthew*, 1.206.

19 Hanson, 'Dreams and Visions,' 1421.

When his mother Mary was engaged to Joseph, but before they had
come together (συνελθεῖν αὐτοὺς), she was found to be pregnant from
the Holy Spirit. Now her husband Joseph, being righteous (δίκαιος) and
not wanting to publicly disgrace her, planned to divorce her privately.
And after he reflected upon these things (ταῦτα δὲ αὐτοῦ
ἐνθυμηθέντος), behold, an angel of the Lord appeared to him in a
dream (ἄγγελος κυρίου κατ᾽ ὄναρ ἐφάνη αὐτῷ) and said, 'Joseph, son
of David, do not be afraid to take Mary as your wife, for the [child]
conceived in her is from the Holy Spirit. She will give birth to a son, and
you will name him Jesus, for he will save his people from their sins. All
this has taken place so that what had been spoken by the Lord through
the prophet would be fulfilled: "Behold, the virgin will conceive and
bear a son, and they will call his name Emmanuel" (which is translated,
"God is with us").' Now when Joseph awoke from sleep (ἐγερθεὶς ...
ἀπὸ τοῦ ὕπνου), he did as the angel of the Lord commanded him and
took his wife. And he did not know her until she had borne a son, and
he named him Jesus.

Given the introductory nature of this dream report, the *scene-setting*
includes the circumstances leading up to the dream.[20] There are two
formal features of the *scene-setting* that are present in this initial
Matthean dream. First, the identity of the dreamer (Joseph) is indicated
along with a sketch of his character (righteous). Other Greco-Roman
dream reports that contain a comment about the dreamer's character
include the following.[21] Strabo recounts the dream of a certain Aristarcha,
whom he identifies as 'one of the most honorable of women' (τῶν
ἐντίμων σφόδρα γυναικῶν).[22] In narrating the dream of the Egyptian
king Sabaco, Diodorus of Sicily comments that he 'in piety and
uprightness far surpassed his predecessors (εὐσεβείᾳ δὲ καὶ χρηστότητι
πολὺ διαφέρων τῶν πρὸ αὐτοῦ).'[23] The description of character could
also be negative. Herodotus describes the dreamer Cambyses as mad
(μαίνομαι), a character flaw that leads to jealousy (φθόνος) of his brother
Smerdis.[24] Some dream reports may not use a specific term or phrase to
describe the character of the dreamer, but the *scene-setting* includes
circumstances that reveal the dreamer's character.[25] Also, as Hanson
notes, the larger context of histories and biographies 'often makes this

---

20   For a similar expansion of the *scene-setting*, see Herodotus, *Hist.* 7.12-14; Josephus, *J. W.* 2.114-116; Plutarch, *Alex.* 26.3.

21   It should be noted that the vision report in Acts 10.1-8 includes a description of Cornelius' character as 'pious and one who fears God' (εὐσεβὴς καὶ φοβούμενος τὸν θεόν).

22   Strabo, *Geogr.* 4.1.4.

23   Diodorus Siculus, *Bib. hist.* 1.65.2 (Oldfather, LCL); cf. 1.65.4.

24   Herodotus, *Hist.* 3.30.

25   For example, see Herodotus, *Hist.* 1.34 and Josephus, *J.W.* 2.114.116.

feature unnecessary.'²⁶ The second feature of the *scene-setting* in Matthew's first dream narrative is the description of the mental state of the dreamer 'reflecting upon these things (ταῦτα ... ἐνθυμηθέντος)'. Dream reports surveyed in the previous chapter that include this feature are the following: Sethos is 'lamenting' (ὀλοφυρόμενον);²⁷ Xerxes is 'giving serious counsel' (βουλὴν διδοὺς πάγχυ) to the advice of Artabanus;²⁸ Callirhoe is 'considering these things' (ταῦτα λογιζομένη) in one dream scene²⁹ and 'lamenting despondently' (δυρομένη ... ἀθύμως) in another;³⁰ Daphnis is 'talking out of his tears and pain' (λέγοντα ... ἐκ τῶν δακρύων καὶ τῆς λύπης);³¹ and Dionysophanes has given 'much thought' (φροντίδα πολλήν).³² Hanson also observes that the mental state of the dreamer could also include prayer,³³ a feature common in Jewish dream reports.³⁴

The *dream terminology* found in the first Matthean dream report is also found in all the references to dreams in Matthew's Gospel: κατ᾽ ὄναρ. BDAG notes that the phrase κατ᾽ ὄναρ first appears in literature around the turn of the first century.³⁵ The phrase also becomes common in inscriptions. Gil Renberg has brought together the largest collection of

---

26 Hanson, 'Dreams and Visions,' 1406 n. 44.
27 Herodotus, *Hist.* 2.141.
28 Herodotus, *Hist.* 7.12-14.
29 Chariton, *Chaer.* 2.9.1-6.
30 Chariton, *Chaer.* 5.5.5-7.
31 Longus, *Daphn.* 2.23.1–24.1.
32 Longus, *Daphn.* 4.34.1-3.
33 Hanson, 'Dreams and Visions,' 1407, references Acts 22.17 and Homer, *Od.* 2.261; cf. also *Acts Pet.* 3.1 Other sources cited by Hanson that include the mental state of the dreamer are Philostratus, *Vit. Apoll.* 4.34; Plutarch, *Eum.* 6.4; *Brut.* 36.4; and Josephus, *A.J.* 11.334. Cf. also Dionysius of Halicarnassus, *Ant. rom.* 1.57.4; Plutarch, *Per.* 13.8; *2 En.* 1.3; *Acts John* 19. The entirety of this evidence refutes Craig Keener's statement that 'the mention of Joseph's anxiety probably has more to do with the story line than with the frequency of citing mental states when relating dreams' (*Commentary on the Gospel of Matthew* [Grand Rapids, Mich.: Eerdmans, 1999], 94 n. 63). All these references to the 'mental states' of the dreamers relate to their respective story lines, and each 'mental state' is particularly suited to its narrative setting – just as dream reports as a whole relate to their particular story lines and narrative settings.This suitability or particularity, however, does not negate the conventional pattern of narrating dreams, which often includes a description of the dreamer's 'mental state.'
34 Cf. Dan. 9.21; *4 Ezra* 3.1-3; 5.121-22; 6.35-37; *1 En.* 13.7; *2 Bar.* 35.1ff; *2 En.* 69.4; 71.24-25; Josephus, *A.J.* 11.326; *L.A.B* 42.2-3.
35 BDAG, 710a. The entry includes references to Strabo, *Geogr.* 4.1.4, *Anth. Pal.* 11.263.1, Diogenes Laertius, *Vit. phil.* 10.32, and Eunapius, *Vit. soph.* 55 as instances of its use.

inscriptions that deal with dreams and waking visions, and the phrase κατ᾽ ὄναρ has the largest representation in the Greek inscriptions.[36]

The *dream proper* is a visitant dream with the dream figure identified as 'an angel of the Lord' (ἄγγελος κυρίου). The ἄγγελος κυρίου reflects the Jewish heritage and symbolic world that informs Matthew's story in particular and the Christian movement in general. Matthew's ἄγγελος κυρίου is not the same as the Old Testament designation for God but is part of the developing angelology of Middle Judaism, particularly the convention of angels appearing in dreams.[37] It is interesting to note, however, that the well-known dream in Homer's *Iliad* that deceives Agamemnon is referred to as the ἄγγελος Διός ('angel/messenger of Zeus').[38] Often in a visitant dream report the position of the dream figure is stated in relation to the dreamer,[39] and sometimes a description of the dream figure is given.[40] Matthew's dream narrative lacks both these features, but this is not uncommon.[41] The message of the dream figure is given in direct discourse, giving encouragement, issuing a command and providing an explanation for the command.

At this point in the dream report, an interpretative issue is raised: is the so-called formula or fulfillment quotation of vv. 22–23 part of the angel's message or a narrative aside?[42] Most interpreters read the formula quotation as an intrusion into the dream report[43] and so interpret it as a

---

36   Gil H. Renberg, ' "Commanded By the Gods": An Epigraphical Study of Dreams and Visions in Greek and Roman Religious Life' (Ph.D. diss., Duke University, 2003), appendix I. See also, Frenschkowski, 'Traum und Traumdeutung im Matthäusevangelium,' 14–21, for a discussion of κατ᾽ ὄναρ.

37   Flannery-Dailey, 'Standing at the Head of Dreamers,' 415–416. Cf. also Davies and Allison, *The Gospel According to Saint Matthew*, 1.206.

38   Homer, *Il.* 2.25.

39   Cf. Herodotus, *Hist.* 2.139; 2.141; Josephus, *J.W.* 2.114; Dionysius of Halicarnassus, *Ant. rom.* 7.68.3; Acts 16.9; 23.11; 27.23; Plutarch, *Arist.* 19.2; Soranus, *Vit. Hipp.* 4.7; Chariton, *Chaer.* 3.7.4; 6.2.2; Longus, *Daphn.* 3.27.1–28.1; *Acts Thom.* 29; *Acts Andr.* 22; 29; *Acts John* 19.

40   Cf. Herodotus, *Hist.* 5.56; 7.12; Tacitus, *Hist.* 4.83; Plutarch, *Alex.* 26.3; Philostratus, *Vit. Apoll.* 4.34; Chariton, *Chaer.* 2.1.2; 2.9.1-6; Longus, *Daphn.* 2.23.1–24.1; *L.A.B.* 9.10.

41   Cf. Herodotus, *Hist.* 3.30; Acts 18.9; Plutarch, *Them.* 30.1-3; *Arist.* 11.5; *Per.* 13.8; *Cor.* 24; Suetonius, *Aug.* 91.2; *Tib.* 74; *Galb.* 4.3; 18.2; Diogenes Laertius, *Vit. Phil.* 1.117; *Life of Aesop* 7; Chariton, *Chaer.* 2.3.5; Longus, *Daphn.* 2.26.5; *Acts Pet.* 1; 30; 1QapGen XXI, 8; *L.A.B.* 23.2-4a; 28.4a.

42   For a brief note that weighs the options, see Davies and Allison, *The Gospel According to Saint Matthew*, 1.211, though they opt for the formula quotation as an 'editorial remark (s).' Consider also Margaret Davies, *Matthew* (Readings: A New Biblical Commentary; Sheffield: JSOT Press, 1993), 33: '*Either the angel or the narrator* goes on to interpret the conception as a fulfillment of a scriptural prophecy from God' (emphasis added).

43   Hanson, 'Dreams and Visions,' 1421, states, 'The report would read smoothly if these two verses were omitted.' A similar sentiment is expressed by Brown, *The Birth of the*

narrative aside, though that terminology is not necessarily used.[44] As intrusive as narrative asides may be, they were common in ancient literature.[45] Moreover, if the consensus is correct that the formula quotation is a narrative aside, Matthew is not alone in inserting a narrator's comment into a dream report. Herodotus has two dream reports that contain narrative asides.[46] In each case, the dreamer experiences a dream about his son. The narrative asides provide the reader with needed information about the dreamer's son, so that the meaning or implication of the dream can be better understood. Plutarch provides a narrative aside in a dream report concerning Alexander's building of Alexandria.[47] The dream figure directs Alexander to build his city on the island of Pharos; the narrative aside explains to the reader that at the time of Alexander's dream Pharos was an island, though presently it had been connected to the mainland by a causeway. Longus also provides narrative asides in two of his dream reports.[48] The first narrative aside informs the reader that the dream figures (Nymphs) are the same Nymphs from earlier in the story whom the dreamer has seen painted on the wall of a cave, where the dreamer had discovered his infant child. Accordingly, it connects the dream scene, which concerns instructions on the rearing of the child, with the previous plot segment. The second narrative aside simply introduces the name of the dreamer, who had been active in the narrative but whose name had not yet been given. Thus, Matthew's insertion of a narrative aside into a dream report is not unique when compared to other dream accounts in Greco-Roman literature, and so

---

Messiah, 144: 'Occurring where it does, the citation in 1.22-23 is intrusive in the flow of the narrative. . . . [Verses] 24–25 is the real continuation of the angelic appearance in 20–21 and that 22–23 is obviously an insertion.'

44   Graham Stanton includes the formula quotation of 1.22-23 in the list of 'theological "asides" or comments' by the evangelist' ('Matthew,' in *It Is Written: Scripture Citing Scripture: Essays in Honour of Barnabas Lindars* [ed. D. A. Carson and H. G. M. Williamson; Cambridge: Cambridge University Press, 1988], 205, 206). See also Brown, *The Birth of the Messiah*, 144 ('intrusive in the flow of the narrative' and 'obviously an insertion'); Krister Stendahl, 'Quis et Unde? An Analysis of Matthew 1–2,' in *The Interpretation of Matthew* (IRT 3; ed. G. Stanton; Philadelphia: Fortress Press, 1983), 60 ('Matthew's interpretive comment'); Davies and Allison, *The Gospel According to Saint Matthew*, 1.211 ('editorial remark(s)'); Janice Capel Anderson, *Matthew's Narrative Web: Over, and Over, and Over Again* (JSOTSup 91; Sheffield: JSOT Press, 1994), 154 ('direct authorial comment'); Jack Dean Kingsbury, *Matthew as Story* (2d ed., rev. and enl.; Philadelphia: Fortress Press, 1988), 44 ('private comments to the reader'); Hagner, *Matthew 1–13*, 20 ('an aside by the evangelist'); and Pierre Bonnard, *L'évangile selon Matthieu* (CNT 1; Geneva: Labor et Fides, 2002), 21 ('le commentaire de Mat.').

45   For a study of narrative asides in ancient literature, see Steven M. Sheeley, *Narrative Asides in Luke-Acts* (JSNTSup 72; Sheffield, JSOT Press, 1992), 40–96.

46   Herodotus, *Hist.* 1.34 and 1.209.

47   Plutarch, *Alex.* 26.3.

48   Longus, *Daphn.* 1.7.1–8.2 and 2.26.5–28.1.

becomes less disruptive than interpreters have suggested. It provides a commentary on the significance of the events taking place in relation to the dream. More significantly, the content of this narrative aside is commonly related to dreams in antiquity: prophecy. This aspect of the formula quotation will be discussed in the next section.

Instead of a narrative aside, however, the formula quotation of Mt. 1.22-23 can be read as part of the angel's message.[49] First, there are other places in Matthew where the formula quotation is part of a character's speech (2.5-6; 26.56), so to have the formula quotation spoken by the angel is not exceptional. Secondly, J. C. Fenton has observed that where the formula quotation is part of a character's speech it contains a verb in the perfect tense (2.5, γέγραπται; 26.56, γέγονεν ἵνα πληρωθῶσιν), whereas the other formula quotations simply have ἵνα πληρωθῇ (2.17; 2.23; 4.14; 8.17; 12.17; 13.35; 27.9 [ἐπληρώθη]).[50] The formula quotation in 1.22 also has a perfect verb (γέγονεν ἵνα πληρωθῇ), which parallels the two instances where the character's speech includes the formula quotation. And thirdly, another factor that suggests that the angel's speech includes the formula quotation is a comparison with the two other dream references with formula quotations in Matthew 2. In 2.13-15 and 2.22-23, Matthew refers to dreams that prompt certain actions; these actions in turn fulfill prophecies, which is stated in a formula quotation at the conclusion of the dream report or reference. The formula quotation in Matthew 1.22-23, however, does not conclude the dream report but is included within it, which may suggest that it is intended to be read as a part of the angel's speech. There are other aspects of the dream report in Mt. 1.18b-25 that may support reading the formula quotation as a continuation of the angel's message, but they will be discussed in the next section.

The final feature of this dream narrative is Joseph's *reaction* and *response*. Joseph's *reaction* is not so much a mental or emotional response but simply the narrator's mentioning his 'awakening from sleep' (ἐγερθεὶς

49 For those few interpreters who read the formula quotation as part of the angel's speech, see J. C. Fenton, 'Matthew and the Divinity of Jesus: Three Questions Concerning Matthew 1.20-23,' in *Papers on the Gospels* (ed. E. A. Livingstone; vol. 2 of *Studia Biblica 1978: Sixth International Congress on Biblical Studies*; JSNTSup 2; Sheffield, JSOT Press, 1980), 79–80; and Theodor Zahn, *Das Evangelium des Matthäus* (Kommentar zum Neuen Testament 1; 2d ed.; Leipzig: A. Deichert, 1905), 78, who notes Irenaeus, *Haer.* 4.23.1 and Photius, *Ad Amphilochium Quaestio* XXV (PG 101.190) as reading the formula quotation as a continuation of the angel's message.

It is interesting to note that even if one reads the quotation formula as part of the angel's message, v. 23 still contains a narrative aside: ὅ ἐστιν μεθερμηνευόμενον μεθ' ἡμῶν ὁ θεός ('which is translated "God with us"').

50 Fenton, 'Matthew and the Divinity of Jesus: Three Questions Concerning Matthew 1.20-23,' 79–80.

... ἀπὸ τοῦ ὕπνου).[51] Joseph *responds* by obeying the angel's command, taking Mary as his wife and naming the child Jesus. The *response* feature of a dream report can either (1) note the immediate response of the dreamer[52], or (2) provide an extended narrative of how the dream or dream-command was fulfilled.[53] The Matthean dream report follows the pattern of the first type: Joseph is portrayed as responding immediately to the dream. Many interpreters make special mention of Joseph's obedient response, suggesting that his response is exceptional and indicative of his 'righteousness' (1.19).[54] Interpretations of Joseph's obedience, however, must be made in light of the conventional form of dream reports in the Greco-Roman literature. Such obedience is a typical feature of the dream report and would be expected by an ancient audience.[55] It is significant, though, that Matthew does describe Joseph's response in the same terms as the dream message,[56] and perhaps the response of Joseph is emphasized in this manner. But this emphasis simply exploits what is already present in the form of the dream report.

The dream of Mt. 1.18b-25 is the most detailed dream narrative in

---

51 For other dream reports that note the dreamer waking up, see Herodotus, *Hist.* 1.34; 1.209; Josephus, *A.J.* 11.328; Diodorus Siculus, *Bib. hist.* 17.103.7; Dionysius of Halicarnassus, *Ant. rom.* 5.54.2; 7.68.3-4; Plutarch, *Alex.* 26.3; Luc. 12.1-2; *Life of Aesop* 9; Acts 16.6-12 [Codex Bezae]; Longus, *Daphn.* 2.23.1–24.1; *Acts Thom.* 29; *Acts Thom.* 91; *Acts Andr.* [M] 29; *L.A.B.* 23.2-4a; Ezek. Trag. 85–86.

52 See esp. Appian, *Bell. civ.* 1.12.105; *Hist. rom.* 8.20.136; Josephus, *A.J.* 11.328; Acts 16.6-10; Plutarch, *Alex.* 26.3; Suetonius, *Aug.* 91.2; Longus, *Daphn.* 2.26.5–28.1; 4.34.1-3; *Acts Pet.* 5; 30. Cf. also Herodotus, *Hist.* 2.141; 3.30; 6.118; Appian, *Hist. rom.* 8.1.1; Diodorus Siculus, *Bib. hist.* 17.103.7; Dionysius of Halicarnassus, *Ant. rom.* 1.56.5; 1.57.4 [2]; Tacitus, *Ann.* 2.14; Acts 18.9-11; Plutarch, *Them.* 30.1-3; Suetonius, *Jul.* 7.2–8.1; Philostratus, *Vit. Apoll.* 4.34; Chariton, *Chaer.* 2.3.5; 6.2.2; *Acts Thom.* 29; 154–155; *Acts John* 18.

53 Cf. Herodotus, *Hist.* 1.34; 1.107-108; 3.124; Plutarch, *Them.* 26.2-4; *Caes.* 63.5-7; Longus, *Daphn.* 2.23.1–24.1; 3.27.1–28.1; *Acts Thom.* 91; *Acts Andr.* [GE] 20.

54 See especially, Gnuse, 'Dream Genre in the Matthean Infancy Narratives,' 113; Flannery-Dailey, 'Standing at the Head of Dreamers,' 406; and Magda Motté, '"Mann des Glaubens": Die Gestalt Josephs nach dem Neuen Testament,' *BibLeb* 11 (1970), 176–189. See also, Robert H. Gundry, *Matthew: A Commentary on His Handbook for a Mixed Church under Persecution* (2d ed.; Grand Rapids, Mich.: Eerdmans, 1994), 25; Davies and Allison, *The Gospel According to Saint Matthew*, 1.218-219; Nolland, *The Gospel of Matthew*, 103; Bonnard, *L'évangile selon Matthieu*, 22.

55 Cf. the references in footnote 52.

56 Note the terminology of the angel's message-command (παραλαβεῖν Μαρίαν τὴν γυναῖκα σου and καλέσεις τὸ ὄνομα αὐτοῦ Ἰησοῦν) is repeated in describing Joseph's response (παρέλαβεν τὴν γυναῖκα αὐτοῦ and ἐκάλεσεν τὸ ὄνομα αὐτοῦ Ἰησοῦν).

It should also be noted that, if Joseph's obedient response is being emphasized, it may also be underscored by his going *beyond* what the dream message dictates. In addition to the specifics of the dream command, Joseph's response also includes the abstinence from sexual relations with Mary until after the child is born (vs. 24). See also Plutarch, *Alex.* 2.4 and Diogenes Laertius, *Vit. phil.* 3.1-2 for examples of husbands abstaining from sexual relations because of the knowledge or suspicion that their wives' pregnancy was of divine origin.

Matthew's Gospel. The two subsequent dream reports in Matthew 2 are not only more terse but also repeat many of the features found in the initial dream report, such as dream terminology, type of dream, dream figure and reaction/response. For this reason, the analysis of the form of these two dream reports is minimal.

The Form of Matthew 2.13-15

> Now after they had departed, an angel of the Lord (ἄγγελος κυρίου) appeared to Joseph in a dream (φαίνεται κατ᾽ ὄναρ) and said, 'Get up, take the child and his mother, and flee to Egypt, and remain there until I tell you; for Herod is about to search for the child to destroy him.' And he woke up (ἐγερθείς) and took the child and his mother by night, and went to Egypt, and remained there until the death of Herod. This was to fulfill what had been spoken by the Lord through the prophet, 'Out of Egypt I have called my son.'

The *scene-setting* is minimal and simply consists of a genitive absolute that connects the dream report with the previous circumstances. Like the dream report in 1.18b-25, Joseph is the dreamer, the dream is a visitant dream and the dream figure is identified as 'an angel of the Lord' (ἄγγελος κυρίου). The message is a command given in direct discourse along with a basis for the command. Joseph is portrayed as 'waking up' and *responding* to the dream figure's message. A formula quotation is given at the end of the dream report, connecting the consequences of the dream with the fulfillment of prophecy.

The Form of Matthew 2.19-21

> When Herod died, behold, an angel of the Lord appeared in a dream (ἄγγελος κυρίου φαίνεται κατ᾽ ὄναρ) to Joseph in Egypt and said, 'Get up, take the child and his mother, and go to the land of Israel, for those who were seeking the child's life are dead.' And he woke up (ἐγερθείς) and took the child and his mother, and went to the land of Israel.

The *scene-setting* feature of this dream narrative provides a temporal reference (death of Herod), the identification of the dreamer (Joseph) and the place of the dream (Egypt). Like the previous dream reports, the *dream proper* is a visitant dream with the dream figure identified as 'an angel of the Lord' (ἄγγελος κυρίου). The dream message is narrated in direct discourse and represents a command. Once again, Joseph is described as 'waking up' and promptly following the directive of the message.

Summary

The dream reports of the Gospel of Matthew represent a conventional, compositional pattern that an ancient audience would find formally comparable to other dream reports in Greco-Roman literature. There is a script as to how dreams are narrated in ancient literature, and the Matthean dreams conform to this literary practice. It should be noted, however, that the dream reports of Matthew are repetitive and lack substantive variation from one another. The dream of 1.18b-25 is the first and most elaborate; the other two dream reports (2.13-15; 2.19-20) not only repeat the type of dream (visitant) but also replicate many of the same features (dream terminology, dream figure and dream response). Other ancient narratives show more diversity in their narration of dreams. Thus, while Matthew reflects a certain amount of uniformity in the way he narrates dreams, the dream reports themselves reflect a conventional form found in Greco-Roman literature; and an ancient audience would bring to Matthew's dream narratives the same literary expectations and values as the dreams found in contemporary literature. It should also be emphasized that there is nothing peculiarly biblical or Jewish about the form of these dreams,[57] as if Matthew was imitating the dream reports of the Jewish scriptures or a particular dream in Jewish tradition (Moses). If anything, Matthew imitates his own dream report, given the repetitive nature of his dreams.

Having analyzed the compositional pattern of Matthew's dreams, I now turn to a study of the functions of the Matthean dreams.

The Functions of the Matthean Dreams and Additional Observations

Not only does the narrative form of the Matthean dreams correspond to the compositional form of other dreams in Greco-Roman literature, but the literary functions of the Matthean dreams also comport to the expectations of an ancient audience. This section describes how the dreams of Matthew function both in the larger matrix of literary dreams and in the particular narrative of Matthew's story of Jesus.

The Dream of Matthew 1.18b-25

The function of the initial Matthean dream (1.18b-25) should first be considered in light of other birth stories and the tradition of encomiastic rhetoric. It was noted in Chapter Three that dreams are a conventional motif for developing the birth *topos* in encomium. After the introductory

---

57 The content of Matthew's dream reports is a different matter and unmistakably reveal a Jewish worldview and heritage (e.g. 'angel of the Lord' and prophecies from Jewish Scripture, as well as the larger narrative context of Matthew's narrative).

proem, an encomium would begin with a discussion about a person's origin, which may then be followed by the topic of birth.[58] Hermogenes describes these *topoi* in the following way:

> Encomiastic topics are (the subject's) nationality (ἔθνος), such as Greek, city (πόλις), such as Athenian, family (γένος), such as Alcmaeonid. You will mention also any marvelous occurrences at birth (περὶ τὴν γένεσιν), for example from dreams (ὀνειράτων) or signs (συμβόλων) or things like that.[59]

Nicolaus states that the 'first heading' of the encomium is 'from origin' (ἀπὸ τοῦ γένους), which includes nationality (ἔθνος), native city (πόλις), and ancestors (προγόνος).[60] He then states, 'After these remarks about origin, we shall come to the circumstances of his birth (ἀπὸ τῆς γενέσεως).'[61] The examples that he then provides for the birth *topos* are the dream of Pericles' mother and the dreams concerning Cyrus' mother. In his treatise on the imperial encomium speech, Menander the Rhetor also reflects this convention of discussing the origin and birth of a person.[62] The origin *topos* can include discussion of native country (πατρίς), city (πόλις) and family (γένος), if these topics are indeed worthy of note. Menander then moves on to discuss the circumstances surrounding the birth (περὶ τῆς γενέσεως); 'and if any divine sign (σύμβολον) occurred at the time of his birth, either on land or in the heavens or on the sea,'[63] it should be mentioned. The dream of Cyrus' mother and Romulus' suckling of the she-wolf are offered as examples. Menander also advises that one should invent (πλάσσω) such signs if it can be done so convincingly. Thus, the Greco-Roman rhetorical tradition indicates that origin and birth are conventional *topoi* of encomiastic rhetoric, which has as its goal the exhibition of a person's virtue, excellence and greatness.[64] This tradition also reveals that when the birth

---

58   Some rhetors do not include the birth *topos*. Theon refers to the origin *topos* as 'good birth' (εὐγένεια) but states that this *topos* will be developed 'either from the goodness of (a man's) city and nationality (ἔθνους) and constitution (πολιτείας), or from ancestors (γονέων) and other relatives' (Theon, *Progym.* 9.15-17 [mod. trans. Kennedy, 50; text Butt]). Theon then moves on to education. Aphthonius instructs that, 'you will state the person's origin (τὸ γένος), which you will divide into national origin (ἔθνος), homeland (πατρίδα), ancestors (προγόνους), and parents (πατέρας)' (Aphthonius, *Progym.* 8 [22] [mod. trans. Kennedy, 108; text Rabe]). The next *topos* that Aphthonius treats is upbringing (ἀνατροφή).

59   Hermogenes, *Progym.* 7.22-24 [15] (trans. Kennedy, 82; text Rabe).

60   Nicolaus, *Progym.* 8 [50] (Kennedy, 156; text Felten).

61   Nicolaus, *Progym.* 8 [51] (Kennedy, 157; text Felten).

62   Menander, Περὶ ἐπιδεικτικῶν 2.369-371 (Russell and Wilson, 78–83).

63   Menander, Περὶ ἐπιδεικτικῶν 2.371 (Russell and Wilson, 80–81).

64   Cf. Theon, *Progym.* 9.1-2 (Kennedy, 50); Hermogenes, *Progym.* 7 [14–15] (Kennedy, 81); Nicolaus, *Progym.* 8 [48–49] (Kennedy, 155); Aphthonius, *Progym.* 8 [21] (Kennedy, 108).

topos is treated dreams are presented as an illustration of how it can be developed.

These comments from the Greek *progymnasmata* are not just prescriptive for compositional exercises, but they also are descriptive of ancient literary practices, as the examples offered come from literary texts not speeches. Thus, the dreams concerning Cyrus' mother come from Herodotus' *Histories*. After a description of the reigns of Cyrus' ancestors (1.95-107), Herodotus describes two dreams associated with the birth of Cyrus. The two dreams were experienced by Cyrus' grandfather Astyages; they were symbolic dreams about his daughter Mandane. The first dream was of Mandane, 'urinating so much that it filled his own city and overflowed all of Asia.'[65] The second dream was similar: 'it seemed that from the pudendum of his daughter came forth a vine, and the vine covered all of Asia.'[66] The dreams signify the future rule and power of Mandane's child, Cyrus. The dream of Pericles' mother is also found in Herodotus as well as Plutarch.[67] Both authors give information about Pericles' origin and then mention a dream that his mother has while pregnant; she dreams that she gives birth to a lion, which portends his future greatness as political and military leader of Athens. This encomiastic pattern of origin and birth dream is also found in Plutarch's *bios* of Alexander the Great.[68] The parents of Alexander, Philip and Olympias, each experience a symbolic dream that signifies Alexander's future greatness. While betrothed (ἁρμόζω) and before 'they came together in the bride-chamber' (συνείρχθησαν εἰς τὸν θάλαμον), Olympias dreams 'that a peal of thunder and a lightning bolt fell upon her womb, and from the lightning strike a great fire was kindled, and then after having burst into flames everywhere it was extinguished.'[69] After the marriage but before the birth of Alexander, Philip dreams that he puts a seal in the image of a lion upon his wife's womb. Dreams are also associated with the births of Augustus[70] and Moses,[71] though these accounts lack a discussion of origin.

The Gospel of Matthew is representative of this literary-rhetorical tradition, beginning with Jesus' ancestry and birth.[72] The origin *topos* (1.1-17) is marked by the initial prescript (1.1), which identifies Jesus as

---

65 Herodotus, *Hist.* 1.107.
66 Herodotus, *Hist.* 1.108.
67 Herodotus, *Hist.* 6.131; Plutarch, *Per.* 3.2.
68 Plutarch, *Alex.* 2.1-3.
69 Plutarch, *Alex.* 2.2.
70 Suetonius, *Aug.* 94.4.
71 *L.A.B.* 9.10; Josephus, *A.J.* 2.212-216.
72 This encomiastic pattern has also been observed by Philip L. Shuler, *A Genre for the Gospels: The Biographical Character of Matthew* (Philadelphia: Fortress Press, 1982), 92–98. Shuler, however, mistakenly interprets the presence of these *topoi* as indicators of genre. For

son of David, son of Abraham (βίβλος γενέσεως Ἰησοῦ Χριστοῦ υἱοῦ Δαυὶδ υἱοῦ Ἀβραάμ), and is developed by the subsequent genealogy (1.2-17). After the genealogy, Matthew turns to the birth of Jesus (1.18-25), even introducing this section with the same term (γένεσις) used by the rhetors who discuss the birth *topos*: 'now the birth of Jesus Christ was thus' (τοῦ δὲ Ἰησοῦ Χριστοῦ ἡ γένεσις οὕτως ἦν; 1.18a).[73] Like the description of the *progymnasmata* and the convention of other ancient writers, Matthew develops the birth *topos* with a dream narrative. While Joseph and Mary are betrothed (μνηστεύω) but 'before they came together' (πρὶν ἢ συνελθεῖν αὐτούς), Joseph experiences a visitant dream that reveals the circumstances of Mary's pregnancy ('that which is conceived in her is from the Holy Spirit'; 1.20) and announces the child's future greatness ('he will save his people from their sins'; 1.21).[74] An ancient audience would hear Matthew's narrative of Jesus in light of the encomiastic pattern and tradition of birth dreams, which proleptically signifies the distinction and honor of the unborn child.

Matthew, however, is not simply writing discursively; his presentation of Jesus is in the form of a narrative. The dream report of Mt. 1.18b-25 is also a literary device that functions in the plot of Matthew's story of Jesus. Mary's pregnancy by the Holy Spirit (ἐκ πνεύματος ἁγίου) creates a situation for Joseph in which he decides to divorce Mary. This decision, however, is never acted upon, because a visitant dream intervenes explaining to Joseph the circumstances surrounding Mary's pregnancy and encouraging him 'to take Mary as his wife' (παραλαβεῖν Μαριὰμ τὴν γυναῖκά σου; 1.20) and to name the child. As is customary of dream reports, Joseph acts according to the message of the dream, taking Mary as his wife and naming the child Jesus. The dream protects Mary and her unborn child from the shame and negative consequences that a divorce and unwed pregnancy might produce. The dream report also functions to solve the anomaly and enigma in the genealogy,[75] where Joseph does not

---

a critique of and correction to Shuler, see Richard A. Burridge, *What Are the Gospels? A Comparison with Graeco-Roman Biography* (2d ed.; Grand Rapids, Mich.: Eerdmans, 2004), 83–86.

73 It should be noted that there is a textual variant for γένεσις in 1.18, though it is well attested by the manuscript tradition: P[1] ℵ B C P W Z Δ Θ f[1] *l* 2211. The term γέννησις is attested by L f[13] 33 Maj. Bruce Metzger notes that γέννησις 'became the customary word used in patristic literature to refer to the Nativity,' thus explaining its appearance in the Byzantine text (Bruce M. Metzger, A *Textual Commentary on the Greek New Testament* [2d ed.; Stuttgart: Deutsche Bibelgesellschaft, 1994], 7).

74 If vv. 22–23 are part of the angel's message, and not a narrative aside, the future greatness of the unborn child is also described in terms of divine presence ('God with us').

75 Stendhal, 'Quis et Unde? An Analysis of Matthew 1–2,' 60–61, though his description of 1.18-25 as an 'enlarged footnote' (61) to the genealogy overstates the relationship. For the relationship between Mt. 1.18-25 and the genealogy, see also L. Cantwell, 'The Parentage of Jesus: Mt 1.18-21,' *NovT* 24 (1982): 304–315.

'beget' (ἐγέννησεν) Jesus but is simply referred to as the husband of Mary (1.16). How is it, then, that the genealogy of Joseph can be claimed for Jesus? The visitant dream commands Joseph to name the child, which would be an act of taking the child as his own.[76]

Therefore, the dream of Mt. 1.18b-25 functions at two levels. First, the dream contributes to the encomiastic pattern of describing the origin and birth of a person. As the motif of the birth *topos*, the dream signifies the future significance and greatness of the yet to be born Jesus. Secondly, the dream is a literary device that functions within the plot of Matthew's story of Jesus. The dream prevents Joseph from divorcing Mary, which in turn protects Mary and her unborn child. The dream also prompts Joseph to take actions that result in Jesus becoming a legitimate heir to Joseph's genealogy.

The dream report of Mt. 1.18b-25 also contains features that are brought to light when read in the larger social and literary contexts of dreams, which the following seeks to demonstrate.

The Formula Quotation: Dreams and Prophecies. In the above discussion of the form of this Matthean dream, it was noted that the formula quotation of 1.22-23 could be read as either a narrative aside or a part of the angel's message. Most interpreters read it as a narrative aside, disrupting the narrative structure of the angel's command (vv. 20–21) and Joseph's faithful response (vv. 24–25). It was noted, however, that narrative asides in dream reports are found in other narrative texts and so Matthew is not unique in providing a narrative aside in a dream report. More importantly, though, is the content of the narrative aside: it announces the fulfillment of prophecy. The connection of dreams and oracles/prophecies in Greco-Roman literature was not uncommon.[77] This association in Josephus and Acts is especially noteworthy. In his *Jewish War*, Josephus describes his decision to surrender to the Romans as being based on the interpretation of his dreams along with his knowledge 'of the prophecies of the sacred books.'[78] In linking these dreams and their interpretation with the prophecies of scripture, Josephus infers that the dreams signify the fulfillment of the biblical prophecies. In *Antiquities*, Josephus recounts a dream of Alexander the Great.[79] Upon seeing the Jewish high priest, Alexander recalls a dream in which he saw a figure

---

76 Davies and Allison, *The Gospel According to Saint Matthew*, 1.209; Nolland, *The Gospel of Matthew*, 98.

77 Cf. Herodotus, *Hist.* 2.139; 3.124; Plutarch, *Them.* 26.2-4; *Arist.* 11.5; Suetonius, *Gal.* 9.2; *Aug.* 94.5.

78 Josephus, *J.W.* 3.351. This example is even more interesting in that the information about Josephus' ability to interpret dreams and his knowledge of the prophecies of scripture is given in a narrative aside.

79 Josephus, *A.J.* 11.333-336.

dressed like the high priest encouraging him not to hesitate but to commence his campaign to conquer Asia. Alexander is convinced that his successful military campaign has been directed by the God of the high priest. The high priest, in turn, shows Alexander the book of Daniel, 'in which it was showing a certain one of the Greeks destroying the rule of the Persians, and Alexander was convinced that he was the one signified [in the book].'[80] The prophecy of Daniel confirms what was already indicated in his dream, and the dream initially provided the impetus and encouragement that contributed to the fulfillment of the prophecy. The dreams in the book of Acts are also related to prophecy. As discussed in Chapter Four, the dreams in the book of Acts are themselves fulfillments of the prophecy of Joel, which was quoted in Peter's speech at the Pentecost event (2.17-20). The dreams, and visions, throughout Acts are signs that the Joel prophecy is being fulfilled in the life and ministry of the church. Thus, Josephus and the book of Acts exhibit a relation between dreams and the fulfillment of prophecy, an association also found in Matthew's Gospel.

Thus, Matthew follows this literary convention of relating dreams and prophecies.[81] If read as a narrative aside, Matthew informs the reader that the dream message contributes to the fulfillment of prophecy. Given this association of dreams and prophecies, the narrative aside becomes even less intrusive. If read as part of the angel's message, the formula quotation takes on an interpretive, revelatory quality, which will now be explored.

Oneirocritic Aspects of Mt. 1.18b-25. The dream report of Mt. 1.18b-25 contains interpretive aspects, which would be familiar to Matthew's readers given the ancient social and literary contexts of dreams. First, ancient interpretation of dreams included a variety of wordplays. Saul Lieberman gives a number of examples from both Greek and rabbinic sources,[82] including the use of homonyms, numerical value of letters, acronyms, the transposing of letters, and division of one word into two parts. An example of this kind of approach to dream interpretation is found in Plutarch's *bios* of Alexander.[83] While making siege against the city of Tyre, Alexander has a dream in which a satyr (σάτυρος) is mocking him. Alexander has difficulty seizing the satyr but eventually succeeds. The dream is then interpreted by the diviners, who base their

---

80   Josephus, *A.J.* 11.337.

81   Cf. also Mt. 2.13-15, 22–23.

82   Saul Lieberman, *Hellenism in Jewish Palestine* (Texts and Studies of the Jewish Theological Seminary of America 18; New York: The Jewish Theological Seminary of America, 1950), 70–78. For a more extensive review of this interpretive aspect, see Scott Noegel, *Nocturnal Ciphers: The Allusive Language of Dreams in the Ancient Near East* (AOS 89; New Haven, Conn.: American Oriental Society, 2007).

83   Plutarch, *Alex.* 24.4-5.

interpretation on the word 'satyr' (σάτυρος); the diviners say, 'Tyre will be yours' (**Σὴ** γενήσεται **Τύρος**). Though the dream of Mt. 1.18-25 is not a symbolic dream requiring interpretation, the dream message includes interpretative wordplays whose presence in a dream report would be familiar to an ancient audience. The angel tells Joseph to name the child Jesus, 'for he will save his people from their sins' (1.21). Interpreters have noted that there is play on the name Jesus ('Iησοῦς) and the activity of salvation.[84] The name 'Iησοῦς is the Greek form of the Hebrew *Yeshua*, which means 'Yahweh is salvation.' Thus, the name Jesus signifies the unborn child's role in God's salvation. This interpretative dimension continues with the announcement that the child will also, according to scripture, be called Emmanuel ('Eμμανουήλ), which is then explicitly stated to mean 'God is with us' (μεθ' ἡμῶν ὁ θεός; 1.23). Thus, the dream report of Mt. 1.18-25 includes interpretative wordplays that were familiar in ancient oneiric material, and these interpretative features contribute to the announcement of the unborn child's significance.[85]

Given this interpretative feature of the angel's message, the angel then takes on the persona of interpreter and revealer. Part of the developing angelology of Middle Judaism, including Christianity, was the role of angels as interpreters of dreams and visions, and dream-vision figures who reveal the divine will. Much of this role is found in apocalyptic literature,[86] but non-apocalyptic literature also contains this motif. For example, in the *Ladder of Jacob* the angel Sariel, who is 'in charge of dreams,' is told to 'go and make Jacob understand the meaning of the dream he has had and explain to him everything he saw.'[87] The angelic role of interpreter is also attested in the Jewish magical tradition found in the magic book *Sepher Ha-Razim*.[88] One of the magic rituals addresses the forty four angels who are 'in charge of dreaming' and includes the request, 'make known to me what is in the heart of N son of N and what is his

---

84 Davies and Allison, *The Gospel According to Saint Matthew*, 1.209-10; Hagner, *Matthew 1–13*, 19–20; Nolland, *The Gospel of Matthew*, 98; Kingsbury, *Matthew as Story*, 45–46; and David E. Garland, *Reading Matthew: A Literary and Theological Commentary* (Macon, Ga.: Smyth & Helwys Publishing, 2001), 23.

85 Cf. *L.A.B.* 42.3, where Samson's mother is visited by an angel in a dream or vision – it is uncertain whether she is sleeping or not – and is told that she will give birth to a son; she is to 'call his name Samson, for this one will be dedicated to your Lord' (Harrington, *OTP*). Harrington notes that 'Ps-Philo may have had in mind a derivation from the Heb. *šmš* (minister, serve) in light of Samson's Nazirite status' (*OTP*, 2.356). Cf. also *Jos. Asen.* 15.7(6), where in a vision an angel tells Aseneth, 'And your name shall no longer be called Aseneth, but your name shall be City of Refuge, because in you many nations will take refuge with the Lord God …' (Burchard, *OTP*).

86 Cf. Dan. 7.16-28; 8.18-26; *T. Levi* 2.7–5.6; *2 Bar.* 55.2ff; *1 En.* 18.14–19.2; 22.1ff; 40.9-10; Rev. 17.3-18.

87 *Lad. Jac.* 3.2 (Lunt, *OTP*).

88 See Chapter Two for a discussion of this text.

desire, and what is the interpretation of his dream and what is his thought.'[89] The whole of *Jubilees*, which is a re-writing of Genesis and part of Exodus, is presented as a revelation to Moses by 'the angel of the presence.'[90] Closer to Matthew's dream report are the dream-vision angels featured in *Joseph and Aseneth* 14.1–15.15, Pseudo-Philo's *Liber antiquitatum biblicarum* (*Biblical Antiquities*) 9.10, and Josephus' *Jewish Antiquities* 2.210-216. The angel of the Lord in the dream report of Mt. 1.18b-25 fits well within this tradition of angels, dreams and revelation. Moreover, this tradition also provides a context in which the fulfillment quotation can be read as part of the angel's message. The angel reveals how the circumstances fulfill prophecy and the manner in which the child will fulfill his salvific role: divine presence (Emmanuel).[91]

The Dream of Mt. 1.18b-25 and the Quotation of Isa. 7.14. In addition to its prophetic function, the quotation of Isa. 7.14 in the message of the dream report (1.23) also reflects a literary praxis found in other literary dreams. In Chapter Three, it was shown that a number of dream reports included quotations or allusions to Homer.[92] In the Jewish tradition of literary dreams, this intertextuality is paralleled by the quotation or echo of the Jewish Scriptures. For example, in Pseudo-Philo's narration of Balaam's dream,[93] the dream message is a highly condensed version of the ancestral narratives that rehearses the blessing and covenant relationship between God and Israel. This quotation and/or allusion to the Jewish Scriptures in a dream is found again in Pseudo-Philo's representation of Joshua's covenant renewal speech.[94] Like Balaam's dream, Joshua's dream rehearses God's past dealings with Israel in a condensed form, but the echoes and allusions to the biblical story are unambiguous. Matthew's quotation of Isa. 7.14 in the dream report of Mt. 1.18b-25 reflects this intertextual quality of dreams, in which dreams are the locus for allusions or quotations of a culture's foundational literature.

The Dream of Mt. 1.18b-25 and Moses Typology? The dream of Mt. 1.18b-25 is often presented as another literary contribution to Matthew's

---

89 *Sepher Ha-Razim* 2.229-30 (Morgan, 42).

90 *Jub.* 1.27–2.1 (Wintermute, *OTP*).

91 For a study of Matthew's soteriology, see David D. Kupp, *Matthew's Emmanuel: Divine Presence and God's People in the First Gospel* (SNTSMS 90; Cambridge: Cambridge University Press, 1996).

92 Cf. Plutarch, *Alex.* 26.3 (quoting *Od.* 4.354-355); Plutarch, *Luc.* 12.1 (allusion to *Od.* 4.335-339); Plato, *Cri.* 44a-44b (quoting *Il.* 9.363); Chariton, *Chaer.* 2.9.6 (quoting *Il.* 23.66-67); Longus, *Daphn.* 3.28.1 (allusion to *Od.* 9.315); Helidorus, *Aeth.* 5.22.1-2 (allusions to *Od.* 13.397ff; 18.67-68; *Il.* 10.261; *Od.* 13.332; 1.1; 19.392ff respectively).

93 *L.A.B.* 18.1-6.

94 *L.A.B.* 23.2-18.

characterization of Jesus as a new Moses.[95] The developing traditions about Moses sometimes included a dream, whether by Pharoah,[96] Moses' sister Miriam,[97] or Moses' father Amram.[98] The closest, and most referenced, parallel to the dream of Mt. 1.18b-25 is the dream of Amram in Josephus' *Jewish Antiquities*. The comparison is usually presented as follows.[99] In Josephus, Moses' father Amram is fearful about his wife's pregnancy because of Pharaoh's campaign to destroy all Hebrew infant males, and so he prays to God. In response to Amram's prayer and faith, God appears to Amram in a dream recounting past dealings with Israel, exhorting him not to fear and telling him of his unborn son's future greatness: 'he shall escape those who are watching to destroy him, and, reared in marvelous wise, he shall deliver the Hebrew race from their bondage in Egypt.'[100] In Matthew, Jesus' father Joseph is troubled about his betrothed wife's pregnancy because they have not yet married and so he decides to divorce her. In response, an angel of the Lord appears to Joseph in a dream explaining the circumstances of the pregnancy and telling him of the unborn child's future greatness: 'he shall save his people from their sins' (1.21). Thus, as the inference goes, the dream of Mt. 1.18b-25 is intended to evoke the tradition of Moses and therefore contribute to Matthew's Moses typology of Jesus.

This sort of comparison, however, must be approached with some caution. Many of the parallels can be attributed to the form and function of the dream report. Dreams are often connected with the birth of a child. For example, one could draw some parallels with the birth of Samson in Pseudo-Philo's *Liber antiquitatum biblicarum* (*Biblical Antiquities*).[101] Samson's mother is despondent because she is barren and so she prays to God. In response to her prayer, an angel appears to her in a dream acknowledging her prayer and announcing the conception and greatness of her son: 'and behold you will conceive and bear a son, and you will call his name Samson, for this one will be dedicated to your Lord.... He will free Israel from the hand of the Philistines.'[102] The 'parallels' between this

---

95 For example, Dale C. Allison, Jr., *A New Moses: A Matthean Typology* (Minneapolis: Fortress Press, 1993), 144–145; Dominic M. Crossan, 'Structure & Theology of Mt. 1.18-2.23,' *Cahiers de Joséphologie* 16 (1968): 1–17; and Frenschkowski, 'Traum und Traumdeutung im Matthäusevangelium,' 27–30.

96 *Tg. Ps.-J.* on Exod. 1.15. For even later sources (medieval), see Crossan, 'Structure & Theology of Mt. 1.18-2.23,' 4–7.

97 *L.A.B.* 9.10.

98 Josephus, *A.J.* 2.210-216.

99 For example, see Allison, *A New Moses*, 144; and Nolland, *The Gospel of Matthew*, 98.

100 Josephus, *A.J.* 2.215-216.

101 *L.A.B.* 42.1-4.

102 *L.A.B.* 42.3 (Harrington, *OTP*)

dream and Joseph's dream are perhaps more striking than those found
with Amram's dream, but any literary imitation or influence is simply
difficult to demonstrate given the literary convention of dreams.[103]
Moreover, the contexts of Amram's dreams and Joseph's dream differ.
The dreams associated with the Moses tradition all come in the context of
Pharaoh's intention to destroy infant males born to the Hebrews. As
shown above, the dream of Joseph is best understood in the context of
encomiastic tradition. The difference of context is even more significant
when one notes that the motif of royal threat is actually found in Matthew
2.[104] If the dream of Joseph is intended to contribute to the Moses
typology of Jesus, this association would have been much more overt in
the context of Matthew 2. If the dream of Mt. 1.18b-25 is read in light of
the Moses story, it is a *retrospective* reading evoked by the *explicit*
parallels of Moses and Jesus found in Matthew 2.

The Dreams of Matthew 2

The dreams of Matthew 2 are best understood by considering first the
literary character of this chapter, which should be read as an amplification
of the birth *topos* that was introduced in 1.18-25. The genitive absolute of
2.1a explicitly links the subsequent narrative with the previous unit (1.18-
25): 'Now when Jesus was born in Bethlehem of Judea in the days of king
Herod' (τοῦ δὲ Ἰησοῦ γεννηθέντος ἐν Βηθλέεμ τῆς Ἰουδαίας ἐν
ἡμέραις Ἡρῴδου τοῦ βασιλέως). Moreover, the birth of Jesus continues
to be the event driving the plot. Having followed a star to Jerusalem as a
sign, the magi ask about the location of 'the one who is born king of the
Jews' (2.2). In turn, Herod is disturbed and also inquires about the place
where 'the Christ is to be born' (2.4). Except for the transitional clause of
2.1a, Jesus is consistently referred to simply as 'the child' (τὸ παιδίον) and

---

103   It is worth quoting Daniel Harrington's conclusion to his comparison of the birth
narratives in Pseudo-Philo, which includes a version of the Moses story, and the New
Testament: 'The parallels show that roughly contemporary writers with differing methods
and concerns used some of the same literary devices and motifs in telling the stories about the
births of their heroes' ('Birth Narratives in Pseudo-Philo's Biblical Antiquities and the
Gospels,' in *To Touch the Text: Biblical and Related Studies in Honor of Joseph A. Fitzmyer,
S.J.* [ed. J. A. Fitzmyer, M. P. Horgan, and P. J. Kobelski; New York: Crossroad, 1989],
324).

104   This motif and the dreams associated with it in Matthew 2 will be discussed in the
next section.

For purposes of the history of scholarship, it is interesting to note that an 'early' Dominic
Crossan explained these differences in context on the possible historicity of the events
surrounding the birth of Jesus: 'One must still look elsewhere for an explanation of
Matthew's entire narrative [sequence]. And among such possible sources must still remain –
history, older traditions of what had actually happened at Jesus' birth' ('Structure &
Theology of Mt. 1.18-2.23,' 15).

always in relation to his mother (2.11, 13, 14, 20, 21). Thus, whereas Mt. 1.18-25 deals primarily with the situation before the birth of Jesus, Matthew 2 recounts events following the birth of Jesus; but both literary units are developments of the birth *topos* that treat the circumstances surrounding Jesus' birth.

As an amplification of the birth *topos*, Matthew 2 represents a conventional 'cultural hypotext':[105] the threat and rescue of a royal child.[106] The plot of this cultural hypotext is the following. A king or ruler becomes aware of the birth of a child that threatens his reign. This perceived threat is prompted by signs that accompany the birth of the child and portend the child's future greatness. The king devises a plan to kill the child, but the plan is thwarted when the divine intervenes, usually guiding an individual or people who have been enlisted by the king to destroy the child not to carry out the king's plan. The child is saved, and the threat to the king is realized when the child grows up. For example, the birth of Cyrus[107] is accompanied by two dreams which are experienced by King Astyages and signify a threat to his reign from his daughter's unborn child. When the child is born, the king commands his servant Harpagus to take the child home and kill it. Unable to bring himself to carry out the command, Harpagus enlists a herdsman to destroy the child. The divine (δαίμων) intercedes, creating a situation where the herdsman takes the child as his own.

Another example is provided by Plutarch who recounts a version of the birth of Romulus and Remus,[108] which is accompanied, even instigated, by a vision and an oracle. The king, Tarchetius, intends to put the pregnant handmaiden to death, but the goddess Hestia appears to him in a dream and forbids him to kill the girl. The king does not murder the handmaiden, but he does keep her busy and close by with the intention of killing her offspring at birth. When the handmaiden gives birth to twins, the king instructs a certain Teratius to kill the twin boys. Teratius exposes the twins beside a river, but a female wolf nurses the babies and birds feed

105   The term 'cultural hypotext' is borrowed from Loveday Alexander, who uses it to describe a cultural story or plot that finds expression in various literary texts. See Loveday C. A. Alexander, 'New Testament Narrative and Ancient Epic,' in *Acts in Its Ancient Literary Context: A Classicist Looks at the Acts of the Apostles* (Library of New Testament Studies 289; London: T&T Clark International, 2005), 169 and 181.

106   Hermann Gunkel, 'The Interpretation of the New Testament,' *The Monist* 13 (1903): 410; and Ulrich Luz, *Matthew 1–7: A Commentary* (trans. W. C. Linss; Minneapolis: Augsburg Fortress, 1989), 129, and 152–155 for a helpful, comparative chart that lists the various literary texts of this cultural hypotext. The most relevant texts for our purposes are Herodotus, *Hist.* 1.107-113 (Cyrus), Plutarch, *Rom.* 2.3-6 (Romulus and Remus); and Josephus, *A.J.* 2.205-227 (Moses); for truncated versions see Herodotus, *Hist.* 5.92 (Cypselus); Suetonius, *Aug.* 94.3 (Augustus) and *Nero* 36 (Nero).

107   Herodotus, *Hist.* 1.107-113.

108   Plutarch, *Rom.* 2.3-6. See also 3.1–4.3 for another version of the story.

them with morsels of food, until the twins are found and taken in by a herdsman.

Even the biblical story of Moses came to be reshaped according to this cultural hypotext. In Josephus' retelling of the Moses story,[109] Pharaoh's decision to destroy all the male Hebrew babies is not based on their growing population, as in the biblical story, but because one of the Egyptian diviners (ἱερογραμματευς) announces to Pharaoh that 'a certain one will be born at that time to the Israelites who will debase the political supremacy of the Egyptians.'[110] This retelling of the Moses story also includes a dream experienced by Moses' father Amram. Though it includes a message about the child's future greatness, the primary purpose of the dream is to encourage Amram, who then is emboldened and takes the proper measures to protect the child (i.e., placing the child in a basket upon the Nile).

Matthew's story of Jesus is also shaped by this cultural hypotext, and it is in this context that the dreams of Matthew 2 function. The birth of Jesus is accompanied by a star, whose significance is discerned by certain diviners (μάγοι) from the East. The diviners come to Jerusalem inquiring about 'the one born king of the Jews' (2.3) in order that they may offer the appropriate gestures of honor (προσκυνέω) to the new born king. The presence and inquiry of the diviners greatly disturbs (ταράσσω) Herod, the present king of the Jews. Under the pretext of also desiring to honor the new born king, Herod instructs the diviners to find the child and then to return and tell him the location of the child. Given the cultural hypotext, an ancient audience would be suspicious of Herod's intentions, a suspicion that is confirmed as the narrative unfolds. After finding and honoring the child, the diviners are 'warned in a dream not to return to Herod' (χρηματισθέντες κατ' ὄναρ μὴ ἀνακάμψαι πρὸς Ἡρῴδην; 2.12). A dream is also experienced by Joseph, the child's father, in which an angel of the Lord directs him to take the child and his mother to Egypt, 'for Herod is about to seek for the child in order to destroy it' (2.13). Herod's plan is thwarted by the obedient responses of both the diviners and Joseph. Though the child is protected, Herod's desperation leads him to have 'all the children' in Bethlehem destroyed (2.16-18). While in Egypt, another dream informs Joseph about Herod's death and directs him to bring the child and his mother back 'to the land of Israel' (2.19). But Herod's son, Archelaus, proves to be a threat as well; Joseph is again 'warned in a dream' (χρηματισθεὶς κατ' ὄναρ; 2.22) and relocates the child and his mother to the region of Galilee, where the child would be safe from Archelaus. Thus, the four dreams of Matthew 2 function in this cultural hypotext of the threat and rescue of a royal child. The dreams are

109   Josephus, *A.J.* 2.212-216.
110   Josephus, *A.J.* 2.205.

divine interventions that thwart the king's plan and protect the child from harm.[111]

Just as the dream of 1.18b-25 functions at two levels, so do the dreams of Matthew 2. Not only do the dreams of Matthew 2 function within the conventional plot of the threat and rescue of a royal child, the dreams also contribute to the specific narrative of Matthew. Two dreams initiate actions that fulfill prophecies: when Joseph is warned of Herod's plot and commanded to flee to Egypt in a dream (2.13), a situation arises that fulfills the prophecy, 'Out of Egypt I called my son' (2.15); and when Joseph fears the reign of Herod's son, Archelaus, a dream directs him to the region of Galilee, where he settles in the city of Nazareth (2.22-23). This circumstance fulfills the prophecy: 'he will be called a Nazaraean.' As in the case of 1.18b-25, the relationship of dreams and prophecies/oracles contributing to the fulfillment of one or the other would be a literary convention familiar to an ancient audience. In another instance, one dream accomplishes the statement announced in another dream; part of the angel's dream message in 2.13-15 is a command for Joseph to stay in Egypt 'until I tell you' (2.13). The dream of 2.19 fulfills this anticipation: while in Egypt the angel appears to Joseph in a dream informing him of Herod's death and directing him to return to his homeland. Thus, in addition to protecting the child from Herod, the dreams of Matthew 2 also prompt plot developments that are specific to Matthew's narrative and literary-theological interests.

There are other aspects of the dreams in Matthew 2 that are brought to light when read in the larger social and literary contexts of dreams in the Greco-Roman world, which the following will illustrate.

The Oneiric Tradition of the Magi. Matthew's inclusion of 'magi from the east' in his story of Jesus would invoke for an ancient audience images of diviners whose craft included various forms of divination, including astrology and dream interpretation.[112] This image would include an estimation of the magi along a spectrum from modest approval to suspicion, though for Matthew's audience a more negative and suspicious opinion is likely.[113] For example, it is the magi who provide the interpretation of the dream that prompts the Persian king Astyages to kill

---

111 For dreams that function as protection, see Josephus, *A.J.* 11.326-335; Plutarch, *Them.* 26.2-4; 30.1-3; Suetonius, *Aug.* 91; Chariton, *Chaer.* 2.9.1-6; Longus, *Daphn.* 2.26.5–28.1; *Acts Andr.* [M 3b-6; L 34] 22.

112 Cf. Herodotus, *Hist.* 1.107-108, 120; 7.37.2-4; Strabo, *Geogr.* 15.3.15; Pliny the Elder, *Nat.* 30.6.16-17; Plutarch, *Quaest. conv.* 4.5.2; *Alex.* 3.4; Cicero, *Div.* 1.23.47.

113 See Mark Allan Powell, 'The Magi as Wise Men: Re-examining a Basic Supposition,' *NTS* 46 (2000): 5-8, for a review of both Greco-Roman and Jewish sources and the conclusion that, 'Matthew's readers are expected to regard magi, generally, not as wise but as fools' (8).

the child Cyrus.[114] In the context of his *bios* of Alexander, Plutarch
recounts how the Persian king, Dareius, was misled by magi who interpret
his dream, 'for favor rather than according to the truth' (πρὸς χάριν ...
μᾶλλον ἢ κατὰ τὸ εἰκός).[115] Matthew, however, plays off these negative
perceptions in his narrative and subverts the audience's expectations.
Though the magi's arrival alerts Herod to the birth of a royal child (2.1-2),
it is the Jewish leaders who interpret the prophecy that sets in motion
Herod's plot to destroy the child (2.3-6). The magi are unknowingly
enlisted in Herod's plan, but on account of a dream they take no part in it
(2.12). This reception of a dream points to another unexpected turn in
Matthew's narrative. Magi are known for interpreting the dreams of
others, but in Matthew's narrative they themselves receive the divine
message. Thus, an ancient audience would bring to Matthew's narrative a
knowledge of the oneiric tradition of the magi, but Matthew subverts this
tradition to contrast the character of the Jewish leaders and, perhaps, to
emphasize the active role of God in the origin of Jesus.

The Dreams of Mt. 2.12 & 2.13-15: A Double-Dream Report? In Chapter
Three, the literary convention of a double-dream report was discussed and
several examples were offered.[116] The double-dream narrative involves
two characters who each have a dream. The two dreams can be identical,
similar or entirely different, but they are connected in some way to
'produce what may be called a "circumstance of mutuality" between the
two dreamers.'[117] Beyond a 'circumstance of mutuality' between the two
dreamers, a double-dream narrative can also produce a 'circumstance of
benefit' for someone beyond the two dreamers. For example, in
Chariton's *Chaereas and Callirhoe* the bandit Theron intends to throw
the heroine Callirhoe overboard. That night, however, he has dream:
'when he fell asleep he saw a dream (κοιμηθεὶς δὲ ἐνύπνιον εἶδε), a closed
door; so he decided to wait for that day.'[118] As a consequence, Theron
delays the drowning of Callirhoe one day, and during that day he becomes
acquainted with a certain Leonas, the administrator (διοικητής) of the
widower Dionysius' household. Sensing an opportunity, Theron proposes
the sale of Callirhoe to Leonas for Dionysius' services. Leonas responds,
'Some god has delivered you to me to be my benefactor. Why, you are

114   Herodotus, *Hist.* 1.107-108.
115   Plutarch, *Alex.* 18.4.
116   Josephus, *A.J.* 11.326-335; Dionysius of Halcarnassus, *Ant. rom.* 1.57.3-4; and Acts
9.10-19; 10.3-16. See also Livy, *Hist. Rome* 8.6.9-11; Tacitus, *Hist.* 4.43-84; Athenaeus, *Deiph.*
13.575; Achilles Tatius, *Leuc. Clit.* 4.1.4-8; Longus, *Daphn.* 1.7.1-3; Heliodorus, *Aeth.* 8.11.1-
9; Petronius, *Sat.* 104; Apuleius, *Metam.* 11.6; *Acts Thom.* 29–34; *Acts John* 18–19.
117   Hanson, 'Dreams and Visions,' 1414–1419.
118   Chariton, *Chaer.* 1.12.5.

setting out before me in reality what I dreamed about (ὠνειροπόλουν)!'[119] At one level, both Theron and Leonas benefit; Theron receives payment for Callirhoe, and Leonas provides a good service for his master by acquiring Callirhoe. Within the plot of the story, however, the dreams function primarily to protect Callirhoe from being killed; she ultimately benefits from the circumstance created by the dreams. Also, as indicated in Chapter Three, the double-vision reports of Acts 9 and 10 function in tandem to serve the greater purpose of the gospel and to motivate the events that will ultimately determine the decision of Gentile inclusion in Acts 15; the Gentiles are the ones who in the end benefit from the visions accorded to Paul, Ananias, Cornelius and Peter.

The dreams of Mt. 2.12 and 2.13-15 may represent this kind of literary elaboration of the dream report. After making obeisance and offering gifts to the child Jesus, the magi are 'warned in a dream not to return to Herod' (χρηματισθέντες κατ' ὄναρ μὴ ἀνακάμψαι πρὸς Ἡρῴδην; 2.12). Though the content or experience of the dream is not narrated, the function of the dream will become apparent: to protect the child from the plot of Herod. Immediately following the reference to the magi's dream and their response ('they departed to their [own] country by another way'), Matthew narrates a dream to Joseph in which the dream figure commands him to 'take the child and his mother and flee to Egypt ... for Herod is about to seek for the child in order to destroy it' (2.13). The two dreams are obviously connected by their similar function to foil the plot of Herod and to safeguard the child Jesus. In addition to their narrative proximity, the dreams are also connected by the second dream (2.13) making explicit what was not stated – but suspected – in the first dream (2.12): Herod's intentions.

Finally, the two dreams may represent a double-dream report based on the narrative presentation of the events occurring simultaneously. In their comments on the Mt. 2.13, Davies and Allison raise the question, 'does the present tense, φαίνεται (cf. 2.19 but contrast 1.20, which has the aorist), imply simultaneity, that is, does it make the angelic appearance concurrent with the magi's departure,'[120] which is repeated in 2.13 as a genitive absolute (ἀναχωρησάντων δὲ αὐτῶν)? In other words, the grammar of 2.13 may intend to communicate the concurrent action of the magi's response to their dream and Joseph's experience of his own dream.

The factor that works against reading the dreams of 2.12 and 2.13-15 as a double-dream narrative is the lack of interaction between the dreamers themselves. Double-dream reports usually entail the two dreamers having

---

119 Chariton, *Chaer.* 1.12.10.

120 Davies and Allison, *The Gospel According to Saint Matthew*, 1.259. Contra Nolland, *The Gospel of Matthew*, 121, who suggests that the historic present is simply a structural marker for beginning a new subsection.

some contact or dealings, even when the dreams create an advantage for a third party. The narrative of Matthew, however, never portrays Joseph and the magi interacting with one another. Notwithstanding this absence of interaction, the dreams of the magi and Joseph reveal several narrative associations and function together to produce a 'circumstance of benefit' for the child Jesus. An ancient audience may very well have read the two dreams as a literary unit.[121]

The Dream of Matthew 27.19

With the dream of Mt. 27.19, the reader is far beyond the narrative of Jesus' birth. This dream is referenced in the context of Jesus' trial before Pilate, which will quickly lead to his torture and crucifixion (27.27-54). Verse 29 reads as follows:

> While [Pilate] was sitting on the judgment seat, his wife sent [word] to him saying, '[Let there be] nothing between you and that innocent man (μηδὲν σοὶ καὶ τῷ δικαίῳ ἐκείνῳ), for today I have suffered many things in a dream on account of him' (πολλὰ γὰρ ἔπαθον σήμερον κατ' ὄναρ δι' αὐτόν).

Just as with the dreams in the infancy narrative, Matthew is unique among the canonical Gospels in relating this incident. Unlike the dreams of the infancy narrative, the meaning and nature of this dream presents the reader with some interpretative ambiguities.

For a reader of Matthew's narrative, the phrase κατ' ὄναρ in 27.19 would certainly evoke the dreams of Matthew 1–2, which functioned principally as divine mediums for the protection of Jesus: protection from illegitimacy (1.18b-25), protection from Herod (2.12, 13-14), and protection from Archelaus (2.22). Is the reader to understand the dream of Pilate's wife in a similar fashion, representing another intervention on God's part to protect Jesus? This understanding, however, would inevitably lead to a conclusion that the divine intervention failed, for Jesus is executed unjustly. Moreover, Matthew's narrative contains three predictions by Jesus himself that 'it is necessary' (δεῖ; 16.21) for him to go to Jerusalem, to suffer, to be killed and to be raised on the third day (16.21; 17.22-23; 20.18-19). The construction of these predictions indicates

---

121   Reading the dreams of Mt. 2.12 and 2.13 as a double-dream report calls into question the regular practice of scholars dividing Mt. 2 exactly between the two dreams (2.1-12 and 2.13-23). For example, see Davies and Allison, *The Gospel According to Saint Matthew*, 1.224 & 1.257; Luz, *Matthew 1–7*, 127 & 141; Margaret Davies, *Matthew*, 35 & 37; Keener, *Commentary on the Gospel of Matthew*, 97 & 106; Nolland, *The Gospel of Matthew*, 103 & 120; Hagner, *Matthew 1–13*, 22 & 32; Joachim Gnilka, *Das Matthäusevangelium* (2 vols.; 2d ed.; HTKNT 1; Freiburg: Herder, 1992), 1.33 & 1.47. Notable exceptions include Kingsbury, *Matthew as Story*, 48; and Daniel J. Harrington, *The Gospel of Matthew* (SP 1; Collegeville, Minn.: Liturgical Press, 1991), 40.

a divine necessity and intention in Jesus' suffering and death.[122] Thus, a reader would sense a different quality about the dream of Pilate's wife than the dreams of the infancy narrative.

The interpretative difficulty is compounded by the fact that the dream is not narrated nor is the meaning of the dream narrated. For example, though the dreams of 2.12 and 2.22 are not narrated, the meaning of the dreams is indicated: the magi are warned not to return to Herod and Joseph is warned to relocate in Galilee. Reference to the dream of Pilate's wife, however, is mentioned as part of her message to Pilate, which is given in direct discourse and contains her inference or interpretation of the dream. The reader is only given the perspective and understanding of Pilate's wife; there is no comment or explanation from an omniscient narrator as to the meaning or purpose of the dream. Questions then arise as to the nature or content of her dream, and what is being emphasized. Was it a visitant dream like those in the infancy narrative revealing Jesus' innocence and warning against a miscarriage of justice?[123] Does she suffer because of some concern that an innocent man might be found guilty? Or, is her suffering related, not to the execution of an innocent man, but to some sense of self-interest?[124] Does she suffer because the dream was a nightmare, portending some catastrophe or revealing the displeasure of the divine?[125] Warren Carter has the unusual interpretation that the message of Pilate's wife actually 'functions as encouragement to Pilate to remove Jesus quickly.' Again, he states, 'No wonder she has suffered much! . . . Her dream seems to have revealed Jesus being faithful to God's saving purposes, and that is clearly bad news for Rome and Pilate!'[126] These questions, and their respective interpreters, simply highlight the

---

122 The predictions in 17.22-23 and 20.18-19 have the future passive form of παραδίδωμι, which most likely reflects and is reminiscent of the divine necessity inherent in the δεῖ of 16.21. See Hagner, *Matthew 14–28*, 479, 507–508, 575.

123 Davies and Allison, *The Gospel According to Saint Matthew*, 3.587, actually use the term χρηματισμός (cf. 2.12, 22), which is not in the text, to describe that Pilate's wife was 'warned (by God) in a dream,' which 'makes her resemble Joseph and the magi, earlier characters to whom God sent reliable dreams.'

124 Nolland, *The Gospel of Matthew*, 1172, states, 'The statement is made in terms of the interests of Pilate and his wife and not in terms of the interests of Jesus. . . . Should we detect a rather narrow self-interest in her language of suffering here?' Cf. Gnilka, *Das Matthäusevangelium*, 2.456: 'Die Sorge der Frau ist auf ihren Mann gerichtet.'

125 Frenschkowski, 'Traum und Traumdeutung im Matthäusevangelium,' 34, states, 'Der Traum der Frau des Pilatus ist als Alptraum gedacht. . . . Alpträume von Herrschenden werden in der gesamten antiken Literatur häufig erzählt; meist künden sie das göttliche Mißfallen bzw. göttliche Strafe an. Manchmal wird in einem weisheitlichen Kontext auch allgemein der Alpträume als Signale der Unsicherheit und Hinfälligkeit unseres Lebens gedacht (Sir. 40,3/6); immer sind sie ein großes Übel von ominöser Bedeutung (Ps. Sal. 6,3).'

126 Warren Carter, *Pontius Pilate: Portraits of a Roman Governor* (Collegeville, Minn.: Liturgical Press, 2003), 94.

vague nature of what Pilate's wife actually experienced in her dream. Although the exact nature of the dream may remain ambiguous, the perspective of an ancient audience and the context of Matthew's narrative provide helpful clues as to dream's literary function.

Although the dream of Mt. 27.19 is not narrated, a feature of the conventional dream form is most apparent: the *reaction/response* of Pilate's wife. The *reaction* of Pilate's wife to the dream is described in terms of 'suffering' (πάσχω). This description would be understood in light of the common motif of fear or being troubled as a dreamer's reaction to a dream. This motif can be found in several of Herodotus' narrations of dreams: 'greatly dreaded the dream' (καταρρωδήσας τὸν ὄνειρον), 'he feared the vision' (διδοικὼς τὴν ὄψιν), 'fears for himself' (δείσας περὶ ἑωυτοῦ), and 'being greatly afraid' (περιδεὴς γενόμενος).[127] In Longus' novel, the bandit general Bryaxis 'was very disturbed' (τεθορυβημένος) by his dream.[128] When Josephus narrates the dream of the Adiabene king, Monobozus, the reaction is one of 'being troubled' (ταραχθείς).[129] It is more likely that an ancient audience would recall the well known dream of Caesar's wife Calpurnia,[130] which is recorded in several sources.[131] Plutarch recounts how on the night before his death, Caesar noticed his wife 'uttering indistinct words and inarticulate groans in her sleep; for it seemed that she was holding her murdered husband in her arms and wailing for him.'[132] The dream is narrated from the viewpoint of Caesar and lacks a full dream report, but the experience of anguish and agony are well expressed in the narration. Calpurnia's dream, of course, was just one ominous sign among others that portended Caesar's death.[133] The dream of Pilate's wife does not portend the death of Jesus, but it does function as one, even the first, of ominous signs connected with the death of Jesus. These signs include the darkness that occurs during the day (27.45), the splitting of the temple curtain (27.51) and the earthquake (27.52). Thus, the suffering of Pilate's wife that results

127   Herodotus, *Hist.* 1.34; 1.107; 3.30; and 7.14 respectively.
128   Longus, *Daphn.* 2.28.1.
129   Josephus, *A.J.* 20.19.
130   Frenschkowski, 'Traum und Traumdeutung im Matthäusevangelium,' 33; and Gnilka, *Das Matthäusevangelium*, 2.456, also note the possible connection with the dream of Caesar's wife.
131   Plutarch, *Caes.* 63.5-7; Suetonius, *Jul.* 81.3; Appian, *Bell. civ.* 2.115; Cassius Dio, *Hist. Rom.* 44.17.1.
132   Plutarch, *Caes.* 63.5.
133   Plutarch reports the dream of Caesar's wife Calpurnia as a part of his larger recounting of the 'wondrous signs and apparitions' (σημεῖα θαυμαστὰ καὶ φάσματα; 63.1). Suetonius reports a number of 'unmistakable signs' (*evidentibus prodigiis*; 81.1) that indicated the murder of Caesar.

from the dream would create for an ancient audience a sense of foreboding.

The dream of Pilate's wife, and the message to Pilate that it initiates, is also a creative literary feature that connects several narrative dimensions in Matthew's story of Jesus; and as will be demonstrated, this feature functions principally in terms of characterization. First, the message initiated by the dream contributes to a scene that parallels themes already introduced in the scene of Judas' remorse and death (27.1-10). Pilate's wife's message to her husband is literally, 'nothing to you and to that righteous one' (μηδὲν σοὶ καὶ τῷ δικαίῳ ἐκείνῳ, 27.19). John Nolland notes the similarity of this expression with the question of the demoniacs to Jesus in Mt. 8.29, 'what is there between us and you' (τί ἡμῖν καὶ σοί), which denotes 'that the parties have [nothing] in common.'[134] Closer in context and circumstance, however, is the response of the chief priests and elders to Judas, who attempts to return the thirty pieces of silver with the confession, 'I have sinned by handing over innocent blood' (ἥμαρτον παραδοὺς αἷμα ἀθῷον; 27.4). The chief priests and elders respond in language comparable to the message of Pilate's wife: 'What [is that] to us (τί πρὸς ἡμᾶς)? See [to it] yourself.' The sentiment is that the chief priests and elders refuse to involve themselves in Judas' remorse and change of mind (μεταμέλομαι; 27.3). Likewise, the message of Pilate's wife is a warning for her husband not to involve himself in the judgment of this innocent man (ὁ δίκαιος; 27.19). The judicial deliberation, though, is already in progress, and Pilate accepts the choice of the crowd: the release of Barabbas and the crucifixion of Jesus (27.20-23). Given the foreboding message with its divinatory origin (i.e., the dream), however, Pilate attempts to absolve himself of his involvement: 'he took water and washed his hands before the crowd saying, "I am innocent of the blood of this one; see [to it] yourselves"' (ἀθῷός εἰμι ἀπὸ τοῦ αἵματος τούτου· ὑμεῖς ὄψεσθε; 27.24).[135] Pilate and Judas are juxtaposed in Matthew 27 as characters who participate in the condemnation of the innocent Jesus, but both also try to absolve themselves of this guilt. Their speech, however, provides a contrast between the two characters. Judas confesses his guilt in betraying 'innocent blood' (αἷμα ἀθῷον). Pilate, on the other hand, announces himself 'innocent' (ἀθῷος). Moreover, Pilate repeats to the crowd the unsympathetic comment that the chief priests and elders made

---

134   Nolland, *The Gospel of Matthew*, 1172.

135   There is a textual variant of this passage, which is accepted by Davies and Allison, *The Gospel According to Saint Matthew* (3.590): 'the blood of this righteous one' (τοῦ δικαίου τούτου; ℵ L W *f*[1, 13] Maj it[c, ff1, g1, l, q] vg syr[h] cop[samss, bo]); cf. τούτου τοῦ δικαίου in A Δ 064 1230 *l*[1231] it[aur, f, h] syr[p,pal]. The reading τούτου, accepted by UBS4 and NA[27], is supported by B D Q it[a, b d, ff2, r1] syr[s].

to Judas: 'See [to it] yourselves' (ὑμεῖς ὄψεσθε, 27.24; cf. 27.4, σὺ ὄψῃ).[136] This negative portrayal of Pilate is underscored by his refusal to heed his wife's warning that was prompted by the dream. Given the divinatory nature of dreams in antiquity, an ancient audience would consider Pilate's unwillingness to heed the warning as impious and foolish.

The dream of Pilate's wife, and the message it prompts, creates another narrative comparison of characters and their actions. In 27.15-18, Pilate is honoring the Passover tradition of releasing a prisoner by presenting before the people the prisoner Barabbas and Jesus. It is during this proceeding that Pilate receives the message from his wife that he should have nothing to do with 'that innocent man, for I have suffered many things in a dream on account of him' (27.19). Immediately upon this statement, Matthew narrates that 'the chief priests and the elders persuaded the crowds that they should request Barabbas and have Jesus killed' (27.20). The narrative arrangement of these actions creates a scene in which Pilate's wife is conveying to her husband a divine gesture of Jesus' innocence, at the same time the Jewish leaders are convincing the crowds to call for Jesus' death. This contrast of characters and actions is highlighted by the fact that Pilate's wife is a Gentile who is made aware of Jesus' innocence and acts on his behalf based on a dream, while the Jewish leaders seek his death. The scene serves as a narrative parallel to the infancy narrative, in which the Gentile magi are made aware of Jesus' birth via a star and act on his behalf based on a dream. The Jewish leaders, however, are complicit with Herod in seeking to destroy the child Jesus. Thus, the dream of Pilate's wife is a literary feature of Matthew's Gospel that creates a narrative intertexture of contrasting characters, repetitive motifs and narrative parallels.

Summary

The dreams of Matthew's Gospel function at several levels. First, the dreams of Matthew are connected with literary-rhetorical motifs or practices with which an ancient audience would be familiar. The first dream of 1.18b-25 corresponds to the function of dreams in the encomiastic tradition of Greco-Roman literary-rhetorical practices. The birth of Jesus is a *topos* in which the dream signifies the future greatness and importance of Jesus. The dreams of Matthew 2 function within the cultural hypotext of the threat and rescue of a royal child. The dreams are the divine means by which the child Jesus is protected from the threat of Herod.

---

136   Cf. Ulrich Luz, *Matthew 21–28: A Commentary* (Hermeneia; Minneapolis: Augsburg Fortress, 2005), 500, who states, 'Matthew has put [Pilate] in a sequence with Judas and the chief priests. He remains like them, even though he tried to hide behind the masquerade of a biblical ritual and to avoid complicity in the guilt of Jesus' fate.'

Second, the Matthean dreams reflect certain literary praxes associated with the literary representation of dreams in Greco-Roman literature. Like other dream reports in Greco-Roman literature, the dream report of Mt. 1.18b-25 is a literary device that facilitates quotations and/or allusions of other texts; in this case, the quotation is from Isa. 14.7. This literary dimension of Matthew's dreams is further evidenced in reading the dreams of Mt. 2.12 and 2.13-15 as a double-dream report; that is a literary device that creates a 'circumstance of benefit' for the child Jesus and his mother.

Third, the Matthean dreams are connected with themes and motifs common in other literary dreams. The dreams of Matthew 1–2 are associated with and participate in the fulfillment of prophecy (1.22-23; 2.15, 23). Three out of the five prophecy fulfillments in Matthew 1–2 are linked to dreams; an ancient audience would find this connection customary. Furthermore, the Matthean dreams are part of the larger presence of divination present in Matthew 1–2, which includes the prophecies, the divinely appointed time (1.17), the divine conception (1.18, 20), and the star (2.2, 10). Paralleling this representation of divination at Jesus' birth, the dream of Pilate's wife introduces a certain ominous tone associated with Jesus' death and should be read along with the foreboding events of the daytime darkness, the destruction of the temple curtain and the earthquake. These functions and qualities of Matthew's dreams demonstrate the First Gospel's participation in the literary conventions and practices of its time.

The Matthean dreams also function within the Gospel's particular narrative presentation of Jesus. So, the dream of 1.18b-25 not only satisfies the general expectations of encomiastic rhetoric, it also resolves the abnormality of the genealogy, in which Joseph is not presented as the father of Jesus. The dream of Pilate's wife is particularly creative in how it contributes to characterization and the repetition of motifs. The dream prompts this Gentile woman to send a message to her husband conveying the innocence of Jesus; this is in contrast to the Jewish leaders who are goading the crowd to call for Jesus' death. The reader would be reminded of the Gentile magi who obey a dream and do not participate in the plot to kill the child Jesus, yet the Jewish leaders share culpability in Herod's plot. The dream and its message also prompt a situation in which Pilate, like Judas, tries to absolve himself of any responsibility in Jesus' death. But unlike Judas, Pilate comes off looking, and sounding, more like the chief priests and elders. In the end, Matthew's narrative of Jesus is literarily enhanced and rhetorically satisfying by his use of dreams.

The Significance of Dreams in Matthew's Portrait of Jesus

This chapter has focused on the literary character of the Matthean dreams, showing both their conventional nature and their specific narrative functions in Matthew's Gospel. It is important, however, to step back and consider how the Matthean dreams contribute to Matthew's overall portrait of Jesus. This consideration begins with a reminder that dreams in the Greco-Roman world constituted one form of divination.[137] Dreams were understood as a means by which the divine enters human affairs in order to bring about the divine will. Thus, an ancient audience would read the Matthean dreams as theological statements about the divine presence and purpose in the person of Jesus.

Matthew 1–2 is especially formative in providing this theological perspective for reading Matthew's story of Jesus. In addition to five dreams, these opening chapters also include the Holy Spirit (1.18, 20), prophecies (1.22; 2.5-6, 15, 17-18, 23) and the star (2.2, 9), creating a kaleidoscope of divine activity; and it is the dreams that unite this pattern. The progenitive activity of the Holy Spirit (1.8) is made known to Joseph in a dream (1.18), which also reveals how the circumstances of that activity fulfill prophecy (1.22-23). In addition to this prophecy, dreams also prompt actions that fulfill other prophecies (2.15, 23). The magi who perceive the significance of the star (2.2, 9) also receive a dream that warns against Herod's plot (2.12). The *genesis* of Jesus (1.1, 18) is nothing less than an act of God, and dreams play a central role in mediating this divine activity.

Dreams as theological acts serve two features of Matthew's portrait of Jesus: Jesus as ruler/king and Jesus as 'God with us.' The titles of Jesus in the Gospel of Matthew are helpful indicators in interpreting Matthew's portrait of Jesus, but the narrative presentation is what puts 'flesh and blood' on the skeletal titles.[138] The importance of Jesus as 'Christ' and 'Son of David' (1.1) with their royal, kingly connotations has been noted by scholars,[139] but it is the narrative of Matthew 1 – 2 and the perspective of the authorial audience that constructs a context in which this royal identity is first communicated. The encomiastic pattern of Matthew 1 and the cultural hypotext of the threat and rescue of a royal child in Matthew 2 are conventional literary-rhetorical patterns that are particularly familiar in texts that narrate the beginnings of great rulers and kings; and dreams are an essential element in both cases in Matthew's Gospel.

---

137   See Chapter Two.

138   See Leander E. Keck, 'Toward a Renewal of New Testament Theology,' *NTS* 32 (1986): 362–377, who seeks to correct biblical studies obsession with christological titles and argues for a more content-oriented approach to New Testament christology.

139   Cf. Warren Carter, *Matthew and Empire: Initial Explorations* (Harrisburg, Penn.: Trinity International Press, 2001), 57–74.

The divinatory nature of dreams invests the narrative of Jesus' beginning with a sense of divine destiny and providence, which in turn underscores Jesus' authority and power. This authority is most fully realized at the end of the Gospel when the resurrected Jesus declares, 'all authority (ἐξουσία) in heaven and upon the earth has been given to me' (28.18).

The divinatory nature of dreams also contributes to the identity of Jesus as 'God with us.' Not only is this knowledge of Jesus' identity revealed in a dream (1.18b-25), but it is also portrayed in the dreams of Matthew 2. The dreams of Matthew 2 are divine interventions that consistently protect the threatened child Jesus. As such, the dreams confirm for the reader the identity of Jesus as 'God with us' by first demonstrating that God is with Jesus. At the end of Matthew's Gospel, the dream of Pilate's wife becomes an important indication of God's presence with Jesus as he stands alone before Pilate, having been betrayed (26.48), deserted (26.56), and denied (26.69ff) by his disciples. As Pilate sits upon the judgment seat (27.19), the dream of Pilate's wife serves as Jesus' divine advocacy and signifies the divine judgment that Jesus is innocent/righteous (δικαίος; 27.19). Dreams are one means of how the unseen, yet very present, character of God is manifested in Matthew's portrait of Jesus as 'God with us.'

Thus, the significance of dreams in Matthew's portrait of Jesus is the way in which dreams as a literary convention contribute to the theological dimension of Matthew's christological narrative.

Conclusion

In this chapter, I have attempted to demonstrate that the dreams of Matthew's Gospel correspond to the form and function of dreams found in other Greco-Roman narratives. With their standard compositional pattern and familiar narrative functions, dreams represent a literary convention in Greco-Roman literature; and the Matthean dreams aptly exemplify this literary tradition. Given this conventional character of dreams, an ancient audience would have certain expectations about how dreams are narrated and how dreams contribute to the narrative itself. An ancient audience hearing Matthew's Gospel would certainly find that the dreams in his *bios* of Jesus meet those literary expectations. An ancient audience would also bring to the reading of Matthew's dreams a belief in the divinatory nature of dreams. This perspective contributes to a theological function of dreams in Matthew's portrait of Jesus.

Chapter Six

CONCLUSION

This volume has offered a reading of the dreams in the Gospel of Matthew as the authorial audience, seeking to understand how an ancient audience would 'make sense' of the Matthean dreams given the larger social and literary contexts of dreams in antiquity. This concluding chapter will summarize the research and results of this reading and will outline implications for further research.

Summary of Research and Results

Reading the Matthean dreams as the authorial audience requires an understanding of the social and literary character of dreams in the Greco-Roman world. Chapter Two described this social context of dreams by considering the social function of dreams and the intellectual tradition about the theory and classification of dreams. In the Greco-Roman world, dreams were understood as a form of divination and so were part of the religious experience and practice of that time. In addition to divinatory practices in general, dreams were also associated with magic and cultic activities – healings, incubation, the establishment of altars and cults, votive offerings and dream interpreters. Because not all dreams proved to be significant (divinatory), theories and classifications of dreams were developed by professional dream interpreters and philosophical traditions. In general, however, the belief and value associated with dreams were one of divine origin and purpose. Dreams were understood as a means by which the divine enters human affairs in order to bring about the divine will. Thus, an ancient audience would bring to the reading of Matthew's dreams a presupposition that dreams signify the activity and intervention of the divine. This perspective revealed a theological function of dreams in Matthew's portrait of Jesus.

In addition to describing the social function of dreams, this dissertation also explored the literary dimension of dreams (Chapters Three and Four), which proved to be most beneficial for my reading of the Matthean dreams (Chapter Five). I referred to this literary character of dreams as the 'script of dreams'; that is, there is a 'script' (form) to how one narrates or reports dreams in ancient literature; and at the same time dreams could be adapted, or 'scripted,' for a range of literary functions. Chapter Three analyzed dreams as a literary convention by noting: (1) the literary form of a dream report, (2) the rhetoric of dreams, and (3) the inventiveness of dreams. As a literary convention in ancient literature, dreams are narrated according to a predictable compositional pattern, which creates a level of expectation for readers. As Chapter Five demonstrated, the narration of dreams in the Gospel of Matthew corresponds to this literary form, fulfilling the expectations of Matthew's authorial audience. It was also argued that Robert Gnuse's thesis that Matthew's dreams are modeled upon the dream reports of Genesis is untenable. A comparison with dream reports in Greco-Roman literature reveals Matthew's utilization of this conventional literary form.

The literary character of dreams was also investigated by considering how dreams are treated in the Greco-Roman rhetorical tradition, especially the compositional exercises known as the *progymnasmata*. In several of these texts, dreams are presented as a motif used to develop the birth *topos* of an encomium. The encomium pattern is evident in Matthew 1 with a genealogy and an account of the circumstances surrounding Jesus' birth, which not only includes a dream but is presented in a dream report proper (Mt. 1.18b-25). Once again, an ancient audience would recognize the encomiastic pattern of Matthew 1 and would find the dream a familiar motif in developing this literary-rhetorical convention.

Dreams as a literary convention were also investigated by exploring the inventiveness of dreams. Ancient sources reveal that dreams were often invented for rhetorical and literary purposes. Although the historicity of reported dreams in ancient literature remains an open question, the inventiveness of dreams does highlight the creative and embellishing aspects of the *literary representation* of dreams. In investigating this creative dimension of literary dreams, two features in scripting dreams were present in Matthew's dreams. First, it was proposed that the dreams of Mt. 2.12 and 2.13-15 could be read as a double-dream report. The double-dream report is an amplification of the dream report in which two dreams create either a 'circumstance of mutuality' for the two dreamers or a 'circumstance of benefit' for a third party. The literary effect of the double-dream report is a more sophisticated and engaging literary device for plot development. The dreams of Mt. 2.12 and 2.13-15 most likely reflect this literary tradition. The other literary feature of dreams represented in the Matthean dreams is the presence of a literary quotation or allusion. Dream reports in Greco-Roman literature sometimes included quotations of or allusions to Homer; the Jewish tradition of reporting dreams includes quotations or allusion to the Jewish scriptures. In the first Matthean dream report (1.18b-25), Matthew quotes Isa. 7.14 as part of the dream message. Though the quotation is the scriptural prophecy fulfilled in the circumstances of Jesus' birth, it also corresponds to the custom of dream reports containing literary quotations.

The functions of the Matthean dreams also correspond to how dreams function in other Greco-Roman narratives. In terms of common motifs or themes associated with dreams, the Matthean dreams signify the future greatness of an individual at his birth, provide protection, occur in relation to a person's death and often occur in relation to prophecies or oracles. In terms of plot and character, the dreams of Matthew's Gospel occur at critical moments, prompt plot development, and contribute to characterization.

This research demonstrates Matthew's use of a conventional literary device and provides one illustration of how the First Gospel participates in the literary praxis of its time. Reading Matthew's dream in light of its Greco-Roman literary context also provides a more nuanced interpretation of these dreams that has not been observed by other interpreters.

Implications for Further Research

This study of dreams in the Gospel of Matthew has several implications for further research. First, an interpretation of Matthew 1–2 would be enhanced by giving more attention to the ancient practice of divination. Dreams represent only one form of divination in Matthew 1–2; there is also the presence of prophecy/oracles and astrology. This constellation of divinatory practices becomes even more intriguing when one considers that Hans-Josef Klauck's *The Religious Context of Early Christianity* includes a chapter on popular religion that discusses dreams, astrology and oracles.[1] Such an awareness of this *religious* context certainly intensifies the sense of divine activity in Matthew's account of Jesus' beginnings. In a similar vein, additional study is needed on the connection between the dream of Pilate's wife and the other omens surrounding the death of Jesus – daytime darkness, temple veil destroyed and earthquake. These other incidents are usually considered separately from the dream of Pilate's wife, but as in the case of other illustrious persons in antiquity, dreams were one omen among others that were associated with their deaths.

Second, this study of dreams has profited from an analysis of the Greco-Roman rhetorical tradition, particularly the *progymnasmata*. Though George A. Kennedy has stated that 'of the four Gospels,

---

1   Hans-Josef Klauck, *The Religious Context of Early Christianity: A Guide to Graeco-Roman Religions* (trans. Brian McNeil; Edinburgh: T & T Clark, 2000), ch. 3.

Matthew's makes the widest use of all aspects of rhetoric,'[2] the First Gospel has not received the kind of rhetorical analyses from which Markan and Lukan studies have benefited. For example, a study of the dream of Pilate's wife has revealed a comparison of characters – Judas, Pilate and the Jewish leaders. This comparison should be studied in light of the rhetorical technique of *synkrisis*, which is a comparison of persons, actions or things, either good or bad. Most often these comparisons are not of persons or actions that are different but that are similar, so that the noble or ignoble quality can be highlighted.[3]

Thirdly, our analysis of dreams in Matthew 1–2 revealed the Gospel of Matthew's participation in common literary conventions, which includes not only dreams but also the encomiastic pattern of Matthew 1 and the cultural hypotext of Matthew 2. These literary practices suggest a shaping of the traditions of Jesus that engages its Greco-Roman milieu. On a smaller scale, we see in the Gospel of Matthew the same kind of literary activity that characterized much of Judaism during the Hellenistic age. Erich Gruen describes this literary enterprise as follows:

> Jews engaged actively with the traditions of Hellas, adapting genres and transforming legends to articulate their own legacy in modes congenial to a Hellenistic setting. At the same time they recreated their past, retold stories in different shapes, and amplified the scriptural corpus itself through the medium of the Greek language and Greek literary forms. In a world where Hellenic culture held an ascendant position, Jews strained to develop their own cultural self-definition, one that would give them a place within the broader Mediterranean world and would also establish their distinctiveness.[4]

The Gospel of Matthew needs to be read within this larger context of the Mediterranean world and within the emerging self-definition of early Christianity,[5] giving attention to how literary strategies and conventions of the First Gospel negotiate these two contexts.[6] I hope that my research, which reveals Matthew's participation in the literary practices of his day,

---

2 George A. Kennedy, *New Testament Interpretation through Rhetorical Criticism* (Chapel Hill, N.C.: University of North Carolina Press, 1984), 101.

3 Cf. Theon, *Progym.* 10 (Kennedy, 52–55).

4 Erich S. Gruen, *Heritage and Hellenism: The Reinvention of Jewish Tradition* (Berkeley, Calif.: University of California Press, 1998), xv.

5 Attention to Christian self-definition in no way negates the more general Jewish identity of early Christianity. For a model of first-century Judaism that includes early Christianity as a form of Judaism, see Gabriele Boccaccini, *Middle Judaism: Jewish Thought, 300 B.C.E to 200 C.E.* (Minneapolis: Fortress Press, 1991), ch. 1.

6 We see the benefit of this kind of perspective with Warren Carter, *Matthew and Empire: Initial Explorations* (Harrisburg, Penn.; Trinity Press International, 2001); and John Riches and David C. Sim, eds., *The Gospel of Matthew in its Roman Imperial Context* (JSNTSup 276; London: T&T Clark International, 2005).

can in some small way contribute to this awareness and appreciation of how Matthew configures the traditions of Jesus in the context of the Greco-Roman world.

Appendix

THE MATTHEAN TRANSFIGURATION AS A DREAM-VISION REPORT[1]

The Gospel of Matthew is the only canonical Gospel that refers to the transfiguration event as a 'vision' (ὅραμα, 17.9). This description creates an understanding of the transfiguration as a visionary experience like dreams. It is important to recognize that in the Greco-Roman world dreams and visions represent very similar phenomena that occur either while one is asleep (dream) or awake (vision). This recognition is evidenced on a funerary altar of a priestess in Thyatira, which has the following inscription: 'If anyone wishes to learn the truth from me let him pray at this altar for what he wishes and he will obtain it through a vision of the night or day (διὰ ὁράματος νυκτὸς καὶ ἡμέρας).'[2] The professional dream interpreter Artemidorus states that 'there is no difference between apparitions that occur during the day and those that appear in a dream, for they predict the same thing.'[3] The resemblance of dreams and waking visions is also evidenced by their literary representation. Hence, in his discussion of the literary form of dreams and vision, John H. Hanson uses the term 'dream-vision' report for the narration of visionary experiences because of 'the difficulty, if not impossibility, of distinguishing [literarily] between a dream and a vision.'[4] Hanson continues:

> Experience, apparently, either confirms or underlies this fluidity, since the ancients themselves could not always distinguish between waking and sleeping in connection with the dream-vision phenomenon. In

---

1 Given the monograph's focus on the Matthean dreams, this appendix is an attempt to extrapolate its analyses and read the Matthean transfiguration as a dream-vision report. There are other narratives in the Gospel of Matthew that could also benefit from an analysis as a dream-vision report: baptism of Jesus (3.13-17), the resurrection appearances (28.8-10, 16-20), and perhaps Jesus' walking on water (14.22-27).

2 Cited in Gil H. Renberg, ' "Commanded By the Gods": An Epigraphical Study of Dreams and Visions in Greek and Roman Religious Life' (Ph.D. diss., Duke University, 2003), 258.

3 Artemidorus, *Onir.* 3.28 (White). Cf. also comments and references by F. T. van Straten, 'Daikrates' Dream: A Votive Relief from Kos, and Some Other Kat'onar Dedications,' *BaBesch* 51 (1976): 14.

4 John S. Hanson, 'Dreams and Visions in the Graeco-Roman World and Early Christianity,' *ANRW* 23.2: 1408.

short, as far as form or content is concerned, dreams and visions cannot readily be separated on the basis of the evidence. The rather rigid modern distinction between the terms dreams (a sleeping phenomenon) and vision (a waking phenomenon) is not paralleled in antiquity, because dreams and visions were narrated in the same manner.[5]

Thus, Matthew's designation ὅραμα for the transfiguration invites a consideration of the transfiguration in Matthew (17.1-9) as a dream-vision report.[6] The following is not a full interpretation of the Matthean transfiguration but seeks to be suggestive in how this literary unit contains the formal features of a vision narrative.

The Form of the Transfiguration

We begin by appropriating Bruce Chilton's assessment of the transfiguration as exhibiting both a generic structure and a narrative structure.[7] Chilton understands the transfiguration as a blending of a divine voice story (*bat qôl*) with the narrative elements of Exodus 24, Moses' experience on Mt. Sinai. The 'generic structure' is the heavenly voice story (*bat qôl*), while the 'narrative structure' is modeled upon Exodus 24. Although these two structures are inseparable in the narration of the transfiguration, it is helpful to consider these two components separately.

Instead of a *bat qôl* story,[8] the generic structure of the transfiguration is best understood according to Matthew's own designation: τὸ ὅραμα ('the vision'; 17.9). As such, we would expect it to conform to the dream-vision report found in the literature of the ancient Mediterranean world. Indeed, Matthew shows his familiarity with this literary form in narrating dreams

5   Hanson, 'Dreams and Visions,' 1408–1409. For other researchers who have reached the same conclusion, see E. R. Dodds, *The Greeks and the Irrational* (Berkeley: University of California Press, 1966), 116 and 125 n. 31; Klaus Burger, 'Visionsberichte Formgeschichtliche Bemerkungen über pagane hellenistische Texte und ihre frühchristlichen Analogien,' in *Studien und Texte zur Formgeschichte* (ed. K. Berger, F. Vouga, M. Wolter, and D. Zeller; TANZ 7; Tübingen: Frande, 1992), 177–225, esp. 204; Shaul Bar, *A Letter That Has Not Been Read: Dreams in the Hebrew Bible* (HUCM 25; trans. Lenn J. Schramm; Cincinnati: Hebrew Union College Press, 2001), 7.

6   Though he does not demonstrate it, Hanson also believes the transfiguration represents a dream-vision report: 'The transfiguration scene may also properly be understood as a dream-vision report' ('Dreams and Visions,' 1422).

7   Bruce D. Chilton, 'Transfiguration,' *ABD* 6.640-642.

8   Chilton's identification of the transfiguration as a *bat qôl* story is based on the rabbinic designation of a heavenly or divine voice that communicates the divine will. There is more to the transfiguration, however, than the voice from heaven; there is also the appearance of Moses and Elijah. Moreover, a Greco-Roman audience also is familiar with a divine voice (cf. Plutarch, *Ages.* 6.5; *Demetr.* 4.3; Herodotus, *Hist.* 6.105-106; Dionysius of Halicarnassus, *Ant. rom.* 1.55.3; Cicero, *Div.* 1.24; Aristides, *Orat.* 50.6; cited in Hanson, 'Dreams and Visions,' 1412 n. 70).

in the infancy narratives (1.18b-25; 2.13-15, 19-21). Thus, a reader of Matthew's Gospel is already predisposed to this literary convention. The formal features of the dream-vision narrative are as follows: (1) *scene-setting*, which may include (a) identification of the dreamer-visionary, (b) place, (c) time, and/or (d) mental state of the dreamer; (2) the *dream-vision proper*, which consists of three types: (a) visitant, (b) symbolic, or (c) auditory; (3) the *reaction* of the dreamer-visionary, which can include waking, amazement, perplexity, fear, etc.; and (4) the *response* of the dreamer-visionary, which is the action that the dreamer-visionary performs as a consequence of the dream-vision experience. A close reading of Matthew's transfiguration scene reveals the presence of these formal features.

The *scene-setting* (17.1) of the transfiguration narrative is provided by an identification of the recipients of the vision (Peter, James, and John)[9], the place ('a high mountain,' ὄρος ὑψηλόν), and the time ('after six days'). It is also noted that they were 'by themselves' (κατ᾽ ἰδίαν). In ancient times, mountains are known as being places of visions and other liminal experiences,[10] and these visionary experiences often take place in a time of seclusion. E. R. Dodds notes three particular instances of visions that 'all occurred in lonely mountainous places, Hesiod's on Helicon, Philippides' on the savage pass of Mount Parthenion, Pindar's during a thunderstorm in the mountains.'[11] References to a 'high mountain' and being 'by themselves' would shape the expectations of an ancient audience to read the subsequent narrative as a visionary account.

The *dream-vision proper* appears to be a combination of the symbolic vision and the auditory vision: the appearance of Moses and Elijah (17.3) and the voice from the cloud (17.5). Whereas a visitant dream-vision (the first type) is the appearance of a dream figure that speaks, the symbolic dream-vision simply describes a scene or set of occurrences. The scene may have divine or human figures, but they are not as direct or central as in the visitant dream-vision. The appearance of Moses and Elijah to the disciples[12] represents this type of dream-vision. Moses and Elijah do not speak to the disciples, and although they are said to converse with Jesus, their presence contributes symbolically to the dream-vision narrative.[13]

---

9 The scene will soon show that it is the disciples, not Jesus, who are the recipients of the vision.

10 K. C. Hanson, 'Transformed on the Mountain,' *Semeia* 67 (1994): 148–170.

11 Dodds, *The Greeks and the Irrational*, 117. For these instances, see respectively Hesiod, *Theog.* 22ff; Herodotus, *Hist.* 6.105; Aristodemus, *Schol. Pind. Pyth.* 3.79 (137).

12 It is a vision to the disciples: 'and behold, Moses and Elijah appeared to them speaking to [Jesus]' (καὶ ἰδοὺ ὤφθη αὐτοῖς Μωϋσῆς καὶ Ἠλίας συλλαλοῦντες μετ᾽ αὐτοῦ; 17.3).

13 It is interesting to note that in Greco-Roman literature it is common for dead people to appear in dreams or visions (Homer, *Il.* 23; Sophocles. *El.* 410–425; Euripides, *Hec.* 1–97;

The disciples, however, are spoken to by a voice from the cloud.[14] This phenomenon corresponds to the auditory dream-vision. Hanson describes this type of dream-vision as follows:

> This type of dream-vision narrative is often referred to as an audition, and is thus distinguished from a dream or vision. But like the terms theophany and angelophany, audition is a designation that is of dubious value. They all refer to what is called in this study a dream-vision proper. It may be suggested that whether a god or angel appears, whether words are only heard and no dream figure appears, when the elements of the full form are present, the narrative should be described as a dream-vision report. It should be noted that not only did no specific terminology for auditions develop, but that even where the dream-vision proper is only auditory visual terminology prevails.[15]

In terms of a combination of a symbolic vision and an auditory vision, Acts 10.9-16 and Exod. 3.1ff (LXX) provide parallels. In Acts 10, Peter has a symbolic vision of a large sheet coming down with all kinds of creatures upon it (10.11-12); he then hears a voice[16] telling him to 'kill and eat' (10.13). After Peter's refusal, the voice comes again saying, 'What God has cleansed you will not call profane' (10.15). In Exodus 3, Moses sees a vision: 'an angel of the Lord appeared to [Moses] (ὤφθη δὲ αὐτῷ ἄγγελος κυρίου) in the flame of a fire out of a bush, and he saw that the fire was burning but the bush was not being consumed' (3.2 [LXX]). After approaching the bush, Moses then hears the Lord call to him (3.4). It is interesting to note that both the visionary experiences of Acts 10 and Exodus 3 are referred to as a vision (ὅραμα; Acts 10.17; Exod. 3.3). In a similar way, the dream-vision proper of the transfiguration contains both the visual appearance of Moses and Elijah and an audible voice from the cloud.

The final feature of the dream-vision report is the *reaction/response* of the dreamer-visionary. In the transfiguration episode there is a *response* to the appearance of Moses and Elijah and a *reaction* to the voice from the

---

Orest. 618–20; *Alc.* 349–56; Aeschylus, *Eum.* 94–104; Ennus, *Annales* 32–48; Cicero, *Republ.* 6.14.14ff; Virgil, *Aen.* 1.341-72, 2.264-60, 5.705-39; [as cited in Flannery-Dailey, 'Standing at the Heads of Dreamers,' 373 n. 120]), but is it is quite uncommon in Jewish literature. The only other example in Jewish literature is 2 Macc. 15.12-16, where Nicanor dreams that the deceased high priest Onias (cf. 3.1-40) prays on behalf of Nicanor and his army; the prophet Jeremiah then appears to encourage Nicanor.

14   'And behold, there was a voice from the cloud (φωνὴ ἐκ τῆς νεφέλη) saying, "This one is my beloved son in whom I am well pleased; listen to him"' (17.5).

15   Hanson, 'Dreams and Visions,' 1411. Hanson lists the following examples of audio dream-visions: Cicero, *Div.* 1.24; Herodotus, *Hist.* 6.105-106; Plutarch, *Demetr.* 4.3; Josephus, *A.J.* 20.8-19; and Aristides, *Orat.* 50.6. See also *T. Job* 42.1 and Diogenes Laertius, *Vit. phil.* 1.115.2.

16   'And a voice came to him' (καὶ ἐγένετο φωνὴ πρὸς αὐτόν; 10.13).

cloud. In response to the appearance of Moses and Elijah conversing with the transfigured Jesus, Peter says to Jesus, 'Lord, it is good that we are here. If you wish, I will make three tents (σκηνάς) here, one for you and one for Moses and one for Elijah' (17.4). A comparison with Mark and Luke shows that Matthew omits the negative assessment of Peter's statement. Mark reads, 'for he did not know what he should say, for they were quite fearful' (9.6); while Luke states, 'not knowing what he was saying' (9.33). Several commentators seem to read Mark's and Luke's negative evaluation of Peter's statement into Matthew's account.[17] An ancient audience, however, might find Peter's response consistent with experiences of dreams or visions. In Chapter Two, it was noted that a number of inscriptions bear witness to the dedication of a temple or setting up an altar in response to a dream or vision.[18] In the Jewish tradition, this kind of response is best known from the patriarch Jacob. In Genesis 28.10-22, Jacob has a dream in which he sees a ladder that reaches to heaven and hears God speaking. He responds to the dream by setting up a sacred pillar (στήλη, 28.18 [LXX]), pouring oil on it, and making a vow. He calls the place Bethel, which becomes an important sanctuary in ancient Israel. Something similar takes place with Isaac and the sanctuary of Beer-sheba (Gen. 26.23-25). The Lord appears to Isaac at night and reiterates the promise first made to Abraham; Isaac responds by building an altar (θυσιαστήριον; 26.25 [LXX]). Peter's willingness to make 'tents' (σκηναί) in response to the vision may represent this kind of gesture.[19] The term σκηνή has cultic associations in both Jewish and Greco-Roman traditions.[20] Peter's response to the appearance of Moses and Elijah is an

---

17   John Nolland, *The Gospel of Matthew: A Commentary on the Greek Text* (NIGTC; Grand Rapids, Mich.: Eerdmans, 2005), 703, is illustrative: 'Peter's attempt to participate in what he sees is inappropriate.' See also, Donald A. Hagner, *Matthew 14–28* (WBC 33B; Dallas: Word, 1995), 493; W. D. Davies and Dale C. Allison, *The Gospel According to Saint Matthew* (3 vols.; ICC; Edinburgh: T & T Clark, 1997), 2.207; 700; David E. Garland, *Reading Matthew: A Literary and Theological Commentary* (Macon, Ga.: Smyth & Helwys Publishing, 2001), 184.

18   Cf. *IPergamon* VII.2, 295 (Renberg, Cat. No. 356); *IG* IV² 1, 561 (Renberg, Cat. No. 44); *IG* IV² 1, 513 (Renberg, Cat. No. 51); *IG* IV² 1, 386 (Renberg, Cat. No. 46); Hugo Hepding, 'Die Arbeiten zu Pergamon 1908–1909, II: Die Inschriften,' *AM* 35 (1910), 359–360 (Renberg, Cat. No. 352 and 353).

19   Though he reads Peter's statement negatively and does not draw on the material that I have provided, cf. Hagner, *Matthew 14–28*, 493: '[Peter] proposes to put up τρεῖς σκηνάς, lit. "three tents," probably little huts made of branches, not for providing the hospitality of overnight lodging or to prolong the experience but possibly as a kind of honorary gesture, a commemoration of this remarkable event, i.e., three shrines or holy places, similar to the OT tent shrine itself, which would symbolize the remarkable communion between heaven and earth represented by these three figures.'

20   BDAG 928a-b; and Liddell & Scott (9th ed.) 1608a.

eagerness to honor the revered figures of Israel's heritage and the now transfigured Jesus who speaks with them.

While Peter is making this proposal to Jesus,[21] a voice from the cloud interrupts with a statement and a command: 'This is my beloved son in whom I am well pleased; listen to him' (17.5). The *reaction* of the disciples is described as 'being greatly afraid' (ἐφοβήθησαν σφόδρα; 17.6). Fear is a common motif in the *reaction* feature of the dream-vision report,[22] and an ancient audience would find the disciples' fear a common reaction to the visionary experience.

Thus, the generic structure of the transfiguration is a dream-vision report, a literary convention with which an ancient audience would be familiar. The transfiguration account, however, also contains what Chilton calls a narrative structure. The narrative structure of the transfiguration is based on Exodus 24 and 34. A comparison of Matthew's transfiguration with Exodus 24 and 34 reveals that the story of the transfiguration is cast in the narrative imagery of the Sinai event. Consider the following associations: mountain (Exod. 24.12, 15; 34.3; Mt. 17.1); after six days (Exod. 24.16; Mt. 17.1); Aaron, Nadab, and Abihu join Moses just as Peter, James, and John join Jesus (Exod. 24.1, 9; Mt. 17.1); a cloud overshadows the mountain (Exod. 24.15; 34.5; Mt. 17.5); a voice speaks from the cloud (Exod. 24.15, 16; Mt. 17.5); and the radiance of Moses and Jesus (Exod. 34.29-30, 35; Mt. 17.2).[23]

This narrative recasting is perhaps best described by what Vernon Robbins calls 'reconfiguration.' As a part of his socio-rhetorical method, Robbins discusses the various ways in which texts may appropriate other texts. Robbins refers to reconfiguration as one way this appropriation takes place. He states:

> Reconfiguration is recounting a situation in a manner that makes the later event 'new' in relation to the previous event. Because the new event is similar to a previous event, the new event replaces or 'outshines' the previous event, making the previous event a 'foreshadowing' of the more recent one.[24]

Thus, as a reconfiguration of Exodus 24 and 34, the narrative structure of the transfiguration is presented as a new Sinai experience. The focus of

---

21   Note the genitive absolute, ἔτι αὐτοῦ λαλοῦντος (17.5).

22   Cf. Herodotus, *Hist.* 1.34 ('greatly dreaded the dream' [καταρρωδήσας τὸν ὄνειρον]); 1.107 ('he feared the vision' [διδοικὼς τὴν ὄψιν]); 3.30 ('fears for himself') [δείσας περὶ ἑωυτοῦ]); 7.14 ('being greatly afraid' [περιδεὴς γενόμενος]); and Josephus, *A.J.* 20.19 ('being troubled' [ταραχθείς]).

23   See Dale C. Allison, Jr., *The New Moses: A Matthean Typology* (Minneapolis: Fortress Press, 1993), 243–244; and Chilton, 'Transfiguration,' 6.640-641.

24   Vernon K. Robbins, *Exploring the Texture of Texts: A Guide to Socio-Rhetorical Interpretation* (Valley Forge, Penn.: Trinity Press International, 1996), 50.

this narrative structure, however, is not on the giving of the law and commandments but on the people, Moses and Jesus. As a matter of fact, references to the law and commandments (Exod. 24.12-14) are absent in the transfiguration; and as Chilton observes, Exodus 24 in its narrative context simply functions as a preamble to the succeeding divine instruction.[25] The effect of the reconfiguration of this introductory material, however, is the unambiguous presentation of the Mosaic character of Jesus, a presentation that Matthew accentuates in his redaction of Mark's transfiguration. These redactions include changing Mark's 'there appeared to them Elijah with Moses' (9.4) to 'Moses and Elijah appeared to them' (17.3), thus emphasizing the presence of Moses. Matthew adds, 'his face shone like the sun' (17.2), which is reminiscent of Exod. 24.29, 'the skin of his face shone.' This reference to shining like the sun seems to reflect a tradition about Moses' radiance, for Philo says that Moses' 'countenance shone like the light of the sun.'[26]

Having dealt separately with the generic structure and the narrative structure of the transfiguration, we can now see how the vision form of the transfiguration promotes the Moses typology of the narrative structure. The meaning of the appearance of Moses and Elijah is ambiguous, which is characteristic of symbolic dream-visions. Hanson states, 'Since the [symbolic] dream-vision proper generally requires interpretation, its meaning can initially seem to be less apparent.'[27] Davies and Allison list no less than twelve interpretations of what Moses and Elijah might represent.[28] The unambiguous voice from the cloud, however, may help in interpreting the presence of Moses and Elijah.

The voice from the cloud states, 'this is my beloved Son in whom I am well pleased; listen to him' (οὗτός ἐστιν ὁ υἱός μου ὁ ἀγαπητός, ἐν ᾧ εὐδόκησα· ἀκούετε αὐτοῦ; 17.5). There is both a statement and a command. The statement is identical to what the voice says at Jesus' baptism (3.17), and it echoes both Ps. 2.7, a royal psalm, and Isa. 42.1, the suffering servant of the Lord. The command, however, is also important, for auditory dream-visions 'most often constitute a command.'[29] It is a direct allusion to Deut. 18.15 (LXX) concerning the prophet like Moses: 'The Lord your God will raise up for you a prophet like me from your brothers; you shall listen to him' (αὐτοῦ ἀκούσεσθε). The Deuteronomy passage goes on to say of the prophet like Moses that, 'I will put the words in his mouth, and he will speak to them whatever I command him. And

25   Chilton, 'Transfiguration,' 6.641.

26   Philo, *Vit. Mos.* 2.70. For other sources giving witness to this tradition, see Allison, *The New Moses*, 244.

27   Hanson, 'Dreams and Visions,' 1412.

28   Davies and Allison, *The Gospel According to Saint Matthew*, 2.698.

29   Hanson, 'Dreams and Visions,' 1411.

whatever person does not listen to whatever that prophet speaks in my name, I will punish him' (18.18-19 [LXX]). The voice from the cloud signifies that Jesus fulfills the expectation of the prophet like Moses.[30] Thus, both the generic structure and the narrative structure of Matthew's transfiguration story present Jesus as a new Moses, particularly the fulfillment of the prophet like Moses.

The Mosaic connection of Jesus is further implied by the following pericope (17.9-13), which explicitly identifies the coming of Elijah with John the Baptist. The ministry of Jesus (the prophet like Moses), which is inaugurated by the ministry of John the Baptist (Elijah), is a fulfillment of the eschatological expectations associated with these two figures.[31] In this case, Matthew's appearance of 'Moses and Elijah'[32] also corroborates his statement that Jesus has not 'come to abolish the law or the prophets ... but to fulfill' (5.17).

In summary, the literary form of the transfiguration in Matthew's Gospel is a dream-vision report whose narrative content is a reconfiguration of Exodus 24 and 34. This narrative reconfiguration casts Jesus in a Moses typology. This Mosaic role of Jesus is furthered defined by the voice from the cloud, which denotes that Jesus fulfills the expectation of the prophet like Moses. This formal analysis of the transfiguration provides a basis for discerning the function of the transfiguration in Matthew's Gospel.

The Function of the Transfiguration

At the macro-level of Matthew's Gospel, the transfiguration contributes to the overall scheme of presenting Jesus as a new Moses.[33] The transfiguration, however, also functions within its immediate narrative context. Once again, the vision form provides a clue as to how the transfiguration functions in Matthew's Gospel. It is important to note that the disciples were the recipients of the transfiguration vision. As

---

30   A messianic expectation of the prophet like Moses is evident in the Dead Sea Scroll 4Q175, which is a *testimonia* of messianic proof-texts. Interestingly, the text represents an expectation of a messiah(s) as a prophet like Moses, a royal *scion* of David, and a high priest. The voice from the cloud indicates that Jesus is a royal son of David, a suffering servant, and a prophet like Moses.

31   Cf. Mal. 4.5-6.

32   Cf. Mark's description of the vision appearance as 'Elijah with Moses' (Ἠλίας σὺν Μωυσεῖ; 9.4).

33   This new Moses typology in the Gospel of Matthew has been reasonably demonstrated by Allison's *The New Moses: A Matthean Typology*.

recipients of the vision, the function of the transfiguration ought to be seen in relation to them.[34]

The immediate narrative context of the transfiguration begins with Peter's confession that Jesus is 'the Christ, the Son of the living God' (16.16). Jesus immediately gives his first prediction of his suffering, death and resurrection (16.21). Peter's response, however, is one of rebuke (16.22); his christological confession is at odds with Jesus' inevitable suffering. Then Jesus teaches about the true nature of discipleship, which entails taking up one's own cross and following his way of suffering (16.24-26). At this point, the transfiguration vision takes place (17.1-9). Except for the redactional changes in the transfiguration story, Matthew has followed Mark's narrative closely.

After the transfiguration, however, Matthew significantly changes his portrayal of the disciples in relation to Jesus' passion predictions. In response to the second passion prediction, Mark says that the disciples 'did not understand and were afraid to ask him' (9.32). Moreover, Mark immediately narrates how the disciples were arguing with one another about who was the greatest (9.33-34). Matthew, on the other hand, says that the disciples 'were greatly distressed' when Jesus predicted his passion for the second time (17.23). Moreover, Matthew does not narrate the argument among the disciples, but he has the disciples come to Jesus and ask, 'Who is the greatest in the kingdom of heaven?' (18.1). In Matthew's Gospel, the second passion prediction does not generate misunderstanding or fear; the disciples simply grieve at the prospect of Jesus' fate. Also, the disciples do not argue among themselves but ask Jesus for his teaching about greatness in the kingdom of heaven.

In Mark, the third passion prediction (10.32-34) is followed by James' and John's request to sit on the left and right of Jesus when he comes into his glory (10.35-37). In Matthew's Gospel, however, this request is not made by James and John but by their mother (20.20-21). Matthew has shifted the imperceptive request from the two disciples who experienced the transfiguration vision to their mother. Before the transfiguration in Matthew's Gospel, Jesus' prediction of suffering and death is met with rebuke; but after the transfiguration, the disciples 'listen to him' and are able to understand Jesus' suffering as part of his messianic mission. Thus, the transfiguration vision functions within Matthew's Gospel to enlighten and enable the disciples in their following Jesus.

In summary, the transfiguration vision confirms the disciples' understanding of Jesus as the Son of the living God ('this is my beloved Son'), but it also intimates that Jesus is the suffering servant ('in whom I am well pleased'). These disciples needed something outside themselves in order to

---

34   Cf. Nolland, *The Gospel of Matthew*, 699: 'Everything is focused on what the chosen disciples are privileged to witness.'

develop as disciples. The revelation that Jesus is the prophet like Moses whose words must be heard is a divine gift to the disciples. Without the vision, they would not be able to hear and understand Jesus' passion predictions, nor could they understand the nature of their own discipleship. Thus, the transfiguration functions as divine enablement. Such an understanding of Matthew's transfiguration corresponds to Charles Talbert's thesis that the Gospel of Matthew is not legalistic.[35] Talbert argues that Matthew's imperatives are controlled by Matthew's indicatives. Over against the Gospel of Mark, the transfiguration is an indicative event that develops the character of the disciples, a development that is explicitly perceived in relation to Jesus' passion predictions.

Conclusion

This appendix has set forth an interpretation of the transfiguration in the Gospel of Matthew based on Matthew's own designation: a vision (ὅραμα, 17.9). As a vision, the transfiguration corresponds to the conventional literary pattern of a dream-vision report, a literary form that would have been familiar to an ancient audience. The dream-vision report constitutes what Chilton calls the generic structure of the transfiguration account. The transfiguration also has a narrative structure, which is reconfiguration of Exodus 24 and 34. The transfiguration functions at two levels. First, it contributes to the Mosaic characterization of Jesus, particularly as 'the prophet like Moses.' Second, the transfiguration functions to develop the character of the disciples within Matthew's narrative. The transfiguration vision enlightens the three disciples in order that they may comprehend the suffering aspect of Jesus' mission.

---

35 Charles H. Talbert, *Reading the Sermon on the Mount: Character Formation and Ethical Decision Making in Matthew 5–7* (Columbia, S.C.: University of South Carolina Press, 2004; repr. Grand Rapids, Mich.: Baker Academic, 2006), 32–43.

BIBLIOGRAPHY

Primary Sources: Texts and Translations

Achilles Tatius. *Leucippe and Clitophon.* Translated by Ebbe Vilborg. Studia Graeca et Latina Gothoburgensia 15. Stockholm: Almqvist & Wiksell, 1962.

The Acts of Andrew and The Acts of Andrew and Matthias in the City of the Cannibals. Introduction and translation by Dennis R. MacDonald. Text and Translations 33. Christian Apocrypha 1. Atlanta, Ga.; Scholars Press, 1990.

Aeschylus. Translated by H. W. Smyth. 2 vols. Loeb Classical Library. Cambridge, Mass.: Harvard University Press, 1936–1938.

Aphthonii progymnasmata. Edited by H. Rabe. *Rhetores Graeci* 10. Leipzig: Teubner, 1926

Aristotle on Sleep and Dreams: A Text and Translation with Introduction, Notes and Glossary. Edited and translated by David Gallop. Warminster, England: Aris and Phillips, 1996.

Arrian. *Anabasis of Alexander.* Translated by E. Iliff Robson. 2 vols. Loeb Classical Library. Cambridge, Mass.: Harvard University Press, 1929.

Artemidorus. *Artemidori Daldiani, Onirocriticon Libri V.* Edited by Roger A. Pack. Leipzig: B. G. Teubner, 1963.

———. *The Interpretation of Dreams.* Translated by Robert J. White. Noyes Classical Studies. Park Ridge, New Jersey: Noyes Press, 1975.

Asclepius: Collection and Interpretation of the Testimonies. Edited by Emma J. Edelstein and Ludwig Edelstein with new introduction by Gary B. Ferngren. Baltimore: Johns Hopkins University Press, 1998.

Charitonis Aphrodisiensis de Chaerea et Callirhoe Amatoriarum Narrationum Libri Octo. Edited by W. E. Blake. Oxford: Clarendon Press, 1938.

Cicero. *De Divinatione.* Translated by William Armistead Falconer. Loeb Classical Library. Cambridge, Mass.: Harvard University Press, 1923.

The Dead Sea Scrolls Translated. By García Martínez Florentino and Wilfred G. E. Watson. Leiden: E. J. Brill, 1994.

Diodorus of Sicily. *The Library of History*. Translated by C. H. Oldfather et al. 12 vols. Loeb Classical Library. Cambridge, Mass.: Harvard University Press, 1933–1967.

Diogenes Laertius, *Lives of Eminent Philosophers*. Translated by R. D. Hicks. 2 vols. Loeb Classical Library. Cambridge, Mass.: Harvard University Press, 1938.

Dionysius of Halicarnassus. *Roman Antiquities*. Translated by Earnest Cary. 7 vols. Loeb Classical Library. Cambridge, Mass.: Harvard University Press, 1937–1950.

Euripides. Translated by A. S. Way. 4 vols. Loeb Classical Library. Cambridge, Mass.: Harvard University Press, 1935–1946.

Graecorum de re onirocritica scriptorum reliquiae. Edited by Darius Del Corno. Milano: Instituto Editoriale Cisalpino, 1969.

The Greek Magical Papyri in Translation, Including the Demotic Spells. 2d ed. Edited by Hans Dieter Betz. Chicago: The University of Chicago Press, 1992.

Hermogenis opera. Edited by H. Rabe. Leipzig: Teubner, 1913.

Herodotus. Translated by A. D. Godley. 4 vols. Loeb Classical Library. Cambridge, Mass.: Harvard University Press, 1920–1925.

Homer. *The Iliad*. Translated by A. T. Murray. 2 vols. Loeb Classical Library. Cambridge, Mass.: Harvard University Press, 1924.

——. *The Odyssey*. Translated by A. T. Murray. 2 vols. Loeb Classical Library. Cambridge, Mass.: Harvard University Press, 1915.

Ioannis Sardiani Commentarium in Aphthonii Progymnasmata. Edited by H. Rabe. Leipzig: Teubner, 1928.

Isocrates. Translated by G. Norlin et al. 3 vols. Loeb Classical Library. Cambridge, Mass.: Harvard University Press, 1929–1954.

Iustini Martyris Apologiae Pro Christianis. Edited by Miroslav Marcovich. Patristische Texte und Studien 38. Berlin: Walter de Gruyter, 1994.

Josephus. Translated by H. St. J. Thackeray et al. 10 vols. Loeb Classical Library. Cambridge, Mass.: Harvard University Press, 1926–1965.

Juvenal. Translated by G. G. Ramsay. Rev. ed. Loeb Classical Library. Cambridge, Mass.: Harvard University Press, 1979.

Kennedy, George A., ed. and trans. *Progymnasmata: Greek Textbooks of Prose Composition and Rhetoric*. Writings from the Greco-Roman World 10. Atlanta: Society of Biblical Literature, 2003.

Longus. *Daphnis and Chloe*. Translated by George Thornley and J. M. Maxwell. Loeb Classical Library. Cambridge, Mass.: Harvard University Press, 1962.

Macrobius. *Commentary on the Dream of Scipio*. Translated by William Harris Stahl. Records of Civilization, Sources and Studies 48. New York: Columbia University Press, 1952.

Menander Rhetor. Edited and Translated by D. A. Russell and N. G. Wilson. Oxford: Oxford University Press, 1981.

The Mishnah. Translated by Herbert Danby. London: Oxford University Press, 1933.

New Testament Apocrypha. Rev. ed. 2 vols. Edited by Wilhelm Schneemelcher. Louisville: Westminster John Knox, 1992.

Nicolai progymnasmata. Edited by J. Felten. *Rhetores Graeci* 11. Leipzig: Teubner, 1913.

The Old Testament Pseudepigrapha. Edited by James H. Charlesworth. 2 vols. New York: Doubleday, 1983.

Ovid. *Metamorphoses*. Translated by Frank Justus Miller. Loeb Classical Library. Cambridge, Mass.: Harvard University Press, 1916.

Papyri Graecae Magicae: Die griechischen Zauberpapyri. 2 vols. Edited and translated by Karl Preisendanz. Stuttgart: Teubner, 1973–1974.

Pausanias. *Description of Greece*. Translated by W. H. S. Jones and H. A. Ormerod. 4 vols. Loeb Classical Library. Cambridge, Mass.: Harvard University Press, 1926.

Philo. *On Dreams*. Translated by F. H. Colson. Vol. 5 *Philo*. Loeb Classical Library. Cambridge, Mass.: Harvard University Press, 1934.

Plato. *The Republic*. Translated by Paul Shorey. 2 vols. Loeb Classical Library. Cambridge, Mass.: Harvard University Press, 1935.

———. *The Timaeus of Plato*. Edited and translated R. D. Archer-Hind. 1888 Repr., Philosophy of Plato and Aristotle; New York: Arno Press, 1973.

Plutarch's Lives. Translated by Bernadotte Perrin. 11 vols. Loeb Classical Library. Cambridge, Mass.: Harvard University Press, 1919.

Quintillian. *Institutio Oratoria*. Translated by H. E. Butler. 4 vols. Loeb Classical Library. Cambridge, Mass.: Harvard University Press, 1920–1922.

Reardon, B. P., ed. *Collected Ancient Greek Novels*. Berkeley: University of California Press, 1989.

Renberg, Gil H. ' "Commanded By the Gods": An Epigraphical Study of Dreams and Visions in Greek and Roman Religious Life.' Ph.D. diss., Duke University, 2003.

Rhetores graeci. Edited by Leonhard von Spengel. 3 vols. Bibliotheca scriptorium graecorum et romanorum teubneriana; Lipsiae: B. G. Teubneri, 1853–1856.

Sepher Ha-Razim: The Book of the Mysteries. Translated by Michael A. Morgan. Society of Biblical Literature Texts and Translations 25. Chico, Calif.: Scholars Press, 1983.

Suetonius. Translated by J. C. Rolfe. 2 vols. Loeb Classical Library. Cambridge, Mass.: Harvard University Press, 1913.

Tertullian, *De Anima*. Edited with introduction and commentary by J. H. Waszink. Amsterdam: J. M. Meulenhoff, 1947.

Theophrastus. *Characters*. Translated by J. M. Edmonds. Loeb Classical Library. Cambridge, Mass.: Harvard University Press, 1929.

Xenophon. *Memorabilia*. Edited on the basis of the Breitenbach-Mücke edition by Josiah Renick Smith. Greek Texts and Commentaries Series. Salem, New Hampshire: AYER Company, 1985. Reprint of College Series of Greek Authors; Boston: Ginn, 1903.

——. *Memorabilia*. Translated and annotated by Amy L. Bonnette. Ithaca: Columbia University Press, 1994.

Xenophon. Translated by Carleton L. Brownson et al. 7 vols. Loeb Classical Library. Cambridge, Mass.: Harvard University Press, 1922.

Xenophon of Ephesus. *Xenophontis Ephesii Ephesiacorum libri V: de amoribus Anthiae et Abrocomae*. Translated by Antonios D. Papanikolaou. Bibliotheca scriptorum Graecorum et Romanorum Teubneriana. Leipzig: Teubner, 1973.

Secondary Sources

Aarde, Andries G van. 'The Evangelium Infantium, the Abandonment of Children, and the Infancy Narrative of Matthew 1 and 2 from a Social Science Perspective.' Pages 435–453 in *Society of Biblical Literature Seminar Papers* 31, 1992.

Alexander, Loveday C. A. 'New Testament Narrative and Ancient Epic.' Pages 165–182 in *Acts in Its Ancient Literary Context: A Classicist Looks at the Acts of the Apostles*. Library of New Testament Studies 289. London: T&T Clark International, 2005.

Alexander, Paul S. 'Incantations and Books of Magic.' Pages 342–79 in vol. 3 of *The History of the Jewish People in the Age of Jesus Christ* by Emil Schürer. Revised and edited by Geza Vermes, Fergus Millar, and Martin Goodman. 3 vols. Edinburgh: T&T Clark, 1986.

Allison, Dale C., Jr. *The New Moses: A Matthean Typology*. Minneapolis: Fortress Press, 1993.

Alter, Robert. *The Art of Biblical Narrative*. New York: Basic Books, 1981.

——. 'How Convention Helps Us Read: The Case of the Bible's Annunciation Type-Scene.' *Prooftexts: A Journal of Jewish Literary History* 3 (1983): 115–130.

Anderson, Janice Capel. *Matthew's Narrative Web: Over, and Over, and Over Again*. Journal for the Study of the New Testament: Supplement Series 91. Sheffield: JSOT Press, 1994.

Arend, Walter. *Die typischen Scenen bei Homer*. Berlin: Weidmann, 1933.

Athanassiadi, Polymnia. 'Dreams, Theurgy and Freelance Divination:

The Testimony of Iamblichus.' *The Journal of Roman Studies* 83 (1993): 115–130.

Aune, David E., ed. *The Gospel of Matthew in Current Study: Studies in Memory of William G. Thompson, S.J.* Grand Rapids: Eerdmans, 2001.

——. 'Magic in Early Christianity.' *ANRW* 23.1.1507-1557. Part 2, *Principat*, 23.1. Edited by Wolfgang Haase. New York: de Gruyter, 1980.

Bakker, Egbert J., Irene J. F. de Jong, and Hans van Wees, eds. *Brill's Companion to Herodotus*. Leiden: Brill, 2002.

Bar, Shaul. *A Letter That Has Not Been Read: Dreams in the Hebrew Bible*. Monographs of the Hebrew Union College 25. Translated by Lenn J. Schramm. Cincinnati: Hebrew Union College Press, 2001.

Barrow, R. H. *Plutarch and His Times*. Bloomington, Ind.: Indiana University Press, 1967.

Barton, S. C. and G. H. R. Horsley. 'A Hellenistic Cult Group and the New Testament Churches,' *Jahrbuch für Antike und Christentum* 24 (1981): 7–41.

Bartsch, Shadi. *Decoding the Ancient Novel: The Reader and the Role of Description in Heliodorus and Achilles Tatius*. Princeton: Princeton University Press, 1989.

Beard, Mary. 'Cicero and Divination: The Formation of a Latin Discourse.' *Journal of Roman Studies* 76 (1986): 33–46.

Behr, C. A. *Aelius Aristides and the Sacred Tales*. Amsterdam: A. M. Hakkert, 1968.

Berchman, Robert M. 'Arcana Mundi: Magic and Divination in the *De Somniis* of Philo of Alexandria.' Pages 115–54 in *Mediators of the Divine: Horizons of Prophecy, Divination, Dreams and Theurgy in Mediterranian Antiquity*. Edited by Robert M. Berchman. South Florida Studies in the History of Judaism 163. Atlanta: Scholars Press, 1998.

Berger, Klaus. 'Visionsberichte Formgeschichtliche Bemerkungen über pagane hellenistische Texte und ihre frühchristlichen Analogien.' Pages 177–225 in *Studien und Texte zur Formgeschichte*. Edited by K. Berger, F. Vouga, M. Wolter, and D. Zeller. Texte und Arbeiten zum neutestamentlichen Zeitalter 7. Tübingen: Frande, 1992.

Bernand, Étienne. *Inscriptions métriques de l'Égypte gréco-romaine: recherches sur la poésie épigrammatique des grecs en Égypte*. Annales littéraires de l'Université de Besançon 98. Paris: Belles lettres, 1969

Best, Thomas F. 'Transfiguration and Discipleship in Matthew.' Ph.D. diss., Graduate Theological Union, 1974.

Betz, Hans Dieter. 'Magic and Mystery in the Greek Magical Papyri.' Pages 244–259 in *Magika Hiera: Ancient Greek Magic and Religion*.

Edited by Christopher A. Faraone and Dirk Obbink. New York: Oxford University Press, 1991.

Blum, Claes. *Studies in the Dream-Book of Artemidorus*. Uppsala: Almqvist & Wiksells, 1939.

Boccaccini, Gabriele. *Middle Judaism: Jewish Thought, 300 B.C.E to 200 C.E.* Minneapolis: Fortress Press, 1991.

Boedeker, Deborah. 'Epic Heritage and Mythical Patterns in Herodotus.' Pages 97–116 in *Brill's Companion to Herodotus*. Edited by Egbert J. Bakker, Irene J. F. de Jong, and Hans van Wees. Leiden: Brill, 2002.

Bonnard, Pierre. *L'évangile selon Matthieu*. Commentaire du Nouveau Testament 1. Geneva: Labor et Fides, 2002.

Boobyer, G. H. 'St. Mark and the Transfiguration.' *Journal of Theological Studies* 41 (1940): 119–40.

Bourke, Myles M. 'Literary Genus of Matthew 1–2.' *Catholic Biblical Quarterly* 22 (1960): 160–175.

Bradley, Keith R. 'Suetonius (Gaius Suetonius Tranquillus).' Pages 1451–1452 in *Oxford Classical Dictionary*. Rev. 3d ed. Edited by S. Hornblower and A. Spawforth. Oxford: Oxford University Press, 2003.

Brayer, Menachem M. 'Psychosomatics, Hermetic Medicine, and Dream Interpretation in the Qumran Literature.' *Jewish Quarterly Review* 60 (1969): 112–127.

Brelich, Angelo. 'The Place of Dreams in the Religious World Concept of the Greeks.' Pages 293–301 in *The Dream and Human Societies*. Edited by G. E. von Grundebaum and Roger Caillois. Berkeley: University of California Press, 1966.

Brenk, Frederick E. 'The Dreams of Plutarch's Lives.' *Latomus* 34 (1975): 336–349.

——. 'An Imperial Heritage: The Religious Spirit of Plutarch of Chaironeia.' *ANRW* 36.1: 248–349. Part 2. *Principat*, 36.1. Edited by Wolfgang Haase. New York: de Gruyter, 1987.

Brown, Raymond E. *The Birth of the Messiah: A Commentary on the Infancy Narratives in the Gospels of Matthew and Luke*. New Updated Ed. Anchor Bible Reference Library. New York: Doubleday, 1993.

——. *The Death of the Messiah: A Commentary on the Passion Narratives in the Four Gospels*. 2 vols. Anchor Bible Reference Library. New York: Doubleday, 1994.

Bultmann, Rudolph. *The History of the Synoptic Problem*. Translated by John Marsh. New York: Harper & Row, Publishers, 1968.

Burridge, Richard A. *What Are the Gospels? A Comparison with Graeco-Roman Biography*. 2d Ed. Grand Rapids: Eerdmans, 2004.

Callaway, Phillip R. 'Exegetische Erwägungen zur Tempelrolle 29.7-10.' *Revue de Qumran* 12 (1985): 95–104.

Cantwell, L. 'The Parentage of Jesus: Mt 1.18-21.' *Novum Testamentum* 24 (1982): 304–315.

Carlston, C. E. 'Transfiguration and Resurrection.' *Journal of Biblical Literature* 80 (1961): 233–40.

Carter, Warren. *Matthew: Storyteller, Interpreter, Evangelist*. Peabody, Mass.: Hendrickson Publishers, 1996.

——. *Matthew and Empire: Initial Explorations*. Harrisburg, Pa.: Trinity Press International, 2001.

——. *Pontius Pilate: Portraits of a Roman Governor*. Collegeville, Minn.: Liturgical Press, 2003.

Cavalletti, S. 'I sogni di San Giuseppe.' *Bibbia e Oriente* 2 (1960): 149–51.

Chilton, Bruce D. 'The Transfiguration: Dominical Assurance and Apostolic Vision.' *New Testament Studies* 27 (1980): 115–24.

——. 'Transfiguration.' Pages 640–2 in vol. 6 of *Anchor Bible Dictionary*. Edited by David Noel Freedman. 6 vols. New York: Doubleday, 1992.

Choi, Mihwa. 'Christianity, Magic, and Difference: Name-Calling and Resistance between the Lines in *Contra Celsum*.' *Semeia* 79 (1997): 75–92.

Corno, Dario Del. 'Dreams and their Interpretation in Ancient Greece.' *Bulletin of the Institute of Classical Studies* 29 (1982): 55–62.

Crossan, Dominic M. 'Structure & Theology of Mt. 1.18-2.23.' *Cahiers de Joséphologie* 16 (1968): 1–17.

Crouch, James E. 'How Early Christians Viewed the Birth of Jesus.' *Bible Review* 7 (1991): 34–38.

Cryer, Frederick H. *Divination in Ancient Israel and its Near Eastern Environment: A Socio-Historical Investigation*. Journal for the Study of the Old Testament Supplemental Series 142. Sheffield: JSOT Press, 1994.

Daniel, Felix Harry. 'The Transfiguration: A Redaction Critical and Traditio-Historical Study.' Ph.D. diss., Vanderbilt University, 1976.

Danker, Frederick William, ed. *A Greek-English Lexicon of the New Testament and Early Christian Literature*. 3d ed. Chicago: The University of Chicago Press, 2000.

Davies, G. J. 'The Prefigurement of the Ascension in the Third Gospel.' *Journal of Theological Studies* 6 (1955): 229–33.

Davies, Margaret. *Matthew*. Sheffield: JSOT Press, 1993.

Davies, W. D. and Dale C. Allison. *A Critical and Exegetical Commentary on The Gospel According to Saint Matthew*. 3 vols. International Critical Commentary. Edinburgh: T & T Clark, 1988–1997.

Davis, Stephen J. *The Cult of Saint Thecla: A Tradition of Women's Piety in Late Antiquity*. The Oxford Early Christian Studies. Oxford: Oxford University Press, 2001.

Day, Michael James. 'The Function of Post-Pentecost Dream/Vision

Reports in Acts.' Ph.D. diss., The Southern Baptist Theological Seminary, 1994.

Derrett, J. Duncan M. 'Further Light on the Narratives of the Nativity.' *Novum Testamentum* 17 (1975): 81–108.

De Vries, Simon J. 'The Vision on the Mount: Moses, Elijah, and Jesus [Presidential Address].' Pages 1–25 in *Proceedings, Eastern Great Lakes Biblical Society* 3, 1983.

Dodd, C. H. 'The Appearances of the Risen Christ: An Essay in Form-Criticism of the Gospels.' Pages 9–35 in *Studies in the Gospels*. Edited by D. E. Nineham. Oxford: Blackwell, 1955.

Dodds, E. R. *The Greeks and the Irrational*. Berkeley: University of California Press, 1966.

Dodson, Derek S. 'Dreams, the Ancient Novels, and the Gospel of Matthew: An Intertextual Study.' *Perspectives in Religious Studies* 29 (2002): 39–52.

——. 'Philo's *De somniis* in the Context of Ancient Dream Theories and Classifications.' *Perspectives in Religious Studies* 30 (2003): 299–312.

Donaldson, T. L. *Jesus on the Mountain*. Sheffield: JSOT Press, 1985.

Duff, Timothy E. *Plutarch's Lives: Exploring Virtue and Vice*. Oxford: Oxford University Press, 1999.

Dulière, W. L. 'La révélation par songe dans l'Évangile de Matthieu.' *Annuaire de l'Institut de philologie et d'histoire orientales et slaves* 13 (1953): 665–69.

Edwards, Mark W. 'Homer and Oral Tradition: the Type-Scene,' *Oral Tradition* 7 (1992): 283–330.

Ehrlich, Ernst L. 'Der Traum in Talmud.' *Zeitschrift für die Neutestamentliche Wissenschaft und die Kunde der älteren Kirche* 47 (1956): 133–45.

Eitrem, Samson. 'Dreams and Divination in Magical Ritual.' Pages 175–87 in *Magika Hiera: Ancient Greek Magic and Religion*. Edited by Christopher A. Faraone and Dirk Obbink. New York: Oxford University Press, 1991.

Evans, Craig A. 'The Genesis Apocryphon and the Rewritten Bible.' *Revue de Qumran* 13 (1988): 153–165.

Fehling, Detlev. *Herodotus and his 'Sources': Citation, Invention, and Narrative Art*. Translated by J. G. Howie. Leeds, Great Britain: Francis Cairns, 1990.

Fenton, J. C. 'Matthew and the Divinity of Jesus: Three Questions Concerning Matthew 1.20-23.' Pages 79–82 in *Papers on the Gospels*. Edited by E. A. Livingstone. Vol. 2 of *Studia Biblica 1978: Sixth International Congress on Biblical Studies*. Journal for the Study of the New Testament Supplement Series 2. Sheffield, JSOT Press, 1980.

Ferguson, Everett. *Backgrounds of Early Christianity*. 3d ed. Grand Rapids: Eerdmans, 2003.

Feldman, Louis H. 'Josephus.' Pages 981–998 in vol. 3 of *Anchor Bible Dictionary*. Edited by D. N. Freedman. 6 vols. New York: Doubleday, 1992.

Festugière, André-Jean. *Personal Religion Among the Greeks*. Berkeley: University of California Press, 1954.

Fisher, Nick. 'Popular Morality in Herodotus.' Pages 199–224 in *Brill's Companion to Herodotus*. Edited by Egbert J. Bakker, Irene J. F. de Jong, and Hans van Wees. Leiden: Brill, 2002.

Fisk, Bruce N. 'Genesis Apocryphon (1QapGen).' Pages 398–401 in *Dictionary of New Testament Background*. Edited by Craig A. Evans and Stanley E. Porter. Downers Grove, Ill.: InterVarsity, 2000.

Fitzmyer, Joseph A. *The Genesis Apocryphon of Qumran Cave I: A Commentary*. 2d rev. ed. Biblica et orientalia 18a. Rome: Biblical Institute Press, 1971.

Flannery-Dailey, Frances Lynn. 'Standing at the Head of Dreamers: A Study of Dreams in Antiquity.' Ph.D. diss., The University of Iowa, 2000.

Fowler, Robert L. 'Greek Magic, Greek Religion.' Pages 317–343 in *Oxford Readings in Greek Religion*. Edited by Richard Buxton. New York: Oxford University Press, 2000.

Fox, Robin Lane. *Pagans and Christians*. New York: Alfred A. Knopf, 1989.

France, Richard T. 'Herod and the Children of Bethlehem.' *Novum Testamentum* 21 (1979): 98–120.

———. *Matthew: Evangelist & Teacher*. New Testament Profiles. Downers Grove, Ill.: InterVarsity Press, 1989.

Frenschkowski, Marco. 'Traum und Traumdeutung im Matthäusevangelium: Einige Beobachtungen.' *Jahrbuch für Antike und Christentum* 41 (1998): 5–47.

Frisch, Peter. *Die Träume bei Herodot*. Beiträge zur klassischen Philologie 27. Meisenheim am Glan: Verlag Anton Hain, 1968.

Gallop, David. 'Dreaming and Waking in Plato.' Pages 187–201 in *Essays in Ancient Greek Philosophy*. Edited by John P. Anton with George L. Kustas. Albany: State University of New York Press, 1971.

Garland, David E. *Reading Matthew: A Literary and Theological Commentary on the First Gospel*. New York: Crossroad, 1993.

Geer, R. 'On the Theories of Dream Interpretation in Artemidorus.' *Classical Journal* 22 (1967): 663–70.

Gerber, Wolfgang. 'Die Metamorphose Jesu.' *Theologische Zeitschrift* 23 (1967): 385–395.

Gevirtz, Marianne Luijken. 'Abram's Dream in the Genesis Apocryphon: Its Motifs and Their Function.' *Maarav* 8 (1992): 229–243.

Gnilka, Joachim. *Das Matthäusevangelium*. 2 vols. 2d ed. Herders theologischer Kommentar zum Neuen Testament 1. Freiburg: Herder, 1992.

Gnuse, Robert. 'Dream Genre in the Matthean Infancy Narratives.' *Novum Testamentum* 32 (1990): 97–120.

———. *Dreams and the Dream Reports in the Writings of Josephus: A Traditio-Historical Analysis.* Arbeiten zur Geschichte des antiken Judentums und des Urchristentums 36. Leiden: E. J. Brill, 1996.

———. *The Dream Theophany of Samuel: Its Structure in Relation to Ancient Near Eastern Dreams and Its Theological Significance.* Lanham, Md.: University Press of America, 1984.

Gollnick, James. *The Religious Dreamworld of Apuleius' Metamorphoses: Recovering a Forgotten Hermeutic.* EdSR 25. Waterloo, Ont.: Wilfrid Laurier University Press, 1999.

Goppelt, Leonhard. *Typos: The Typological Interpretation of the Old Testament in the New.* Translated by Donald H. Madvig. Grand Rapids: Eerdmans, 1982.

Gould, John P. A. 'Herodotus.' Pages 696–698 in *Oxford Classical Dictionary.* Rev. 3d ed. Edited by S. Hornblower and A. Spawforth. Oxford: Oxford University Press, 2003.

Graf, Fritz. 'Inkubation.' Pages 1006–7 in vol. 5 of *Der neue Pauly: Enzyklopädie der Antike.* Edited by H. Cancik and H. Schneider. Stuttgart: J. B. Metzler, 1998.

Gruen, Erich S. *Heritage and Hellenism: The Reinvention of Jewish Tradition.* Berkeley: University of California Press, 1998.

Gundry, Robert H. *Matthew: A Commentary on His Handbook for a Mixed Church under Persecution.* 2d ed. Grand Rapids, Mich.: Eerdmans, 1994.

Gunkel, Hermann. 'The Interpretation of the New Testament.' *The Monist* 13 (1903): 398–455.

Gunn, David M. 'Thematic Composition and Homeric Authorship.' *Harvard Studies in Classical Philology* 75 (1971): 1–31.

Hagner, Donald A. *Matthew.* Word Biblical Commentary 33A–33B. Dallas: Word, 1993–1995.

Hamilton, J. R. *Plutarch: Alexander.* 2d ed. London: Bristol Classical Press, 1999.

Hansen, Hanne Lavér. '"The Truth without Nonsense": Remarks on Artemidorus' *Interpretation of Dreams.*' Pages 57–66 in *Divination and Portents in the Roman World.* Odense University Classical Studies 21. Edited by Robin Lorsch Wildfang and Jacob Isager. Odense University Press, 2000.

Hanson, John S. 'Dreams and Visions in the Graeco-Roman World and Early Christianity.' *ANRW* 23.2.1395-1427. *Principat,* 23.2. Edited by Wolfgang Haase. New York: de Gruyter, 1980.

Hanson, K. C. 'Transformed on the Mountain.' *Semeia* 67 (1994): 147–170.

Harrington, Daniel J. 'Birth Narratives in Pseudo-Philo's Biblical Antiquities and the Gospels.' Pages 316–325 in *To Touch the Text: Biblical and Related Studies in Honor of Joseph A. Fitzmyer, S.J.* Edited by Joseph A. Fitzmyer, Maurya P. Horgan, and Paul J. Kobelski. New York: Crossroad, 1989.

——. *The Gospel of Matthew.* Sacra Pagina 1. Collegeville, Minn.: Liturgical Press, 1991.

Harris, Monford. *Studies in Jewish Dream Interpretation.* Northvale, New Jersey: Jason Aronson Inc., 1994.

Harrison, Thomas. *Divinity and History: The Religion of Herodotus.* Oxford Classical Monograph. New York: Clarendon Press, 2000.

Heil, John Paul. *The Transfiguration of Jesus: Narrative Meaning and Function of Mark 9.2-8, Matt 17.1-6, and Luke 9.28-36.* Analecta biblica 144. Roma: Editrice Pontificio Istituto Biblico, 2000.

Heininger, Bernhard. *Paulus als Visionär: Eine religionsgeschichtliche Studie.* Herders biblische Studien 9. Freiburg: Herder, 1996.

Hepding, Hugo. 'Die Arbeiten zu Pergamon 1908–1909, II: Die Inschriften.' *Annales du Midi* 35 (1910), 359–360.

Hock, Ronald F., J. Bradley Chance, and Judith Perkins, eds. *Ancient Fiction and Early Christian Narrative.* Society of Biblical Literature Symposium Series 6. Atlanta: Scholars Press, 1998.

Hock, Ronald F. 'Why New Testament Scholars Should Read Ancient Novels.' Pages 121–38 in *Ancient Fiction and Early Christian Narrative.* Edited by Ronald F. Hock, J. Bradley Chance, and Judith Perkins. Society of Biblical Literature Symposium Series 6. Atlanta: Scholars Press, 1998.

——. 'Why We Should Read the Commentaries on Aphthonius' Progymnasmata.' Paper presented at the annual meeting of the Society of Biblical Literature. Philadelphia, Pa., 19 November 2005.

Hooker, Morna D. '"What Doest Thou Here, Elijah?" A Look at St. Mark's Account of the Transfiguration.' Pages 59–70 in *The Glory of Christ in the New Testament: Studies in Christology.* Edited by L. D. Hurst and N. T. Wright. Oxford: Clarendon Press, 1987.

Hopfner, Theodor. *Griechisch-ägyptischer Offenbarungszauber.* 2 vols. 1921. Repr., Amsterdam: A. M. Hakkert, 1974.

Horsley, G. H. R. *New Documents Illustrating Early Christianity: A Review of the Greek Inscriptions and Papyri published in 1976.* North Ryde, Australia: Macquarie University, 1981.

Horst, P. W. van der. 'Moses' Throne Vision in Ezekiel the Dramatist.' *Journal of Jewish Studies* 34 (1983): 21–29.

Husser, Jean-Marie. *Dreams and Dream Narratives in the Biblical World.*

The Biblical Seminar 63. Translated by Jill M. Munro. Sheffield: Sheffield Academic Press, 1999.

Immerwahr, Henry R. 'Historical Action in Herodotus.' *Transactions and Proceedings of the American Philological Association* 85 (1954): 16–54.

Jacobson, Howard. *A Commentary on Pseudo-Philo's Liber antiquitatum biblicarum.* 2 vols. Arbeiten zur Geschichte des antiken Judentums und des Urchristentums 31. Leiden: E.J. Brill, 1996.

Janowitz, Naomi. *Magic in the Roman World: Pagans, Jews and Christians.* Religion in the First Christian Centuries. London: Routledge, 2001.

Jauss, Hans Robert. *Toward an Aesthetic of Reception.* Translated by T. Bahti. Vol. 2 of *Theory and History of Literature.* Edited by W. Godzich and J. Schulte-Sasse. Minneapolis: University of Minnesota Press, 1982.

Jeffers, Ann. *Magic and Divination in Ancient Palestine and Syria.* Studies in the History and Culture of the Ancient Near East 8. Leiden: E. J. Brill, 1996.

Kany-Turpin, José and Pierre Pellegrin. 'Cicero and the Aristotelian Theory of Divination by Dreams.' Pages 220–245 in *Cicero's Knowledge of the Peripatos.* Rutgers University Studies in Classical Humanities 4. Edited by William W. Fortenbaugh and Peter Steinmetz. New Brunswick, New Jersey: Transaction Publishers, 1989.

Keck, Leander E. 'Toward a Renewal of New Testament Theology.' *New Testament Studies* 32 (1986): 362–377.

Kee, Howard Clark. 'The Transfiguration in Mark: Epiphany or Apocalyptic Vision?' Pages 135–52 in *Understanding the Sacred Text: Essays in Honor of Morton S. Enslin on the Hebrew Bible and Christian Beginnings.* Edited by John Reumann. Valley Forge, Pa.: Judson Press, 1972.

Keener, Craig S. *Commentary on the Gospel of Matthew.* Grand Rapids, Mich.: Eerdmans, 1999.

Kennedy, George A. *New Testament Interpretation through Rhetorical Criticism.* Chapel Hill, N.C.: University of North Carolina Press, 1984.

Kenny, A. 'The Transfiguration and the Agony in the Garden.' *Catholic Biblical Quarterly* 19 (1957): 444–52.

Kessels, A. H. M. 'Ancient Systems of Dream-Classification.' *Mnemosyne* 22 (1969): 389–424.

——. 'Dreams in Apollonius' *Argonautica.*' Pages 155–173 in *Actus: Studies in Honour of H. L. W. Nelson.* Edited by H. L. W. Nelson, J. den Boeft, and A. H. M. Kessels. Utrecht: Instituut vor Klassieke Talen, 1982.

——. *Studies on the Dream in Greek Literature*. Utrech: HES Publishers, 1978.

Kingsbury, Jack Dean. *Matthew as Story*. 2d ed., rev. and enl. Philadelphia: Fortress Press, 1988.

Kittel, G., and G. Friedrich, eds. *Theological Dictionary of the New Testament*. Translated by G. W. Bromiley. 10 vols. Grand Rapids: Eerdmans, 1964–1976.

Klauck, Hans-Josef. *The Religious Context of Early Christianity: A Guide to Graeco-Roman Religions*. Studies of the New Testament and Its World. Translated by Brian McNeil. Edinburgh: T & T Clark, 2000.

Klijn, A. F. J. *The Acts of Thomas: Introduction, Text, and Commentary*. 2d rev. ed. Supplements to Novum Testamentum 108. Leiden: Brill, 2003.

Kupp, David D. *Matthew's Emmanuel: Divine Presence and God's People in the First Gospel*. Society for New Testament Studies Monograph Series 90. Cambridge: Cambridge University Press, 1996.

Lake, Keely Kristen. 'Vergil's Dreams and Their Literary Predecessors.' Ph.D. diss., University of Iowa, 2001.

Lampe, G. W. H. and K. J. Woollcombe. *Essays on Typology*. Studies in Biblical Theology 22. London: SCM Press, 1957.

Lange, Armin. 'The Essene Position on Magic and Divination.' Pages 377–435 in *Legal Texts and Legal Issues: Proceedings of the Second Meeting of the International Organization for Qumran Studies, Cambridge, 1995*. Studies on the Texts of the Desert of Judah 23. Edited by Moshe Bernstein, Florentino García Martínez, and John Kampen. Leiden: Brill, 1997.

Latacz, Joachim. 'Funktionen des Traums in der antiken Literatur.' Pages 10–31 in *Traum und Träumen: Traumanalysen in Wissenschaft, Religion und Kunst*. Edited by Therese Wagner-Simon and Gaetano Benedetti. Göttingen: Vandenhoeck & Ruprecht, 1984.

Leuci, Victor Alexander. 'Dream-Technical Terms in the Greco-Roman World.' Ph.D. diss., University of Missouri-Columbia, 1993.

Lewis, Naphtali. *The Interpretation of Dreams and Portents*. Toronto: Hakkert, 1976.

Lewis, R. G. 'Suetonius' "Caesares" and Their Literary Antecedents.' *ANRW* 33.5.3623-3674. Part 2, *Principat*, 33.5. Edited by Wolfgang Haase. New York: de Gruyter, 1991.

Lieberman, Saul. *Hellenism in Jewish Palestine*. Texts and Studies of the Jewish Theological Seminary of America 18. New York: The Jewish Theological Seminary of America, 1950.

Lieshout, R. G. A. van. *Greeks on Dreams*. Utrecht: HES Publishers, 1980.

Lipton, Diana. *Revisions of the Night: Politics and Promises in the Patriarchal Dreams of Genesis*. Journal for the Study of the Old

Testament Supplemental Series 288. Sheffield: Sheffield Academic Press, 1999.

Luz, Ulrich. *Matthew 1–7: A Commentary*. Translated by W. C. Linss. Minneapolis: Augsburg Fortress, 1989.

——. *Matthew 8–20: A Commentary*. Hermeneia. Translated by James E. Crouch. Minneapolis: Fortress Press, 2001.

——. *Matthew 21–28: A Commentary*. Hermeneia. Translated by James E. Crouch. Minneapolis: Fortress Press, 2005.

MacAlister, Suzanne. *Dreams and Suicides: The Greek Novel from Antiquity to the Byzantine Empire*. New York: Routledge, 1996.

MacDonald, Ronald R. *Does the New Testament Imitate Homer?: Four Cases from the Acts of the Apostles*. New Haven: Yale University Press, 2003.

——. *The Homeric Epics and the Gospel of Mark*. New Haven: Yale University Press, 2000.

——. ed. *Mimesis and Intertextuality in Antiquity and Christianity*. Studies in Antiquity and Christianity. Harrisburg, Pa.: Trinity Press International, 2001.

MacMullen, Ramsay. *Paganism in the Roman Empire*. New Haven: Yale University Press, 1981.

Martin, Luther H. 'Artemidorus: Dream Theory in Late Antiquity.' *The Second Century* 8 (1991): 97–108.

——. *Hellenistic Religions: An Introduction*. Oxford: Oxford University Press, 1987.

Mason, Steve. *Josephus and the New Testament*. 2d ed. Peabody, Mass.: Hendrickson Publishers, 2003.

——. *Life of Josephus: Translation and Commentary*. Vol. 9 of *Flavius Josephus: Translation and Commentary*. Edited by S. Mason. Leiden: Brill, 2001.

Meister, Klaus. 'Herodotos.' Pages 470–475 in vol. 5 of *Der neue Pauly: Enzyklopädie der Antike*. Edited by H. Cancik and H. Schneider. Stuttgart: J. B. Metzler, 1998.

Menken, Maarten J. J. *Matthew's Bible: The Old Testament Text of the Evangelist*. Bibliotheca ephemeridum theologicarum lovaniensium 173. Leuven: Leuven University Press, 2004.

Messer, William Stuart. *The Dream in Homer and Greek Tragedy*. Columbia University Studies in Classical Philology. New York: Columbia University Press, 1918.

Metzger, Bruce M. *A Textual Commentary on the Greek New Testament*. 2d ed. Stuggart: German Bible Society, 1994.

Meyer, Marvin, and Richard Smith, eds. *Ancient Christian Magic: Coptic Texts of Ritual Power*. San Francisco: HarperSanFrancisco, 1994.

Milavec, Aaron. 'Matthew's Integration of Sexual and Divine Begetting.' *Biblical Theology Bulletin* 8 (1978): 108–116.

Miller, John B. F. *'Convinced that God has called us': Dreams, Visions, and the Perception of God's Will in Luke-Acts.* Biblical Interpretation Series 85. Leiden: Brill, 2007.

Miller, Patricia Cox. *Dreams in Late Antiquity: Studies in the Imagination of a Culture.* Princeton: Princeton University Press, 1994.

——. 'Dreams in Patristic Literature: Divine Sense or Pagan Nonsense?' *Studia Patristica* 18, 2 (1989): 185–89.

Morgan, Michael A. Introduction to *Sepher Ha-Razim: The Book of the Mysteries.* Translated by Michael A. Morgan. Society of Biblical Literature Texts and Translations 25. Chico, Calif.: Scholars Press, 1983.

Morris, James F. ' "Dream Scenes" in Homer: A Study in Variation.' *Transactions of the American Philological Association* 113 (1983): 39–54.

Moses, A. D. A. *Matthew's Transfiguration Story and Jewish-Christian Controversy.* Journal for the Study of the New Testament Supplement Series 122. Sheffield: Sheffield Academic Press, 1996.

Motté, Magda. ' "Mann des Glaubens": Die Gestalt Josephs nach dem Neuen Testament,' *Bibel und Leben* 11 (1970), 176–189.

Murphy, Frederick J. *Pseudo-Philo: Rewriting the Bible.* New York: Oxford University Press, 1993.

Murphy-O'Connor, Jerome. 'What Really Happened at the Transfiguration: A Literary Critic Deepens Our Understanding.' *Bible Review* 3 (1987): 8–21.

Neihoff, Maren. 'A Dream which is Not Interpreted is like a Letter which is Not Read: Biblical Dream Interpretation, Pesher Habakkuk in Midrash.' *Journal of Jewish Studies* 43 (1992): 58–84.

Nickelsburg, George W. E. 'The Bible Rewritten and Expanded.' Pages 89–156 in *Jewish Writings of the Second Temple Period: Apocrypha, Pseudepigrapha, Qumran Sectarian Writings, Philo, Josephus.* Edited by Michael E. Stone. Vol. 2 of *The Literature of the Jewish People in the Period of the Second Temple and the Talmud.* Compendia rerum iudaicarum ad Novum Testamentum Section Two. The Netherlands: Van Gorcum, Assen, 1984.

Nilsson, Martin P. *Greek Popular Religion.* The American Council of Learned Societies New Series 1; New York: Columbia University Press, 1940.

Noegel, Scott. 'Dreams and Dream Interpreters in Mesopotamia and in the Hebrew Bible [Old Testament].' Pages 45–71 in *Dreams: A Reader on Religious, Cultural, and Psychological Dimensions of Dreaming.* Edited by Kelly Bulkeley. New York: Palgrave, 2001.

——. *Nocturnal Ciphers: The Allusive Language of Dreams in the Ancient Near East.* American Oriental Series 89. New Haven, Conn.: American Oriental Society, 2007.

Nolland, John. *The Gospel of Matthew*. New International Greek Testament Commentary. Grand Rapids: Eerdmans, 2005.

North, John. 'Diviners and Divination at Rome.' Pages 49–71 in *Pagan Priests: Religion and Power in the Ancient World*. Edited by Mary Beard and John North. London: Duckworth, 1990.

Oberhelman, Steven M. 'Dreams in Graeco-Roman Medicine.' *ANRW* 37.1: 121–56. *Principat* 37.1. Edited by W. Haase. Berlin: Walter de Gruyter, 1993.

———. 'A Survey of Dreams in Ancient Greece.' *The Classical Bulletin* 55 (1979): 6–40.

Oevermann, Susanne. 'Der Traum im Sefer Hassidim (ms Parma).' *Henoch* 12 (1990): 19–51.

Oppenheim, Leo. *The Interpretation of Dreams in the Ancient Near East: With a Translation of an Assyrian Dream-Book*. Transactions of the American Philosophical Society, n.s., 46. Philadelphia: American Philosophical Society, 1956.

Parman, Susan. *Dream and Culture: An Anthropological Study of the Western Intellectual Tradition*. New York: Praeger Publishers, 1991.

Pedersen, Sigfred. 'Die Proklamation Jesu als des eschatologischen Offenbarungsträgers (Mt 17.1-13).' *Novum Testamentum* 17 (1975): 241–64.

Pelling, Christopher. 'Tragical Dreamer: Some Dreams in the Roman Historians.' *Greece & Rome* 44 (1997): 197–213.

Penner, James A. 'Revelation and Discipleship in Matthew's Transfiguration Account.' *Bibliotheca Sacra* 152 (1995): 201–10.

Penney, Douglas L., and Michael O. Wise. 'By the Power of Beelzebub: An Aramaic Incantation Formula from Qumran (4Q560).' *Journal of Biblical Literature* 113 (1994): 627–650.

Perry, John Michael. *Exploring the Transfiguration Story*. Exploring Scripture Series. Kansas City, Missouri: Sheed & Ward, 1993.

Pervo, Richard I. *Profit with Delight: The Literary Genre of Acts of the Apostles*. Philadelphia: Fortress Press, 1987.

Pitre, Brant. 'Rewritten Bible.' Pages 410–414 in *The Westminster Dictionary of New Testament and Early Christian Literature and Rhetoric*, by David E. Aune. Louisville, Ky.: Westminster John Knox, 2003.

Plastira-Valkanou, Maria. 'Dreams in Xenophon Ephesius.' *Symbolae Osloenses* 76 (2001): 137–149.

Powell, Mark Allan. *What is Narrative Criticism?* Guides to Biblical Scholarship. Minneapolis: Fortress Press, 1990.

———. 'The Magi as Wise Men: Re-examining a Basic Supposition.' *New Testament Studies* 46 (2000): 1–20.

Prabhu, George M. Soares. *The Formula Quotations in the Infancy*

Narrative of Matthew: An Enquiry into the Tradition History of Mt. 1–2. Analecta biblica 63. Rome: Biblical Institute Press, 1976.

Price, S. R. F. 'The Future of Dreams: From Freud to Artemidorus.' *Past and Present* 113 (1986): 3–37.

Rabinowitz. Peter J. 'Truth in Fiction: A Reexamination of Audiences.' *Critical Inquiry* 4 (1977): 121–141.

——. 'Whirl without End: Audience-Oriented Criticism.' Pages 81–100 in *Contemporary Literary Theory*. Edited by G. D. Atkins and L. Morrow. Amherst, Mass.: The University of Massachusetts Press, 1989.

Rasmussen, Susanne William. 'Cicero's Stand on Prodigies. A Non-existent Dilemma?' Pages 9–24 in *Divination and Portents in the Roman World*. Edited by Robin Lorsch Wildfang and Jacob Isager. Odense University Classical Studies 21. Odense: Odense University Press, 2000.

Reckford, Kenneth J. 'Catharsis and Dream-Interpretation in Aristophanes' *Wasps.*' *Transactions of the American Philological Association* 107 (1977): 283–312.

Reider, Glenn A. 'Epiphany and Prophecy in Dreams in the Homeric Epics.' Ph.D. diss., Boston University, 1989.

Renberg, Gil H. ' "Commanded By the Gods": An Epigraphical Study of Dreams and Visions in Greek and Roman Religious Life.' Ph.D. diss., Duke University, 2003.

Riches, John, and David C. Sim, eds. *The Gospel of Matthew in its Roman Imperial Context*. Journal for the Study of the New Testament: Supplement Series 276. London: T&T Clark International, 2005.

Robbins, Vernon K. *Exploring the Texture of Texts: A Guide to Socio-Rhetorical Interpretation*. Valley Forge, Pa.: Trinity Press International, 1996.

Russell, Donald Andrew Frank Moore. 'Plutarch.' Pages 1200–1201 in *Oxford Classical Dictionary*. Rev. 3d ed. Edited by S. Hornblower and A. Spawforth. Oxford: Oxford University Press, 2003.

Sandnes, Karl Olav. '*Imitatio Homeri?*: An Appraisal of Dennis R. MacDonald's "Mimesis Criticism".' *Journal of Biblical Literature* 124 (2005): 715–732.

Scardigli, Barbara, ed. *Essays on Plutarch's Lives*. Oxford: Clarendon Press, 1995.

Schofield, Malcolm. 'Cicero for and against Divination.' *Journal of Roman Studies* 76 (1986): 47–65.

Scott, Bernard Brandon. 'The Birth of the Reader.' *Semeia* 52 (1990): 83–102.

Segal, Alan F. 'Hellenistic Magic: Some Questions.' Pages 349–75 in *Studies in Gnosticism and Hellenistic Religions*. Edited by R. Van Den Brock and M. J. Vermaseren. Leiden: E. J. Brill, 1981.

Sheeley, Steven M. *Narrative Asides in Luke-Acts*. Journal for the Study of the New Testament Supplement Series 72. Sheffield, JSOT Press, 1992.

Shuler, Philip L. *A Genre for the Gospels: The Biographical Character of Matthew*. Philadelphia: Fortress Press, 1982.

Shulman, David and Guy G. Stroumsa, eds. *Dream Cultures: Explorations in the Comparative History of Dreaming*. New York: Oxford University Press, 1999.

Smith, Morton. 'The Origin and History of the Transfiguration Story.' *Union Seminary Quarterly Review* 36 (1980): 39–44.

Spawforth, Antony J. S. 'tourism.' Page 1535 in *The Oxford Classical Dictionary*. Edited by Simon Hornblower and Antony Spawforth. 3d ed. Oxford: Oxford University Press, 1996.

Stanton, Graham N. *A Gospel for a New People: Studies in Matthew*. Louisville: Westminster/John Knox Press, 1993.

——, ed. *The Interpretation of Matthew*. Issues in Religion and Theology 3. Philadelphia: Fortress Press, 1983.

——. 'Matthew.' Pages 205–219 in *It Is Written: Scripture Citing Scripture: Essays in Honour of Barnabas Lindars*. Edited by D. A. Carson and H. G. M. Williamson. Cambridge: Cambridge University Press, 1988.

Stemberger, Brigitte. 'Der Traum in der rabbinischen Literatur.' *Kairos* 18 (1976): 1–42.

Stendahl, Krister. 'Quis et Unde? An Analysis of Matthew 1–2.' Pages 56–66 in *The Interpretation of Matthew*. Issues in Religion and Theology 3. Edited by G. Stanton. Philadelphia: Fortress Press, 1983.

Sterling, Gregory E. *Historiography and Self-definition: Josephos, Luke-Acts, and Apologetic Historiography*. Supplements to Novum Testamentum 64. Leiden: Brill, 1992.

Stramare, Tarcisio. 'I sogni di S. Giuseppe.' *Cahiers de Joséphologie* 19 (1971): 104–22.

van Straten, F. T. 'Daikrates' Dream: A Votive Relief from Kos, and Some Other Kat'onar Dedications.' *Bulletin antieke Beschavung* 51 (1976): 1–38.

Stroumsa, Guy G. *Barbarian Philosophy: The Religious Revolution of Early Christianity*. Wissenschaftliche Untersuchungen zum Neuen Testament 112. Tübingen: Mohr Siebeck, 1999.

Talbert, Charles H. *Literary Patterns, Theological Themes, and the Genre of Luke-Acts*. Missoula, Mont.: Scholars Press, 1974.

——. *Reading Acts: A Literary and Theological Commentary on The Acts of the Apostles*. New York: Crossroad, 1997.

——. *Reading Luke-Acts in its Mediterranean Milieu*. Supplements to Novum Testamentum 107. Leiden: Brill, 2003.

——. *Reading the Sermon on the Mount: Character Formation and Ethical*

Decision Making in Matthew 5–7. Columbia, S.C.: University of South Carolina Press, 2004. Repr. Grand Rapids, Mich.: Baker Academic, 2006.

Tannehill, Robert C. *The Acts of the Apostles.* Vol. 2 of *The Narrative Unity of Luke-Acts: A Literary Interpretation.* Minneapolis: Fortress Press, 1990.

Thrall, Margaret E. 'Elijah and Moses in Mark's Account of the Transfiguration.' *New Testament Studies* 16 (1969–70): 305–17.

Trites, Allison A. 'The Transfiguration in the Theology of Luke: Some Redactional Links.' Pages 71–81 in *The Glory of Christ in the New Testament: Studies in Christology.* Edited by L. D. Hurst and N. T. Wright. Oxford: Clarendon Press, 1987.

Viviano, Benedict T. 'The Genres of Matthew 1–2: Light from 1 Timothy 1.4.' *Revue Biblique* 97 (1990): 31–53.

Walde, Christine. *Die Traumdarstellungen in der griechisch-römischen Dichtung.* Leipzig: K. G. Saur München, 2001.

Wallace-Hadrill, Andrew. *Suetonius.* 2d ed. London: Bristol Classical Press, 1995.

Waszink, J. H. *Tertulliani De Animia.* Amsterdam: J. M. Meulenhoff, 1947.

Weaver, Dorothy Jean. 'Rewriting the Messianic Script: Matthew's Account of the Birth of Jesus.' *Interpretation* 54 (2000): 376–385.

West, Stephanie. 'And it Came to Pass that Pharaoh Dreamed: Notes on Herodotus 1.139, 141.' *The Classical Quarterly* 37 (1987): 262–271.

Wikenhauser, Alfred. 'Die Traumgesichte des Neuen Testaments in religionsgeschichtlicher Sicht.' Pages 320–333 in *Pisciculi: Studien zur Religion und Kultur des Altertums.* Edited by Franz Joseph Dölger. Antike und Christentum 1. Münster: Aschendorff, 1939.

——. 'Doppelträume,' *Biblica* 29 (1948): 100–111.

Wildfang, Robin Lorsch. 'The Propaganda of Omens: Six Dreams Involving Augustus.' Pages 43–56 in *Divination and Portents in the Roman World.* Odense University Classical Studies 21. Edited by Robin Lorsch Wildfang and Jacob Isager. Odense: Odense University Press, 2000.

Winkler, John J. 'The Constraints of Eros.' Pages 214–243 in *Magika Hiera: Ancient Greek Magic and Religion.* Edited by C. A. Faraone and D. Obbink. New York: Oxford University Press, 1991.

Wimsatt, W. K., and M. C. Beardsley. 'The Intentional Fallacy.' Pages 1–13 in *On Literary Intention.* Edited by D. Newton-deMolina. Edinburgh: Edinburgh University Press, 1976.

Wolfson, Harry Austryn. *Philo: Foundations of Religious Philosophy in Judaism, Christianity, and Islam.* Rev. ed. 2 vols. Cambridge, Mass.: Harvard University Press, 1948.

Zahn, Theodor. *Das Evangelium des Matthäus.* Kommentar zum Neuen Testament 1. 2d ed. Leipzig: A. Deichert, 1905.

INDEX OF ANCIENT REFERENCES